THE OLD ENGLISH HOMILY
& ITS BACKGROUNDS

THE OLD ENGLISH HOMILY & ITS
BACKGROUNDS ❦ EDITED WITH AN
INTRODUCTION BY PAUL E. SZARMACH
& BERNARD F. HUPPÉ ❦ STATE
UNIVERSITY OF NEW YORK PRESS ❦
ALBANY, 1978

First published in 1978 by
State University of New York Press
Albany, New York 12246

Printed in the United States of America

Library of Congress Cataloging in Publication Data

Main entry under title:

The Old English homily and its backgrounds.

Includes bibliographical references.
1. Anglo-Saxon literature—History and criticism.
2. Preaching—History—England. I. Szarmach, Paul E.
II. Huppé, Bernard Felix, 1911–
PR226.04   829   77-21447
ISBN 0-87395-376-2

CONTENTS

ABBREVIATIONS & SHORT TITLES

BH	Morris, Richard, ed., *The Bickling Homilies,* EETS Original Series 58, 63, 73 (Oxford, 1874, 1876, 1880). Repr. as one in 1967.
CCL	*Corpus Christianorum, Series Latina*
CH I, CH II	Thorpe, Benjamin, ed., *The Homilies of the Anglo-Saxon Church,* 2 vols. (London, 1844–46).
EEMF	Early English Manuscripts in Facsimile
EETS	Early English Text Society
Ker, *Catalogue*	Ker, Neil R. *Catalogue of Manuscripts Containing Anglo-Saxon* (Oxford, 1957).
LS I, LS II	Skeat, Walter W., ed. *Aelfric's Lives of the Saints,* EETS 76, 82, 94, 114 (1881–1900). Repr. in 2 vols. 1966.
Napier 49, etc.	Napier, Arthur S., ed. *Wulfstan, Sammlung der ihm zugeschriebenen Homilien* (Berlin, 1883). Repr. with bibliographical supplement by Klaus Ostheeren 1967. [Works cited by arabic number]
PL	Migne, J. P. *Patrologia Latina* (Paris, 1844–91). [Citations by volume and column]
SS I, SS II	Pope, John C., ed. *Homilies of Aelfric: A Supplementary Collection,* EETS 259, 260 (1967–68).

INTRODUCTION

Old English classical prose may lay claim to an importance and distinction equal to that of Old English poetry, but whereas the latter is the subject of enthusiastic study, the former, and much larger, corpus has suffered neglect. The annual bibliographies of the Modern Language Association, for example, list only a few articles on the major prose writers of the period over the last several years, and many of these are limited to a study of source material. Ker's *Catalogue* may be an eloquent witness to the influence and importance of Aelfric, yet in modern times there has appeared but one critical book on his achievement. The Clemoes-Godden critical edition of the *Catholic Homilies,* sure to become standard, has not yet seen print, and Pope's *Supplementary Series* is only now beginning to have influence.

An important subject, demanding interdisciplinary study, reasonably requires that scholars from various disciplines, who are united in their concern with developing the subject, collaborate in a joint attempt to show its importance and to stimulate interest in its study. The present collection of original essays responds to this demand as a contemporary contribution to an understanding of the Old English homily and the masterly achievement of Aelfric. The first essays provide the background necessary to evaluation through study of the historical, ecclesiastical, and literary contexts which permitted and encouraged the flourishing of prose in the late tenth century. The latter essays deal with the literature itself through functional study of style and structure, structure, and theme, while employing source criticism, descriptive analysis, and comparison. Such issues as the relationship of prose and poetry, the importance of the Latin tradition both in form and content, the question of originality, and the concept of *curiosa felicitas* are explored.

Although the collaborators break much new ground, this collection is intended to serve only as a beginning for the contemporary discussion of Old English prose, not as a definitive statement. Not only is this collection the first collaborative effort in this long-neglected subject, but virtually every essay also points out explicitly or implicitly the depth and breadth of the subject and the massive work still left untouched.

In the light of the interdisciplinary character involved in the study of Old English prose, it is appropriate to begin the collection with an essay on "Church and Society in England in the Age of Aelfric." P. A. Stafford gives an overview of the interrelationship between the ecclesiastical and political orders in the later Anglo-Saxon period that helps explain how the efflorescence of prose could become a historical possibility. Using evidence from charters, she shows that the king and a small group of aristocrats endowed the monasteries on a comparatively lavish scale. Such generosity reflects the belief that the church was the bridge between the human and the divine. Thus, as Stafford says, "There was no clear line of demarcation between the concerns of the king and the concerns of the bishops. . . ." (p. 18) Bishops and abbots were royal counselors and judges as well as diplomats and defenders of the realm. When Aelfric, Wulfstan, and their anonymous contemporaries write, they serve both church and kingdom for practical ends of education. In Wulfstan's writings on law and status, for example, one of the major recurring themes is the right ordering of society to bring about a harmonious whole. As archbishop in the backward North, Wulfstan tried to establish a society that resembled the more orderly South and Midlands. Not all efforts to influence society were unblushing successes, but even antimonastic reactions had the tendency to forge stronger alliances between monks and kings. The church aided the king by creating and propagandizing his role, and in so doing remade the king in its own image. Laws became homilies, and homilies supported the laws. The development of an organized cultural establishment that produced a coherent body of religious and intellectual prose was only a natural result. Continuing detailed study of the interaction between church and state promises important results.

Milton McC. Gatch and Cyril A. Smetana complement Stafford's essay on the historical context in their respective discussions of the continental and Latin homilies that furnish touchstones and sources. Gatch describes the place of Old English homilies in the history of European vernacular preaching and considers possible English influence on the vernacular texts that appeared in the twelfth century. He finds that except for possible missionary activity in early times pastoral concern for vernacular preaching first became apparent in the Carolingian era. Early ninth-century councils promulgated canons that required bishops to have homiliaries whose contents might be translated in *rusticam Romanam linguam aut Thiotiscam,* but these canons did not in fact require written vernacular homilies. The few witnesses to German prose before the eleventh century do not compare to the Anglo-Saxon achievement. The Celtic church did apparently commit catechetical or instructional teaching to written form, but the evidence makes it unlikely that any early Irish vernacular preaching texts existed. After the Anglo-Saxon period, however, there are numerous vernacular collections that, though reminiscent of the Blickling Homilies and the Vercelli Book, still do not equal the achievement of Aelfric. In Norway and Iceland there is evidence for the direct influence of Old English homilies, but more comparative work needs to be done in Scandinavian and French material. Gatch concludes that the "Age of Aelfric" is an incorrect label for this period because Aelfric was unique in providing a cycle of exegetical addresses *ad populum* for the Temporale and because no subsequent author followed his example. Why this should be is a question, among others, which calls for further intensive study.

Developing his early work on the Latin sources of Aelfric, Father Smetana presents a descriptive analysis of Paul the Deacon's Homiliary. Paul's two-volume anthology of readings from the Fathers for liturgical occasions became the standard for the western church and, as is well known, is a major direct source for Aelfric and other Anglo-Saxon writers. The official homiliary of the Carolingian kings, Paul's collection of 244 homilies quickly replaced earlier collections in an official sense and superseded them in a religious sense by its comprehensiveness. Paul drew heavily on Bede, Maximus of Turin, Leo the Great, and Gregory the Great. From Augustine he chose sparingly, but judiciously. Other Fathers, such as Jerome, Ambrose, John Chrysostom, and Isidore, are less well represented. The flowers that Paul collected exist in a number of manuscripts in English

libraries from the time of Aelfric and Wulfstan. Further study to
determine if these manuscripts were made and used in England is
needed to give an indication of what Anglo-Saxon homilists may
have had at hand.

Malcolm Godden's essay on "Aelfric and the Vernacular Prose
Tradition" provides an easy transition from the consideration of
backgrounds to the treatment of prose texts. Godden places Aelfric
in Anglo-Saxon literary history by reviewing Aelfric's relationship
to earlier English writings and by assessing his later influence.
Aelfric's comments and remarks suggest that he knew a number of
works full of *gedwyld* ("heresy," "folly"), particularly works which
now merit the term *"apocrypha."* It appears that Aelfric has in
mind such collections as Vercelli and Blickling, but his unapproving
reference to the *Visio Pauli* is clear and unambiguous. Aelfric does
know and approve of the "Alfredian" rendering of Bede's *Historia
Ecclesiastica* and of Alfred's translations of the *Pastoral Care,* the
Consolation of Philosophy, and the *Dialogues.* It is not unreason-
able, moreover, to see Aelfric as a continuator of Alfred's scholarly
and intellectual tradition. Aelfric follows similar authorities, shows
the same respect for history. He demonstrates a comparable scholarly approach to the Bible, and moreover transforms the formal,
literary style he inherited. If the number and chronological spread
of the manuscripts are proof, then Aelfric had a wide reputation.
The text of his works, however, ultimately suffered radical rewriting by later hands who generally sought to simplify content or to
modernize linguistic forms. The sets of homilies he had issued soon
suffered interpolation. In effect Aelfric's writing became a useful
quarry for succeeding generations, who adapted his work for their
own purposes. Such adaptations may often be untrue to Aelfric's
original intentions, but in the main Aelfric's attempt to foster
Christian learning succeeded.

Bernard F. Huppé, although he had completed his study before
he had read Godden's essay, abbreviated and modified his introduction to indicate the consistency of his findings with those of Godden.
He suggests that Alfred modelled his *Preface to the Pastoral Care*
upon some current form of the epistle, a matter, as he indicates,
which requires further study and promises important results. But
in employing the form of the epistle, Alfred in fact created a

distinctive prose style. Alfred employed the devices of the Latin rhetoricians, but was concerned to achieve an "English" style. In so doing he appeared to employ the most striking devices of Old English poetry, as it has come down to us, particularly in his use of structural, incremental repetition, of prosopopoeia, of word play. Huppé argues that Aelfric would certainly have been moved and inspired by Alfred's work, and suggests that his *Preface to Genesis* may reveal his knowledge of, and response to, Alfred's *Preface*. The evidence of the continuity of an Alfredian tradition to the time of Aelfric should serve as a call to further investigation.

What Huppé suggests about Alfred's awareness and use of poetic rhetoric is the subject of Douglas R. Letson's study of "The Poetic Content of the Revival Homily." Letson argues that style, particularly poetic style, in the service of Christian substance characterizes not only Wulfstan but also Aelfric and many of the anonymous homilists. These writers do not observe the distinction between prose and poetry as rigidly as modern scholars do, and Letson attempts to describe and explain the convergence of the two modes. He sees Augustine's *De Doctrina Christiana* as an important authority for later Old English prose, in particular Augustine's recommendation of the limited use of rhythm and rhyme. The long tradition of homilists who also wrote poetry, the precedents of including prose and poetry together in miscellanies, and the practice of borrowing from vernacular and Latin poetry were also important factors in the convergence of modes. Letson argues that the Revival homilist, sharing the same goal as the Christian poet, used the same elements of design: alliteration, occasional rhyme, rhetorical catalogues, balance of thought and expression, etc. He shows, for example, how thematic interlace, a structural approach associated with Old English poetry, animates the pericope in Aelfric's homily for the Third Sunday after Epiphany. Letson's arguments therefore provide a basis for convincing students of Old English Christian poetry that prose merits their equal concern. Both modes serve the same Christian culture.

Next Ann Eljenholm Nichols turns to a close study of Aelfric's "plain" style. She cites five Friday homilies for Lent as evidence that this style derives from his method of abbreviation. In her comparison with Augustinian sources she finds that Aelfric generally avoids word play, rejects complex imagery, and deletes such features of Augustinian style as rhetorical questions, first-person transitions, and exhortations. Since a given passage could come from memory rather than rewriting, pericope translations provide the most valid examples of syntactical abbreviation. These translations also demonstrate Aelfric's syntactical freedom and his self-assurance in the techniques of embedding and splicing. Nevertheless abbreviation does not appear to be an end in itself for Aelfric does develop and amplify his sources at times. Nichols ends with the suggestion that Aelfric has a conscious and intuitive sense of decorum, perhaps patristic in inspiration, that needs further definition and study.

Keith Tandy argues that Aelfric's *Lives of the Saints* is a part of this same achievement, a proposition with which all who have read the *Lives* must agree, but Tandy's contribution to the collection is particularly significant for another reason. His study of verbal aspect is one of the first to apply the modes of modern linquistic to the work of Aelfric. After establishing that Aelfric knew what verbal aspect is and how it operates, Tandy demonstrates that Aelfric uses verbal aspect as a narrative structure in two selections from the *Lives,* the homily on the Nativity and the life of St. Eugenia. In the former Aelfric distinguishes between men and beasts through aspect, while in the latter he develops a contrast between pagans and Christians. Pagans perform punctual, inceptive, perfective acts; Christians act, change, and grow. These dichotomous spiritual values of the narrative derive from a range of aspectual features and from variations of agentive features of verbs. Tandy's modern linguistic analysis announces a new way to approach Aelfric and serves as a model for future inquiries.

As Aelfric's reputation continues to grow quietly, that of his contemporary Wulfstan seems to diminish correspondingly. Raachel Jurovics provides a basis for a revised estimate of the archbishop's prose by her consideration of the moral purposes of *Sermo Lupi,* long considered Wulfstan's masterpiece, however uncharacteristic of his work some think it to be. She applies the ecclesiastical, legal, and patristic themes in the earlier essays by Stafford and Gatch to a specific literary text, thus making those interdisciplinary connections that allow for a total view of a work in its cultural context.

The topicality of the sermon, i.e., *ad Anglos quando Danes maxime persecuti sunt eos,* the major theme of moral regeneration, and the minor themes of national vices all proceed from Wulfstan's acceptance of his episcopal responsibility, which, in turn, becomes a major theme running through his other homilies and his episcopal letters. When Wulfstan seeks to move his English audience to virtue, he gives expression to the Christian rhetorical tradition that ultimately originated with Cicero but received its full form from Augustine's *De doctrina christiana,* a matter also given emphasis by Letson. In this rhetoric, style serves content. Jurovics explains how Augustinian rhetoric appears in both the structural and verbal features of the *Sermo Lupi* and how throughout Wulfstan's impassioned sermon every stylistic detail supports the rhetorical strategy. Jurovics's detailed discussion helps absolve Wulfstan from the charge of mannerism and argues that Christian persuasion, not emotionalism, is the goal sought for and achieved in *Sermo Lupi.*

The remaining essays in the collection discuss the tradition of anonymous homilies that preceded the work of Aelfric and Wulfstan. Marcia Dalbey focuses on the Lenten Homilies in Blickling to show the parenetic and didactic intent of the whole homiliary. In her comparison of the Blickling Homilies with the sources, the homilists become practical teachers interested in moving their audience to the Christian moral life but either uninterested in explaining dogma and mystery or unable to do so. The homily for the First Sunday in Lent, whose partial source is Gregory's *Homilia XVI in Evangelia,* is an important example. Gregory presents a detailed, coherent, and clear explanation of the meaning of the forty days in Lent; the Blickling homilist omits many of the logical connections between the points of analysis that are in Gregory, thus producing an emotional appeal for right conduct but a somewhat confused explanation of the forty days. The success in exhortation rather than in exegesis characterizes the Lenten homilies and reflects the overriding concern of the compiler of the collection. Paul E. Szarmach presents the first literary analysis of the prose contents of the Vercelli Book, one of the four major Old English manuscripts. Employing the generic distinctions *sermo, homilia,* and *vita,* he describes the stylistic and structural features of several Vercelli "homilies." In

the type of sermon known as the *Kompilationspredigt* he shows
that literary evidence as well as textual evidence points to a concentric design wherein a number of introductory motifs or themes
prepare for a narrative or dramatic center. This center itself may
appear independently with its own title or rubric. The *homiliae*
proper in the Vercelli Book have a different coherence because of
their necessary relationship to a biblical passage. The homily on the
Epiphany has a unique personal voice, while the homily on the Purification seems to be a blend of features from both the genres of
sermo and *homilia*. The *vitae* in the collection, Martin and Guthlac,
call for source comparisons with the Latin and for literary comparisons with other Old English versions. The selective method of
the author of the Vercelli Martin shows some skill, but the Vercelli
Guthlac may be only a scribal afterthought that may have importance only for textual critics. Nevertheless these earlier writers
on the whole argue for a strong and confident tradition that explains
why Aelfric and Wulfstan are such accomplished writers.

These original essays on Old English prose hopefully begin a
major reconsideration of this long-neglected body of writing that
may even ultimately effect the reconsideration of Old English
poetry as well. Letson's point that prose and poetry are not rigid
categories for Old English writers must be acknowledged. As for
the prose itself, these essays say many things. They reaffirm the
importance in religious prose of the Latin tradition and its correlative, the vernacular tradition. They emphasize that knowledge
drawn from history, church history, the papal chancery, theology,
and textual criticism is important to an understanding of the whole
of later English prose and to the elucidation of specific works and
passages. The reliance on contemporary methods of literary analysis
shows how fruitful those techniques can be, especially when joined
with historical concerns. There are cautions here as well, e.g., the
importance of the precise use of terminology, the need to be wary
and aware of texts and editions. Although few of the essays are
directly devoted to Aelfric, throughout this whole collection there
is a significant theme that receives particular attention: Aelfric is
the measure of excellence. Questions of attribution aside, Aelfric is
the major author of the period by virtue of every posible criterion.
In different ways many of the essays either assess Aelfric's cultural

preeminence directly, or if they do not directly demonstrate Aelfric's art, use Aelfric as the touchstone. In the last analysis this collection asks students of Old English Literature to review their understanding of their subject by considering once again the important achievement of Aelfric and the Old English homily.

The editors would like to thank Mrs. Dorothy Huber, the secretary of the Center for Medieval and Early Renaissance Studies at the State University of New York at Binghamton, for her hard work in the preparation of the manuscript for publication. Paul E. Szarmach wishes to acknowledge with thanks that the Research Foundation of the State University of New York generously supported the research work on his article and much of the writing with a 1972 Summer Research Fellowship.

P. A. STAFFORD ❧ CHURCH & SOCIETY IN THE AGE OF AELFRIC

At the end of the tenth century the most spectacular theme in the history of England was the revival of Viking attacks. A century which had opened with the final victories of Alfred and Edward the Elder closed with their descendant, Aethelred, facing renewed invasions from the north. Although it was not at first apparent, these attacks differed significantly from the earlier series. They were to have a very different outcome. In 1014 a Danish king, Swein, was accepted by the English nobility, and Aethelred, the representative of the native dynasty, was in flight to the Viking-French duchy of Normandy. In 1017 the Danish Cnut was established on the throne.

And yet in many ways what is impressive is not the disruption but the continuities of the age. The work, for example, of a man like Wulfstan of York spans the reigns of Aethelred and Cnut; he developed his ideas on kingship and the necessary ordering of society for Anglo-Saxon and Danish king alike and produced some of his most systematic statements post 1017.[1] For the late tenth and early eleventh centuries were witnessing the impact on England of a movement no less important than the Danish attack, namely the great revival of organized monastic life. Not only in England, but widely in western Europe, this revival had profound significance for religious organization, for art and learning, as well as for political and economic development. In the wake of this revival England was experiencing a minor renaissance, in which Aelfric and Wulfstan are only the most famous names. The ideas of this movement and their implications for religious and political life were being worked out at precisely the same time as the Viking attacks, and the accession of Cnut had no immediate impact upon them.

The English monastic revival is part of a wider movement for monastic reform in the tenth century. Neither "reform" nor "revival" is really an accurate description of the movement. It was not primarily a reform of laxity, nor yet a simple revival of an earlier form of monasticism, which had decayed, though there are elements of both. Rather the tenth century movement was the culmination of the spread of the Benedictine rule, fostered by the Carolingians and coming to such splendid fruition at Cluny, Gorze, and Brogne.[2]

The European revival has recently been the subject of much study, and it is increasingly seen as at once a religious and political phenomenon. The essential spirituality, especially of the Cluniac reform, has been recognized as a truly spontaneous growth to meet the real spiritual needs of the tenth century, and in this it has been contrasted with the imperially led and directed Carolingian movement.[3] But at the same time other scholars have been stressing the political and social importance of the monasteries. One extreme sees the monasteries as initiating a new stage of feudalism,[4] and it does seem certain that they were important in providing the new feudal classes with a new cultural pattern.[5] Many scholars are now revealing the importance of the monasteries in the development of political power,[6] while the economic significance of their estates has long been realized.[7] In the life and organization of the church itself the monasteries not only had an impact on the episcopate, on church reform, and learning, but they also played a role in winning the mass of the people to the church through their acquisition of relics, their popular Saints' lives, and their homilies.[8] Since these reevaluations of the English reform movement are still in progress, what follows can be no more than an interim statement on this large subject.

The immediate links of the English movement were with Lotharingia rather than with Cluny. During his exile on the continent Dunstan had spent his time at Ghent, a monastery reformed by the Lotharingian Gerard of Brogne. Links with Ghent remained important after his return to England, money and prayers were requested on both sides, and the monks of Ghent were present and assisted at the drawing up of the *Regularis Concordia*.[9] His fellow reformer Oswald learned his monasticism at a Cluniac school in the abbey of Fleury and links between Fleury and Oswald's abbeys, especially with Ramsey, long continued.[10] But the main influence on the English reform, at least in the English rule, seems to have been from Ghent.[11] The deciding factor here may well have been Dunstan. His influence at the royal court dated back to the reign of Athelstan, and it was Dunstan who received the prestigious position of archbishop of Canterbury.[12] But the greater similarities between the English and Lotharingian reforms is probably to be understood more in political terms. Cluny, although founded by a layman, Duke William of Aquitaine, emphasized its total freedom from secular control. This desire for autonomy arises out of the feudal disintegration in France, specifically the lack of any strong central authority to protect the monks. The Lotharingian movement grew up within the domains of the Ottonian emperors, and the emperors were instrumental in spreading the movement through generous grants of land to the new foundations. The result was a close relationship between monks and ruler, more akin to that which had existed under the Carolingians than to the total freedom of the Cluniac houses. The political similarities between England, with her strong monarchy, and East Frankia helped to further closely parallel reform movements. And for England, as we shall see, Carolingian practice and example were very important.

The reform and refoundation of English monasticism belongs largely to the reign of Edgar (959–75). He worked more closely in partnership with the reformers than any other tenth-century king and generously endowed the abbeys which they had founded.[13] His promonastic reputation seems to have been established before his accession, since the leading reformers, Oda and Dunstan, were supporting him against his brother Edwig in the succession crisis of (956–58).[14] Most of the new foundations were made during Edgar's reign. The only houses reformed before this were Glastonbury (c.943) and Abingdon (c.954), while relatively few of the monasteries were founded or reformed after his death. Tavistock, Cerne, Eynsham, Sherborne, and Christ Church Canterbury belong to the reign of his son, Aethelred II; Bury, Coventry, and Gloucester were established later in the eleventh century. Compare this with some twenty and more houses founded in the brief sixteen years of Edgar's reign and the involvement of that king in the reform is apparent.

The movement was confined to England south of the Humber and was concentrated in the Fens, the Severn Valley, and to the south of the Thames. There is a link here with the patrons of the monasteries (see below) and especially with the chief areas of

wealth and power of the Old English kings. But the absence of reformed houses in the diocese of York is strange, especially in view
of the successive rule as archbishop of York of Oswald and Wulfstan, one a prominent reformer and the other often considered one
of the greatest products of the revival. All the cathedral chapters of
southern England were reformed along monastic lines, the priests
driven out and the monks brought in.[15] But there is no evidence
of an attempt to reform the York chapter, nor the minsters
of Ripon, Beverley, and Southwell, all of which came under the
sway of the archbishop of York. One possible reason was poverty,
a reason also suggested to account for the joining of the York and
Worcester dioceses in the tenth century.[16] If the York diocese was
already poor by the mid-tenth century, it was to suffer further
losses during the latter half of the century. Oswald's list of lands
lost by York during the time of Earl Thored [17] is one certain example
of what may have been a regular occurrence. It may also indicate a
hostility towards the church on the part of laymen, or at best a
lack of complete sympathy. Benedictine monasteries were wealthy
institutions, with estates large enough to support the monks from
rents and renders. At the time of Domesday Book, for example,
the great southern monasteries owned lands worth one-sixth of the
survey's total valuation. The wealthiest among them could hold its
own in relation to almost any of the lay magnates.[18] In the north the
church does not seem to have had this sort of wealth, nor were there
any number of lay patrons prepared to endow the monasteries. As a
result the monastic movement did not spread north until after the
Norman Conquest, and we shall find Wulfstan more concerned with
the standards which should govern *all* the clergy and not solely
with monks.

When it was allowed to take root, the new monasticism transformed the English church. The numbers of monks increased in relation to the rest of the clergy, a situation graphically revealed in
the witness lists of royal charters where abbots figure prominently.
The monks were required to live a common life in the abbey,
celibate and sharing all things in common. In these respects they
were to differ from the canons who had often filled their places
prior to the reform, for the canons had often kept separate house-
holds, dividing the property of the foundation between them as if it

had been their own inheritance, as in part it probably was.[19] The new communal life was to be orderly and dominated by the liturgy which was such a central feature of the tenth-century reforms. The *Regularis Concordia,* the rule drawn up for the English monks and nuns, has the same elaborate regulation of the canonical hours and the daily round of prayers as its continental counterparts, but it lays more stress than any of them on prayers for the king and the royal family.[20] Indeed the *Regularis Concordia* makes the association of king and monks very clear. It is King Edgar who is said to desire reform and uniformity in the rule of life of the monks, lest any dissension over the rule to be followed should bring the monks into disrepute.[21] It is with his advice and consent that abbots and abbesses are to be elected.[22] Lay dominance (*saecularium prioratum*) is to be avoided for fear of the "utter loss and ruin" which it brought in the past, but it is made clear that this does not refer to the king and queen. "The sovereign power of the king and queen—and that only—should ever be besought with confident petition, both for the safeguarding of holy places and for the increase of the goods of the church."[23] In other words the king is the major patron and protector of the monasteries. It is the domination of the local aristocracy which is to be guarded against, and the alliance with the king was in part intended to combat the interference of local lords.

These statements should not be taken to mean that the revival proceeded without any help from the aristocracy. The monasteries which were to live under this rule were founded and endowed by the king and a very small group of great magnates. Indeed wherever the rule mentions prayers for the royal family, it also speaks of those to be said for benefactors (see note 20). During the tenth century a small group of great families had risen to preeminence, profiting largely from the extension of royal power during that century. They were all closely bound to the king by office, by blood, and by marriage.[24] These families or at least some of them feature prominently as monastery founders. The family of Athelstan Half-King in East Anglia is perhaps the best example.[25] This family, which controlled the ealdormanry of East Anglia for three generations, was important in the endowment first of Glastonbury, and then of Oswald's fenland abbeys of Ramsey, Thorney, and Peter-

borough. It should be noticed that they were supporters of particular abbeys rather than of monasticism in general. Ely, for
example, certainly did not remember them as friends.[26] This involvement with particular abbeys does not imply the sort of secular lord-
ship against which the Rule warned, though there were possible
dangers.[27] It was a family investment in the prayers of the monks
as well as an important proof of social position (see notes 4 and 5).
Such secular protection was sought and valued by the monks, and
could be critically important, as during the reaction against monasticism on the death of Edgar, when the East Mercian monasteries
were saved precisely by the families of their founders.[28] Ely remem-
bered Aethelwine of East Anglia as an enemy, but it had its own
aristocratic benefactor, Brihtnoth, ealdorman of Essex, and his
wife Aelflaed.[29] Abbot Aelfric's two abbeys of Cerne and Eynsham
were endowed by another family, that of Aethelmaer, ealdorman of
West Wessex, son of ealdorman Aethelweard the chronicler and
descendants of King Aethelred I, brother of King Alfred.[30]
Tavistock Abbey was the foundation of Ordulf, a great thane of the
southwest, uncle of King Aethelred II and son of ealdorman
Ordgar.[31] The only north midlands monastery, that of Burton-on-
Trent, was founded by the thane Wulfric Spott.[32] His was a family
whose loyalty had long been cultivated by the kings of Wessex, and
at the time of the foundation his brother Aelfhelm was ealdorman
at York.[33] The monastic revival was thus a movement fostered by
the king and a small circle of the great nobility. In the cases of
Aethelwine, Brihtnoth, and Aethelmaer, their foundations were all
within the area of their political power;[34] in the case of Wulfric
Spott his monastery occupied a key position in the north midlands.
Whilst not necessarily implying that the revival was solely political
in nature, the identity of its chief patrons underlines how closely it
must have been involved in the concerns and plans of this ruling
group.

This same involvement is suggested by the enemies whom the
monks made as well as by the friends. For the monks were not
universally popular. Throughout the early history of the revival
there was feeling both for and against among the nobility, and the
vacillations of kings such as Athelstan and Edmund and the apparent opposition of Edwig suggest that kings too were not neces-

sarily wholehearted supporters. This feeling came to a head on the death of Edgar in 975, when a succession crisis was again complicated by antimonastic reaction.[35] Prominent in the reaction was Aelfhere, ealdorman of Mercia, a leading member of the nobility. His opinions of monks were shared by Edwin of Sussex, who also took part against the monks in these years, and by Aelfric, ealdorman of East Wessex, whose harassment of Glastonbury was later to be rebuked by the pope.[36] The reaction saw attacks on monastic property at all levels of society.[37] The hostility is not surprising. The church had many ways of helping secular rulers. It had developed theories of rule and kingship which made it incumbent on the king to help the church. Its moral power in such an age of faith was formidable. But there was never universal agreement in practice on such questions. To many of the great nobles the advancing power of the church could only seem a threat to their own, the extravagance of the king to the monasteries a threat to his own position. Moreover in a land-hungry society the monks were great engrossers of land, threatening men's inheritance.[38]

The foundation of a Benedictine house was a great expense. Whether we look at Domesday and their estates in the mid-eleventh century, or at the tenth-century foundations themselves, the scale is impressive. Eynsham, founded by Aethelmaer in 1005, was far from being one of the largest abbeys. Yet its foundation charter shows that Aethelmaer endowed it with lands in Eynsham, Shipton-on-Cherwell, Shifford, Mickleton, Burton, Marle Cliff, Bentley, Yarnton, Esher, Ditton, and Ramsleigh, a total of well over ninety-two hides of land (not all the estates are given a value in hides). Some of the estates he had inherited; some he had acquired from relatives, such as Lawling in Essex, which his kinswoman Aelflaed, wife of ealdorman Brithnoth, had left to him in her will;[39] some were grants made to him by the king, as in the case of Thames Ditton;[40] some came from other members of his family, Ramsleigh for instance was given to him by his relative Wulfwyn, Mickleton by ealdorman Brihtnoth; some he had purchased from the king, as Marle Cliff and Bentley. The foundation of Eynsham had been built up by Aethelmaer and it represented a substantial investment of land on the part of him and his family. Cerne and Eynsham together cannot have amounted to a negligible amount of

his family property. The will of Wulfric Spott records a similar
massive endowment of Burton Abbey. The king was no less
prodigal towards the monasteries. The reign of Aethelred, not the
first flush of monastic fervor, has a total of 43 charters granted
in favor of monastic houses out of a total of 111 for the entire
reign. Of course not all are genuine, and some are royal confirma-
tions of other men's gifts, like the Eynsham charter. But in all
those cases where a genuine grant survives, the king was alienating
some rights and dues in the monastery's favor. We have evidence
here for a prodigal use of royal and noble resources which again
suggests the existence of important reasons why the king and the
great magnates near to him thought it worth their while to endow
the monks on such a lavish scale.

The church played a very important role in early medieval
society. The relationship between the human and the divine was
seen as a very real one. Men felt a need to harmonize that relationship if their affairs were to prosper, and the church was the
essential bridge, the interpreter of the divine will and the placater
of divine wrath. The church could and did exercise political powers
of an administrative and executive kind. But its involvement in
political affairs should not be seen solely in this practical light. It
was the church which helped man establish on earth that reflection
of the divine order which alone would guarantee peace and prosperity. There was no clear line of demarcation between the concerns of the king and the concerns of the great bishops, which is
scarcely surprising when one considers the extent to which the
church had formulated these concerns.[41] Both had as a prime aim
the ordering of society according to the divine model. It is no surprise, therefore, to discover an interest in the role of kings in the
writings of Aelfric, a passion for law in the work of Wulfstan.
These were in the best traditions of church/king relations, especially as they had developed during Carolingian times. The king
might thus be expected to endow and protect institutions inextri-
cably involved with his own purposes and the great men most
closely bound to him to further those ends as well as ensuring
their own.

From a very concrete point of view it was the church which
prayed for the souls of its members and secured for them eternal

salvation. In this the role of monks and monasteries was very important. Although the idea of individual guilt, repentance, and penance was known in the early penitentials, there was still room for a more corporate view, for the idea that penance and prayer could be performed vicariously. The monasteries could act as powerhouses of prayer in society, the monks could pray for all. The role which the monks could play in relation to penance is brought out in some of Wulfstan's own statements on this subject. At the end of the penitential known as *Pseudo-Theodore,* with which Wulfstan was certainly familiar,[42] under a heading "De poenitentiarum diversitate," is a discussion of methods of lightening the load of penance on men who will no longer tolerate such harsh penances. And the methods largely consist of prayers and almsdeeds. That such prayers could be said by others, and not necessarily by the penitent himself, is made clear in Wulfstan's own reflections on penance in the same manuscript,[43] where he explains how a rich man may lighten his penance by fasting, almsdeeds, and having others say masses and prayers for him. Such functions on the part of the monks help explain the numerous benefactions, especially when coupled with the exhortations to penance which fill the works of both Wulfstan and Aelfric. The monks were seen as an elite force fighting the spiritual battles of others. And they were respected as warriors, as spiritual warriors, in a fighting age.[44] The parish priests, more humble in social origin and function, never shared their glory. The tenth and eleventh centuries saw the definition of the threefold division of medieval society. It has been suggested that this was not simply a division of society, but the definition of three elites, of the three most important groups in the minds of social theorists: the free peasants who colonized the land, the knight who fought to protect it, and the monk who prayed for its spiritual well-being.[45] It is interesting, therefore, to find two of the earliest clearly formulated references to this division in the works of Aelfric.[46] For all these reasons men endowed the church, and for the same reasons it was monks who were the main beneficiaries of this endowment.

The growth and reform of monasticism also had practical uses for the king. This was first an alliance with the wealth and influence of the church, a wealth which it was acquiring from sources

other than the king. It was also a way of guaranteeing loyalty, a
virtue in which some churchmen had shown themselves lacking.
The great bishops were normally drawn from among the nobility,
and as such their loyalty to the king was not automatic. The most
famous example of a rebellious bishop is Wulfstan I of York, who
helped lead a northern rebellion against West Saxon control in the
reign of Edred.[47] Bishops held too much power to be ignored by
the king, who kept close control over their appointment. But the
problems of finding suitably loyal *candidates* remained. Here the
new monasteries were a help. The literature which emerged from
the reformed abbeys was permeated with an ideology of loyalty
and obedience. The life of the monks was, as we have seen, centered
round a theme of prayer for the royal family. There was constant
gratitude for royal benevolence and protection. The loyalty of the
abbeys as owners of land and wielders of political power in their
own right was assured. But these loyal monks were also useful to
the king as potentially loyal bishops. The abbeys were an effective
school in the benefits of royal friendship to the church and as such
a good training ground for bishops. Monastic bishops dominated
the English church from the reign of Edgar until well into the
eleventh century.[48] During the reign of Aethelred, for example,
twenty-nine of the bishops who held office were previously monks
or abbots, over two-thirds of the total, and in many of the remaining ones we lack precise information. In this way not only did the
king benefit from the loyalty of former monks, but the English
church felt the influence of the monasteries in a much wider movement of reform.[49]

Indeed the monasticism which grew up in tenth-century England
was, like the church in general, far from being an ivory-tower
development. Abbots and monks were prominent in royal councils.
The witness lists of charters in the reigns of Edgar and Aethelred
show abbots surrounding the king on all occasions, as well as the
bishops who had always been present. Formal occasions when the
great men of the kingdom assembled around the king must have
had an overwhelmingly ecclesiastical air, attended as they could
be, by two archbishops, a dozen or more bishops, and anything up
to eighteen abbots with their retinues.[50] These guardians of the
divine will were natural royal councillors, and in far more than

ecclesiastical matters. In preamble after preamble to the laws reference is made to the witan "ge gehadode ge laewede" (V Atr) who had discussed and approved the enactment. The bishop's joint presidency, together with the ealdorman, of the shire court is well known. Ordinances concerning the coinage from the reign of Aethelred call on the bishop with other royal officials to be on the watch for false moneyers and traders with irregular coin.[51] Churchmen took part in royal judgments and might be entrusted with the task of communicating them, as on one occasion Abbot Aelfhere did to the shire court of Berkshire.[52] Their activities may often seem indistinguishable from those of the great magnates whom they resemble in wealth and power. Aescwig trained as a monk at the Old Minster, Winchester, and then as bishop of Dorchester was one of the leaders of the fyrd which fought against the Danes in 992; with him as joint leader were not only ealdormen Aelfric and Thored, but also bishop Aelfstan, probably the bishop of Rochester of that name.[53] Sigeric, who was first monk at Glastonbury, then abbot of St. Augustine's, bishop of Ramsbury, and finally archbishop of Canterbury, was instrumental as archbishop in making peace with the Viking host in 994. The treaty which survives as the so-called second law code of Aethelred, mentions the archbishop together with ealdormen Aelfric and Aethelweard as the three rulers of England south of the Thames,[54] and it seems possible that the archbishop did exercise control similar to that of an ealdorman in Kent.[55] Where ecclesiastics have left wills, their similarity to the nobles is again apparent. The will of Aelfric, who was archbishop of Canterbury after Sigeric, has survived.[56] Aelfric's ecclesiastical career is reflected in the will with his bequests to Abingdon, St. Alban's, and Christ Church, but so too are his secular concerns, for amongst his miscellaneous possessions is a fully armed long ship, which is to be used in the defense of Kent if need arise. But what such wills reveal in addition to secular involvement and a position analogous to that of the lay magnates is the extent to which these monastically trained men have been separated from their original backgrounds. Bequests to family feature, but not prominently. The monastic order itself has largely taken the place of family affiliations, and it is just this which made such men potentially good royal servants.

Wulfstan of York is one of the best examples of how churchmen could be involved in all contemporary concerns of the society.
His interest in law and his importance in the law-making of
Aethelred and Cnut has been amply demonstrated,[57] though the
picture of his total control over the king in these activities may
have been overdrawn.[58] None of the Anglo-Saxon laws would
have been preserved for us, were it not for the interest of men
like Wulfstan. Here the monastic revival and its aftermath are of
great importance, since most of the collections of law were made
at about this time, not only those which we associate with the
name of Wulfstan, but also the important collection on which the
Textus Roffensis was later based.[59] Wulfstan's political ideas and
writings are related, as we shall see, to his general role as a royal
adviser and to his special position in the north. Some of the
homilies and homiletic literature associated with his name suggest
the function of preaching for secular purposes, transmitting laws,[60]
royal orders, and the message of obedience and loyalty to the king.
The *Sermo Lupi* provides only the most obvious example of the
pulpit in the service of the king.[61] At the side of Wulfstan Aelfric,
abbot of the lesser monasteries of Cerne and Eynsham, tends to
appear as a scholar recluse and has been presented as such. But
this is not really true. "Pure" scholarship, divorced from practical
purposes, was rare in the tenth century. As Clemoes has pointed out,
Aelfric's writings have a definite educative program.[62] In addition
to his homilies, saints' lives and so on, all of which should be seen
in the context of Christian education, he produced more overtly
practical works; a rule of life for his own monks at Eynsham [63]
and pastoral letters for Bishops Wulfsige of Sherborne and Wulfstan of York.[64] And throughout his work there is continual reference to royal power, its origins, its scope, and to the needs of a
Christian society. Aelfric's writings were produced in the service
of the church and kingdom of his day. The fact that he often attended royal councils is only the simplest expression of his involvement.

The very range of documentation which survives from the late
tenth century, largely as a result of the revival, measures the broad
impact of monasticism on society and of monastic involvement in
it. The bulk of our surviving Anglo-Saxon land charters date from

the mid-tenth century onwards.[65] These charters were themselves the product of monastic scriptoria.[66] As the abbeys built up their landed endowments, many of them produced accounts of their acquisitions and of the litigation in which they became involved. Our first surviving English cartulary, the Worcester cartulary, dates from this period and is associated by Neil Ker with Wulfstan.[67] The *Liber Eliensis,* though not a cartulary, preserves a systematic account of the building-up of the abbey's endowment.[68] The second volume of this post-Conquest work contains detailed accounts of bequests and acquisitions from the time of the abbey's revival until well into the eleventh century. Much of it takes the form of accounts of litigation, into which the monks were so often drawn. These accounts are analogous to the vernacular accounts of court cases, which are again a novel phenomenon of this period. Some have survived separately, some have been copied into Gospel books, and often in the reign of Aethelred they were actually copied into the body of a Latin charter.[69] Similar records of endowments and litigation survive from Peterborough and Ramsey.[70] The growth of this court-centered literature must surely be related to the endless litigation which arose as a result of the revival itself and the land transactions which accompanied it. It has recently been argued that such of these documents as relate to the running of estates jut out as the mere tip of an iceberg of lost documentation on estate management and administration in general.[71] The Carolingian parallels which Campbell proposes are especially interesting in view of the arguments below about other similarities with Carolingian Frankia. It has certainly long been recognized that the monks were efficient estate managers,[72] and long-standing estate practices can be dated back to this period.[73] The impact of the monks on the economic and social life of their day is shown not simply by the content of these documents, but by their mere existence.

It is against the background of this total involvement that we should understand the ideas and writings of the major figures of the revival, for it is misleading to make distinctions between their theory and practice which would have been foreign to them. Take for example the question of status and its definition in the work of Wulfstan. This is a recurring theme. It is prominent in his mature work on political order, the *Institutes of Polity Civil and Ecclesi-astical*,[74] which is concerned with the various ranks of society and their positions and functions. Much more precisely, it is the theme of the pieces specifically concerned with status, *Had Geðyncðo, Mirce, Norðleoda Laga* and the *Northumbrian Priests' Law*.[75] The *Canons enacted under King Edgar*[76] are a rule of life for priests but touch upon the same theme. And general references to the position of various groups and the importance of their filling those positions correctly feature throughout Wulfstan's work, most notably in the *Sermo Lupi* and in the laws associated with him.[77] His specific concern in these works is first with the clergy; he attempts to define the position of various ranks of the clergy (*Had*), to equate them with their secular equivalents (as in *Norðleda laga* for bishops and archbishops), and to raise the status of priests. A priest who lives worthily should rank as a mass thane, with the same wergeld as a secular thane.[78] But Wulf-stan is also concerned with lay society not only in the general sense of defining functions, as in the *Institutes,* but also in the laying down of precise criteria for the enjoyment of thanely status in *Norðleoda laga* and *Geðyncðo*. Indeed the clearest statements on the status of the Old English nobility and on the five hides of land which was one condition of that status come from Wulfstan's pen.

All these specific regulations and definitions should be compared with Wulfstan's general position as it appears in the *Sermo Lupi,* for instance. This work castigates the English, explaining that God has allowed the heathen to punish them because of their sins, especially because the different ranks of society fail to perform their duty and to give due honor and respect to the church. The answer is penance and a return to an orderly existence. Inciden-tally we can see here how Wulfstan's concern with penance meshes with his political ideas. Wulfstan suggests that a dislocation of the essential *order* of society has caused the troubles of the English and only by restoring that order can peace be restored. But if order is to be restored, it must first be defined and promulgated, hence the work of Wulfstan in general and specifically his concern with law.

Wulfstan's general ideas of political theory were common in the early Middle Ages, and he certainly could have found them in his

Carolingian predecessors; namely, he thought that earthly society in order to prosper must reflect the divine order and that the major aim of government was to produce this order.[79] But Wulfstan's thought also reflects his position as archbishop of York. Some of his work is designed to regulate northern society on the southern pattern and to raise the status of the northern clergy, which especially needed reform. The lower standards which accompanied the poverty of the north are brought out clearly in a comparison between the pastoral letters which Aelfric wrote for Wulfstan and for Wulfsige, bishop of Sherborne.[80] The letter for Wulfstan concentrates on fundamentals, such as cleanliness of altar vessels and respect for the church building, and on the basic Christian morality. In the absence of monasticism Wulfstan was concerned to reform the secular clergy, and to do this he produced for them a rule of life, in many ways approximating monasticism, that stressed community, orderliness of behavior, and a rule of common conduct. His specific recommendations for northern lay society reflected its very different pattern.[81] The Yorkshire Domesday, for example, shows a host of freemen holding tiny portions of land, yet calling themselves thanes. Wulfstan asserted that the possession of military equipment in itself was insufficient grounds for such thanely status and affirmed the land requirements for it in an attempt to regulate this northern society along lines closer to those of the south and midlands. And all his definitions of thanely status stress another point, the necessity of royal service in order to enjoy noble position. In this enhancement of royal power Wulfstan reveals a typical concern for the growth of royal authority.

Wulfstan must have felt a need to redefine the position of the clergy and of the church and ecclesiastical property [82] in the wake of the great upheaval which the revival represents. In simple numbers and in sheer landed wealth the church was much more prominent in 1000 than it had been in 900. Because this prominence could bring problems, there was need for a new statement of the church's place in society, and Wulfstan provided the first such statement since the time of Aethelberht of Kent.

With Wulfstan there is the need to regularize, to codify, to provide the basis of order which is present in the work of so many

great ecclesiastics in the ninth and tenth centuries and which was
such an important legacy of the Carolingian past. At the same
time, and in no way divorced from this, are the concerns of a
northern archbishop coping with the aftermath of the monastic
revival. In his work on status, as in all his work, Wulfstan is
severely practical even at his most theoretical, a product of his
own political and intellectual world.

Both Aelfric and Wulfstan wished to define and interpret the
king's role. Aware of their kings' illustrious lineage, they praise
Alfred and Athelstan, successful warrior kings, but especially
Edgar, the friend of monks.[83] However, these kings were not held
up to the reigning king, Aethelred, primarily because he was
judged an incompetent follower of great traditions, as is sometimes
suggested.[84] Rather they are holding up to the king a mirror of
action in the time-honored fashion. Nor does it seem that Aelfric
and Wulfstan are merely passing on existing traditions, important
though those traditions are for their work.[85] There is evidence to
suggest that they were molding them in a new way,[86] especially in
stressing elements of holy kingship. Like the Carolingians, they
stress the importance of the king maintaining the social order,
defining and promulgating laws in the interest of that order, and
of "translating into reality Christian doctrine." [87] But an essential
element in Carolingian ideas had been the ideal of warrior kingship
on the Old Testament model,[88] an ideal necessary for the extension
of Christendom. In the light of this intellectual inheritance the
views of Aelfric are particularly interesting. It is Edgar, the pious
king, who is praised more than Alfred. And the days of Edgar
were happy and peaceful precisely because he furthered Christendom and fostered monasticism, the connection between this and his
political triumphs is explicit.[89] Aelfric chooses to write the lives of
holy kings like Oswald, whose victories are related to his faith,[90]
and Edmund, who guides his people in righteousness and throws
away his weapons to accept martyrdom rather than submit to the
heathen.[91] There is obviously a military element here, but the rest
of Aelfric's writing on this subject suggests that it is the holy
king whom he is praising. The king is described in religious terms:
he is Christ's messenger to the Christian people; [92] it is the duty
of others to fight his battles for him, since the king now shares

with the church the function of upholding his armies by prayer;[93] the role of the king as shepherd of the Christian flock is a direct parallel of that of Christ.[94] The warrior image is not totally eclipsed; like Christ, for example, the king will lay down his life, if necessary, for his people. But the emphasis has shifted. Increasingly the military problems are seen as an outcome of failure to live up to the image of Christian kingship. Of *De octo vitiis et de duodecim abusivis* Aelfric translates the section on the *Rex Iniquus* in full.[95] The rule of a wise and pious king will be directly reflected in the state of his people, Aelfric says elsewhere.[96] These statements should not be thought simply to reflect the reigning king's incompetence and the consequent difficulty of stressing warrior kingship. They seem to represent something more fundamental, viz., a real shift of emphasis in the definition of kingship. The "holy king" as an ideal triumphed following the monastic revival, and it is in the works of Aelfric that this change is especially evident.

The church was a great aid to the king in the creation and propagation of his role. It was in fact the most effective propaganda machine of its day. It should be noted, for instance, that most of the ideas mentioned above appear in sermons some of which were certainly designed to be preached before the *witan* (see notes 93 and 94). The literary and artistic models of the day, both owing much to ecclesiastical inspiration, production, and patronage, are drenched in royal imagery. Christ is portrayed dressed as a king, while the Christ in majesty with its royal pose is a favored theme.[97] The revival produced a minor crop of lives of saintly kings, those in the works of Aelfric already referred to, the *Life of Saint Edmund*,[98] which Dunstan commissioned Abbo of Fleury to write, and the *Passio Sancti Edwardi*.[99] The first surviving English work of political theory, Wulfstan's *Institutes of Polity*, inevitably concerns the king. We have already seen Aelfric reworking the old Irish tract on political life, the *De duodecim abusivis saeculi*, wherein he gives more prominence to the king than the original does and takes the opportunity to stress that the king is above criticism or removal. Statements of a broadly "political" nature, usually concerned with the place of the king, are scattered through many of contemporary works. Over and above the literary and artistic image the church was deeply

involved in creating the visible liturgical image of the coronation.
The church had already added religious elements to the old secular
king-making ceremonies. Here more than anywhere it could
publicize to the world the king's special position above all other
laymen. He alone received anointing, like the clergy. The ceremony, performed in church by two archbishops and a concourse of
bishops and abbots on a king dressed in ecclesiastical fashion, pro-
claimed to the world his special role in the sight of God.[100] It also
clearly demonstrated that the king in this role had to rely on the
church. Present work on the coronation *ordines* does not suggest
that they underwent any special evolution as a result of the
monastic revival.[101] But the second anointing of Edgar at Bath in
his thirtieth year was almost certainly a carefully stage-managed
event to underline the new relations between king and church and
to form part of an elaborate political theatre in that year which
included the ritual rowing on the Dee, the submission of the king
of the Scots, and probably the reform of the coinage.[102] This
masterly concurrence of events cannot have been without ecclesiastical inspiration.

The religious symbolism was mirrored in what are generally
considered purely secular affairs. The Old English monarchy ruled
over a kingdom the growing wealth of which was reflected in a
flourishing coinage,[103] and whose whole organization King Edgar
remodeled. If we look at the various issues minted during the
reigns of Edgar and his son Aethelred, we find that the pattern
which differentiated one issue from another was with only one
exception religious: Small Cross, Long Cross, Hand of God,
Agnus Dei. Only one issue, the Helmet coinage of Aethelred,
shows a secular militaristic imagery. Even in these universal
symbols of royal power, the coins used throughout the kingdom,
the king is associated in the eyes of his subjects with the divine.

The king surrounded by his ecclesiastical councillors was a
potent symbol of his relations with the church. This close proximity to the king in his council helps explain why the church could
hope for success in molding the king in their image. The importance of these councillors was recognized. Wulfstan wrote at least
one sermon to be preached before the witan reminding them of
their duties.[104] Both he and Aelfric were acutely aware that the

church must speak out and fulfil its role of counsel. Bishops and priests are the *bydelas* who must set a good example to all.[105] The exaltation of the bishop's role in Wulfstan's writings has recently been demonstrated.[106] But the most explicit statement on the point is Aelfric's sermon for the Sunday after the Ascension.[107] The gospel of the day describes the imminent arrival of the Holy Ghost, whose spirit will fill the apostles and their consequent mission in the world, with all its social and political consequences. The apostles were *Cristes bydelas*. When the Holy Ghost came down on them, they were given great wisdom, so that they could preach to kings and ealdormen. This is a general homily on counsel, but it is primarily an admonition to the bishops and abbots, those ecclesiastical councillors who should follow the apostles' example. It is their special function to advise and admonish, just as the king's special function is to rule. Like many of the late Carolingian writers, Aelfric accords a high place to the church in political affairs; but unlike them, he does not use it to undermine the position of the king in any way.[108] In England after the revival the king and the monks lived in great harmony.

Perhaps nowhere did the joint concerns of king and church come together so closely and clearly as in the laws. The Anglo-Saxon monarchy maintained a tradition of law-giving from the first arrival of Christianity with Augustine through to the reign of the last convert king, Cnut. It was an area of royal activity in which the church always played the greatest part.[109] The first written English laws appear at the same time as Augustine in Kent; the last to survive are those of Cnut, so closely associated with the work of Archbishop Wulfstan. Throughout the intervening period it was the church which was responsible for preserving the Anglo-Saxon laws. Some instances show that the laws owe their written form to the interest of ecclesiastics, for whom law was the principal way to create and maintain an orderly society. It is not always clear that the laws were originally issued in written form or intended to be anything more than simple orders or instructions. Their survival in any form is often solely due to the church. The role of Wulfstan in the laws of Aethelred and Cnut should be seen against this background. Wulfstan was certainly an important councillor to both these kings and may,

especially in the case of Cnut's codification, have been responsible
for the decision to issue certain laws. But the surviving texts of
V to X Aethelred and I and II Cnut have been shown to be
couched in such perfect Wulfstan phraseology and so deeply concerned with his own especial interests that he would appear to
have written them in their entirety. [110] And so he doubtless had,
though not in the accepted sense. For what we seem to see in many
of these cases is Wulfstan committing to writing orders which the
king may have issued in very different form. Wulfstan worked
these commands into a homiletic form together with other material
which was purely his own. Often several versions of the same
orders have survived to perplex historians, as in the case of V and
VI Aethelred. The indications are that Wulfstan intended to use
the reworked material as sermons, which gives yet another un-
expected insight into the methods of promulgating Anglo-Saxon
law.[111] It is surely more than a coincidence that these codes are
associated so closely in time with the similarly discursive IV
Edgar, which may well have fulfilled the same function. The
repercussions of the revival were thus wide indeed.

Aethelred issued at least two codes concerned solely with ecclesiastical matters. VII Aethelred calls for penance to placate the
wrath of God and so avert the Viking menace; and VIII Aethelred
concerns the behavior of monks and priests, Sunday buying and
selling, the nonpayment of tithes, and similar religious offenses.
VII Aethelred is unique among Old English laws, though there is
a similar spirit in IV Edgar, issued in time of plague and again
designed to quell divine wrath. Few clearer indications exist that
the age totally confused the religious and the secular than this
royal command to prayer and penance as a remedy for the ills of
the Viking invasion. It is wrong to see it as simply a weak king's
response to an overwhelming situation. It was a wholly natural
reaction for men accustomed to believe in a sympathy between the
affairs of God and man and aware of the need to maintain a
harmony between them. The threats of doom if God's laws were
not obeyed were not mere idle thunderings.

The eighth code of Aethelred was aimed at offenses against
ecclesiastical law. Such throwing of royal prestige behind their
enforcement has a long ancestry; in England it stretches back to

the seventh century and the laws of Wihtred of Kent. During the tenth century many kings issued ecclesiastical ordinances separate from their secular codes. As the preamble to VI Aethelred suggests, these codes might emerge from meetings with a large but not exclusively, clerical element. The Latin paraphrase of this code calls its articles the synodal decrees from a meeting at Pentecost, where Archbishops Aelfheah and Wulfstan dominated amongst great men of England, and when the archbishops had much to say "as if divinely inspired" about the restoration of true religious worship and about the improvement of secular affairs. Meetings such as these, equally concerned with crime and sin, could produce commands relating to both. The tidy-minded churchmen who committed them to writing might sort them out one from the other into separate secular and ecclesiastical codes, but we should not assume too clear a distinction in origin or intention. VIII Aethelred has ancestors of the same nature in I Athelstan, I Edmund, II Edgar, and later, II Cnut. In spite of their concern with tithes, burial dues, the status of churches, and the behavior of vagrant monks, the orders were issued in the king's name. And it is not merely a question of guaranteeing enforcement. Like the Carolingians and Ottonians, the Anglo-Saxon kings took very seriously their own part in the alliance with the church; they did not see it as a subordinate or secondary role. It was their duty, as much as that of the church, to ensure the people's safety. They too wished to ensure that society was orderly and pleasing to God, just as their pagan ancestors had sought to preserve the luck of the tribe through their personal actions. This might often involve interference with the church itself to be certain that the church too was living as it should. The remarks placed in the mouth of Edgar in the *Regularis Concordia* about his desire to regulate the lives of all monks, lest their deviations be a source of scandal, are not a cover for what was in reality the concern of the monks alone. They are a serious statement of the role which the king saw himself playing in the reform. It was a role which could involve much interference in the church's own affairs, an interference still welcomed rather than resented by a church seeking powerful allies.

In this close relationship between church and society, and especially between church and king, the English situation is very

like that which existed in other strong monarchies in the early
Middle Ages. The Carolingians in the eighth and ninth centuries
and the Ottonians in the tenth and eleventh show many parallels.
All three are instances of the close cooperation between kings and
churchmen and in all three the use of organized monasticism was
crucial. The contribution of the church to the Carolingians was
indispensable. In the eighth century it helped establish their right
to rule, while at the height of their power both Charlemagne and
Louis the Pious worked with their bishops and abbots to achieve
the realization of a Christian empire, a total renewal of society.[112]
It is not surprising that close analysis of the works of Wulfstan
has revealed his knowledge of Carolingian authors and his debt to
their ideas.[113] The late Old English monarchy has lately been seen
as a continuation of Carolingian kingship, its methods, and
ideals.[114] Their Ottonian contemporaries were even more consciously renewing the Carolingian Empire [115] and used a similar
alliance with the church. The eleventh century saw changes in
ideas and practice which would destroy the harmony between
church and king, but around the year 1000 these changes were not
apparent in England. The mutual benefit of the alliance was still
uppermost. Kings could still see the advancement of church power
as in some ways an advancement of their own, and an archbishop
could see no contradiction in drafting a law code to be preached
as a homily and ending it with the words:

> Let us do as is necessary for us, let us take as our example
> what former rulers wisely decreed, Athelstan and Edmund,
> and Edgar who came last—how they honored God and kept
> God's tribute as long as they lived.
> And let us love one God with our inmost heart and heed
> God's law as well as ever we can.
> And let us zealously honor the true Christian religion and
> utterly despise all heathen practice.
> And let us loyally support one royal lord. . . .
>   (VIII Aethelred 43–44)

NOTES

1. See, e.g., his codifications of Anglo-Saxon law, I and II Cnut, and his work of political theory, the *Institutes of Polity, Civil and Ecclesiastical,* ed. Karl Jost, Swiss studies in English, 47 (Bern, 1959), the final draft of which seems to have been written after the accession of Cnut.

2. The standard account of the revival is still David M.Knowles, *Monastic Order in England,* 2nd ed. (Cambridge, 1966), but much important work has been done by Eric John. A number of John's essays are collected in *Orbis Britanniae* (Leicester, 1966). On Cluny, see Joan Evans, *Monastic Life at Cluny* (Oxford, 1931). On the Lotharingian movement, Kassius Hallinger, *Gorze-Cluny,* 2 vols. (Rome, 1950–51).

3. Rafaello Morghen, "Riforma monastica e Spiritualita Cluniacense," *Spiritualita Cluniacense, Convegni del Centro di studi sulla spiritualita medievale, 1958* (Todi, 1960), pp. 33–56.

4. E. Werner, *Die gesellschaftlichen Grundlagen der Klosterreform im 11 Jht.* (Berlin, 1953), an essentially Marxist approach.

5. G. Duby, "Les origines de la chevalerie," *Ordinamenti Militaria nell'alto medioevo, Settimane di studio del Centro Italiano di studi sull'alto medioevo* 15 (Spoleto, 1968), pp. 739–61, and "The Diffusion of Cultural Patterns in Feudal Society," *Past and Present* 39 (1968) : 3–10.

6. Jean F. Lemarignier, "Structures monastiques et structures politiques dans la France de la fin du Xe et des debuts du XIe siecle," *Settimane di studi del Centro Italiano di studi sull'alto medioevo* 4 (Spoleto, 1957) ; cf. David C. Douglas, *William the Conqueror* (London, 1964), pp. 105–33.

7. The most recent general statement of their European significance is in G. Duby, *Warriors and Peasants* (London, 1974).

8. On these last points, see especially B. Topfer "Reliquienkult und Pilgerbewegung zur zeit der Klosterreform im

burgundisch-aquitanischen gebiet," *Vom Mittelalter zur
Neuzeit,* ed. H. Sproemberg and H. Kretzschmar (Berlin,
1956), pp. 420–39. On the Cluniacs and reform, see
H.E.J. Cowdrey, *The Cluniacs and the Gregorian Reform*
(Oxford, 1970).

9. *Regularis Concordia,* tr. Thomas Symons (London, 1953),
   p. 3, and p. li.

10. See, e.g., *Memorials of St. Dunstan,* ed. William Stubbs, Rolls
    Series 63 (1874), pp. 376–77 and 378–80, two letters from
    Fleury thanking Dunstan for his kindness to Abbo,
    requesting the return of books loaned, and commenting on
    the life of Edmund which Abbo had promised to write.

11. *Regularis Concordia,* p. li.

12. J. Armitage Robinson, *Life and Times of Saint Dunstan*
    (Oxford, 1923) is still useful for the basic facts of
    Dunstan's career.

13. The role of Edgar and the possible motives for his actions
    have been discussed by Eric John, "The King and the
    Monks in the Tenth Century Revival," *Orbis Britanniae*
    (Leicester, 1966), pp. 154–80.

14. See my "Royal Government in the Reign of Aethelred II,"
    (Phil. thesis, Oxford University, 1973), pp. 106–11.

15. For a description of this process at Winchester, see John,
    "The Beginning of the Benedictine Reform in England,"
    Orbis Britanniae, especially pp. 249–54.

16. On the northern diocese in the tenth century, see the excellent
    study by Dorothy Whitelock, "Dealings of the Kings of
    England with the North in the Tenth and Eleventh
    Centuries," *Anglo Saxons, Studies in Some Aspects of
    Their History and Culture Presented to Bruce Dickins,*
    ed. Peter A.M. Clemoes (London, 1959), pp. 70–88.

17. A.J. Robertson, *Anglo-Saxon Charters* (Cambridge, 1956),
    no. 54.

18. Statistics of the Wealth of the Benedictine Abbeys in Knowles,
    pp. 164–73.

20. *Regularis Concordia,* pp. 5, 13, 14, 16, 21, 22.

21. Ibid., pp. 2–3.

22. Ibid., p. 6.

23. Ibid., p. 7.
24. This aristocracy is more fully discussed in Stafford, "Royal Government," Chapter VI, Royal Servants, and Chapter VII, Royal Governance and the Old English Nobility. The relationships between royalty and nobility are brought out in the genealogical tables, pp. 436–37.
25. A detailed discussion of this family is in Cyril Hart, "Athelstan Half-King and His Family," *Anglo-Saxon England* 2 (1973) : 115–44.
26. *Liber Eliensis,* ed. E.O. Blake, Camden Society, Series 3, vol. 92 (1962), Book II, chap. 7, pp. 79–80.
27. This became apparent later in the eleventh century. See the eventual dominance of the family of the Mercian ealdorman over these monasteries, *Anglo-Saxon Chronicle* MS E. s.a. 1066. Leofric, nephew of Leofric of Mercia, was abbot of Peterborough, Burton, Coventry, Crowland, and Thorney.
28. On the reaction in general, see D.J.V. Fisher, "The Anti-Monastic Reaction in the Reign of Edward the Martyr," *Cambridge Historical Journal* 10 (1952) : 254ff. On the precise saving of the Fenland monasteries, see *Vita Oswaldi,* in *Historians of the Church of York and Its Archbishops,* ed. J. Raine, Rolls Series 71 (1879–94), Vol. I, pp. 443–45.
29. Aelfflaed's will is in Dorothy Whitelock, *Anglo-Saxon Wills* (Cambridge, 1930) no. 15. *Liber Eliensis* Bk. II, chap. 62, pp. 133–36 records Brihtnoth's gift of fourteen estates to Ely, and chap. 63 p. 136 his wife's gift of four estates.
30. On the family of Aethelweard, see the introduction to the *Chronicle of Aethelweard,* ed. A. Campbell (London, 1952). The foundation charters are printed J.M. Kemble, *Codex Diplomaticus Aevi Saxonici* (London, 1839–48), Cerne no. 656, Eynsham no. 714. A better edition of the latter is in the *Eynsham Cartulary* ed. H.E. Salter, *Oxford Historical Society* 49 (1907), pp. 19–28.
31. Foundation charter printed H.P.R. Finberg, *Tavistock Abbey* (Cambridge, 1951), pp. 278–83.
32. *O.S. Facsimiles* Vol. III, Anglesey 2, Kemble 710.
33. On the general position of this family of the North, see White-

lock, "Dealings . . . ," pp. 80–87. A more specific study of the importance of this family is Peter H. Sawyer, "The Charters of Burton Abbey and the Unification of England," *Northern History,* 10 (1975) : 28–39.

34. The probable exception, Eynsham, does not seem to have been in Aethelmaer's ealdormanry of West Wessex, though the bounds of his jurisdiction are not certain.

35. See note 28, and also Stafford, "Royal Government," chap. I, Succession to the Throne, especially pp. 91–100. I do not believe that the succession crisis and reaction against monasticism were as distinct as Fisher suggests.

36. The letter is printed *Memorials of Saint Dunstan,* ed. William Stubbs, Rolls Series 63 (1874), pp. 396–97.

37. *Liber Eliensis,* Book II, chap. 11, pp. 84–91.

38. E. John, "King and the Monks. . . . ," takes a similar line to this but stresses the overt political role of the monasteries more.

39. Whitelock, *Wills* no. 15. Aethelmaer gave this and other lands to his son-in-law to acquire Eynsham.

40. Sawyer *Handlist* no. 847, printed Cyril Hart, *Early Charters of Eastern England* (Leicester, 1966), pp. 186–87.

41. An excellent introduction to this vast subject is R.W. Southern, *Western Society and the Church in the Middle Ages* (London, 1969). On the church's political theory and its role in relation to kingship, see W. Ullmann, *The Carolingian Renaissance and the Idea of Kingship* (London, 1969) and J.M. Wallace-Hadrill, *Early Germanic Kingship in England and on the Continent* (Oxford, 1971).

42. It is copied in CCCC 265, a MS discussed in detail by M. Bateson, "A Worcester Cathedral Book of Ecclesiastical Collections made c. A.D. 1000," *English Historical Review* 10 (1895) : 712–31. Printed B. Thorpe, *Ancient Laws and Institutes,* vol. II (London, 1840), pp. 1–62.

43. *Be Mightigum Mannum* printed by Thorpe as part of *The Canons Enacted under King Edgar.*

44. On warrior monks and the cultural patterns of the feudal aristocracy, see G. Duby (note 5).

45. J. Le Goff, "Note sur une société tripartie, ideologie monarchique et renouveau économique dans la chrétienté du IXe au XIIe

siècles," *L'Europe aux IXe–XIIe siècles, Aux origines des États nationaux* (Warsaw, 1968), pp. 63ff.

46. His first reference is in the story of the Maccabees, *LS* 25, pp. 121–25: The second is in the letter to the thane Sigewulf, "On the Old and New Testament," *Old English Version of the Heptateuch,* ed. S.J. Crawford EETS 160 (1922), 1207ff.

47. *Anglo-Saxon Chronicle* s.a.

48. For a list of monastic bishops, see Knowles, *Monastic Order,* Appendix IV, pp. 697–701.

49. See R.R. Darlington, "Ecclesiastical Reform in the Late Old English Period," *English Historical Review* 51 (1936): 385–428, which brings out the importance of these monastic bishops for general reform.

50. See, e.g., Kemble, *Codex Diplomaticus,* 684, a grant to Abingdon in 993 or the foundation charters of Eynsham and Burton, notes 30 and 32.

51. IV Aethelred 8.

52. Robertson, *Anglo-Saxon Charters* no. 66.

53. *Anglo-Saxon Chronicle* Ms C s.a., 992.

54. II Aethelred Preamble.

55. See Stafford, "Royal Government," pp. 282–83.

56. Whitelock, *Wills,* no. 18.

57. Dorothy Whitelock, "Archbishop Wulfstan, Homilist and Statesman," *Transaction of the Royal Historical Society* ser. IV, 24 (1942): 25–45; "Wulfstan and the Laws of Cnut," *Engish Historical Review* 63 (1948): 433–52; "Wulfstan's Authorship of Cnut's Laws," *English Historical Review* 69 (1955): 72–85; Dorothy Bethurum, "Six Anonymous Old English Codes," *Journal of English and Germanic Philology* 49 (1950): 449–63.

58. See Stafford, "Royal Government," chapter on Laws and Lawmaking.

59. Ed. Peter H. Sawyer, EEMF 7 and 8 (Copenhagen, 1957 and 1962). The regnal list on folios 7v–8v ends with the name of Aethelred, which suggests an original compilation in his reign.

60. See Stafford, "Royal Government," chapter on Laws for this interpretation of the laws associated with Wulfstan.

K. Sisam, "The Relationship of Aethelred's Codes V and
VI," *Studies in the History of Old English Literature*
(Oxford, 953), pp. 278–87, also feels that VI Aethelred
may have been a sermon intended to be preached before the
higher clergy.

61. *Sermo Lupi ad Anglos,* ed. Dorothy Whitelock, 3rd ed. (London, 1963).

62. Peter A.M. Clemoes, "The Chronology of Aelfric's Works,"
Anglo Saxons, Studies . . . presented to Dickins, pp. 212–47. See Godden, below.

63. The so-called "Letter to the Monks of Eynsham," ed.
M. Bateson, *Computus Rolls of the Obedientiaries of
St. Swithun's Priory, Winchester,* ed. G.W. Kitchin, Hants
Record Society (1892), Appendix VII, pp. 171ff.

64. B. Fehr, *Die Hirtenbriefe Aelfrics* (Hamburg, 1914), nos. 1, 2a, 2, 3, II & III.

65. See Sawyer, *Handlist of Anglo-Saxon Charters* (London, 1968). Well over 900 of the 1539 charters listed are post 950.

66. P. Chaplais, "The Anglo-Saxon Chancery, from the Diploma
to the Writ," *Journal of the Society of Archivists* 3, 4
(1966) : 160ff.

67. This is the early part of *Hemingi Chartularium Ecclesie
Wigorniensis,* ed. T. Hearne (Oxford, 1723). For Ker's
study of this, see *Studies in Medieval History presented to
F.M. Powicke,* ed. R.W. Hunt, W.A. Pantin, and R.W.
Southern (Oxford, 1948), pp. 49ff. For his identification of
the hand of Wulfstan in the MS, see "The Handwriting of
Archbishop Wulfstan," *England Before the Conquest:
Studies in Primary Sources presented to D. Whitelock,* ed.
Peter A.M. Clemoes and Kathleen Hughes (Cambridge, 1971), pp. 315–31.

68. *Liber Eliensis,* ed. E.O. Blake, Book II.

69. I have discussed these documents, their nature and significance,
in greater detail in "Royal Government," pp. 62–70. For
examples of them, see Robertson, *Charters,* nos. 59, 63, 66, 69, etc.

70. For Peterborough, see Robertson, *Charters* no. 40. Details of
Ramsey benefactions are contained in *Chronicon Ramesiensis,* ed. W.D. Macray, Rolls Series 83 (1886).

71. J. Campbell, "Observations on English Government from the Tenth Century to the Eleventh," *Transaction of the Royal Historical Society* Ser. 5, 25 (1975), pp. 38–54.

72. See R.V. Lennard, *Rural England* (Oxford, 1959) *passim*, but especially pp. 130–41. Although his arguments are for the mid-eleventh century, the estate structures which he discusses are already fully formed.

73. E. Miller, *The Abbey and Bishopric of Ely* (Cambridge, 1941), pp. 38–39 dates the farming system to the time of Abbot Leofsige 1029–35.

74. Ed. and printed Jost, note 1.

75. Printed F. Liebermann, *Die Gesetze der Angelsächsen* (Halle, 1903–16), Vol. I, pp. 458–68 and pp. 380 ff. The pieces on status are discussed by Bethurum "Six Old English Codes. . . ."

76. Ed. and printed Roger Fowler, EETS 266 (1972).

77. E. g., V Aethelred 4.

78. V Aethelred 9.1, VI Aethelred 5.3, VIII Aethelred 28, I Cnut 2, *Canons* 68b.

79. See Ullmann and Wallace-Hadrill (note 41); also J.M. Wallace Hadrill, "Via Regia of the Carolingian Age," *Trends in Medieval Political Theory,* ed. B. Smalley (Oxford, 1965), pp. 22–41, rpt. in his *Early Medieval History* (London, 1975), pp. 181–200.

80. As note 64.

81. See G.W.S. Barrow, "Northern English Society in the Early Middle Ages," *Northern History* 4 (1969): 1ff. and Glanville R. Jones, "Basic Patterns of Settlement Distribution in Northern England," *The Advancement of Science* 18 (1961): 192–200.

82. See also here *Grið,* printed Liebermann, *Die Gesetze der Angelsächsen,* Vol. I, pp. 470–73.

83. Aelfric in the homily on Judges in the *Old English Heptateuch* and the Life of St. Swithun, LS 21, and Wulfstan's panegyric on Edgar in *Anglo-Saxon Chronicle* MS D s.a. 963 and at the end of VIII Aethelred.

84. By, e.g., W. Braekman, "Wyrdwriteras: An unpublished Aelfricean text in MS Hatton 115," *Revue Belge de Philologie et d'Histoire* 44 (1960): 959–70 and also ed.

Pope, SS 2, pp. 725–33; and cf. the views of Dorothy Bethurum, "Regnum et Sacerdotium in the early eleventh century," *England Before the Conquest,* especially pp. 137–39.

85. See, e.g., Karl Jost, "Einige Wulfstantexte und ihre Quellen," *Anglia* 56 (1932): 265–315; M. Bateson "Letter to the Monks of Eynsham," D. Bethurum, *Homilies of Wulfstan* (Oxford, 1957), pp. 1–8.

86. See Joel T. Rosenthal, "Edward the Confessor and Robert the Pious: Eleventh Century Kingship and Biography," *Medieval Studies* 23 (1971): 7–20. In "Regnum and Sacerdotium" Bethurum also notices a shift of emphasis, though she feels that Wulfstan's stress on the growing power of the church is more important.

87. W. Ullmann, *Short History of the Papacy* (London, 1972), p. 98.

88. J.M. Wallace Hadrill, "Via Regia . . ."

89. See Life of St. Swithun, LS 21, p. 468.

90. LS 26, p. 132.

91. LS 32, p. 320.

92. VIII Aethelred 2.1.

93. E.g.; "Wyrdwriteras us secgað. . . ." ed. Pope, SS 22.

94. *Dominica Post Ascensionem Domini,* ed. Pope, SS 9, 46ff.

95. Ed. Richard Morris, *Old English Homilies,* Series I, Part 2, EETS 34 (1868), Appendix pp. 296–304.

96. *De Letania Maiore,* CH II, ed. B. Thorpe, pp. 314ff. especially p. 318.

97. Among many examples, see the figure of Christ, Trinity Coll Cambridge Ms B 10.4 reproduced in D. Talbot Rice, *English Art 871–1100* (Oxford, 1932), no. 62, and compare the figure of Edgar in Cotton Tiberius A.iii f.2b reproduced as the frontispiece in Symons's *Regularis Concordia.*

98. Passio S. Edmundi, *Memorials of St. Edmond's Abbey,* ed. T. Arnold, Rolls Series 96 (1890), vol. I.

99. *Edward, King and Martyr,* ed. C. Fell, Leeds Texts and Monographs, New Series, no. 3 (Leeds, 1971).

100. Coronation of King Edgar described in *Vita Oswaldi,* pp. 436–38.

101. C.A. Bouman, *Sacring and Crowning: the Development of the Latin Ritual for the Anointing of Kings and the Coronation of an Emperor before the Eleventh Century* (Groningen, 1957) ; P.E. Schramm, "Die Kronung bei den Westfranken und Angelsächsen von 878 bis um 1000," *Zeitschrift der Savigny-Stiftung fur Rechtsgeschichte, Kanonistische Abteilung* 23 (1939) : 117–268; P.L. Ward, "An Early Version of the Anglo-Saxon Coronation Ceremony," *English Historical Review* 57 (1942) : 345–61. J. Nelson, "National Synods, Kingship as Office and Royal Anointing: An Early Medieval Syndrome," *Studies in Church History* 7, ed. G.J. Cuming and D. Baker (Cambridge, 1971), pp. 41–59 associates the rite of anointing with the upsurge of synodal activity and feels that Edgar's anointing did mark a new departure, though it is not clear how. For the question of whether it was a first or second coronation, see E. John, *Orbis Britanniae,* pp. 276–88, and H.G. Richardson and G.O. Sayles, *The Governance of England* (Edinburgh, 1963), pp. 397–412.

102. *Anglo-Saxon Chronicle* MS C & D & E s.a. 973, Florence of Worcester vol. i pp. 142–3 ; Roger of Wendover s.a. 975 ; R.H.M. Dolley and D.M. Metcalf, "The Reform of the English Coinage Under Eadgar," *Anglo-Saxon Coins,* ed, R.H.M. Dolley (London, 1961), pp. 136–168, especially p. 152.

103. The literature on this subject is vast. *Anglo-Saxon Coins,* edited by Dolley, is the best starting point. Recent volumes of the *British Numismatic Journal* and the *Numismatic Chronicle* contain much more on the subject.

104. Napier 50 and 51 both seem to have been sermons intended to be preached before the witan.

105. Aelfric, *De Letania Maiore,* p. 319, Wulfstan, *Be Biscophadum,* Bethurum Homily no. XVII, p. 243.

106. Bethurum, "Regnum and Sacerdotium."

107. Ed. Pope SS I. If we do not accept that lines 20–82 are "tangential," the whole fits together well as a work on **counsel.**

108. Ullmann, *Carolingian Renaissance and the Idea of Kingship,*

Lecture V "The King's Stunted Sovereignty," especially
pp. 114–121 stressing the importance of men like Hincmar
in developing the idea of clerical restriction on the king.

109. Much of what follows is based on my "Royal Government"
chapter on Laws and Law-making.

110. See note 57 and Jost, *Wulfstanstudien,* Swiss Studies in
English 23 (Bern, 1950).

111. I have discussed this question fully in my "Royal Government," pp. 247–59.

112. See Ullmann, *Carolingian Renaissance,* and F.L. Ganshof,
"The Church and the Royal Power in the Frankish Monarchy
Under Pippin III and Charlemagne," *Carolingians and the
Frankish Monarchy* (London, 1971), pp. 205–39, where he
demonstrates the kings' awareness of their role in relation
to the church.

113. See note 85.

114. J. Campbell, "Observations on English Government. . . ."

115. P.E. Schramm, "Gli imperatori della casa di Sassonia alla luce
della simbolistica dello Stato," *Renovatio Imperii,* Atti della
giornata internazionale di studio per il millenaria, Ravenna,
1961, Societa di Studi Romagnoli (Faenza, 1963), pp. 15–
40.

MILTON McC. GATCH ❦ THE ACHIEVEMENT OF AELFRIC & HIS COLLEAGUES IN EUROPEAN PERSPECTIVE

It is a curious fact that the Old English vernacular preaching texts have never achieved an international reputation; they have not even been viewed in a perspective broader than the insular. They have, of course, been studied with an eye to exposing their Latin sources. In recent years several works have enhanced our appreciation of the two most important sermon writers, Aelfric, abbot of Eynsham, and Wulfstan, archbishop of York. Within a few years editors now at work on inadequately studied anonymous homilies in the Blickling and Vercelli manuscripts, as well as a number of other less well-known collections, will have done a similar service for that anonymous, but remarkably productive, company of English homily writers from the mid-tenth century to the Conquest and beyond.[1] Yet with the exception of a few essays on their influence on early Norse preaching, there have been no studies of these English preachers' materials which attempt to view them in their European setting. Rarely has anyone from beyond the eastern shore of the Channel examined them, other than specialists in English or Germanic philology, and these few continental philologists tend to view the sermons as narrowly as their English and American colleagues. Scholars have been aware of the references to preaching and teaching in the vernacular in ecclesiastical legislation of the Carolingian period, but the question of how the actual achievement of churchmen elsewhere in Europe measures against that of the Anglo-Saxons has not been pursued in a sustained way.

Recently I have had occasion to discuss one aspect of this wider setting, the place of the homilies in liturgical history, and have concluded that the Old English authors' intentions for their writings were both more varied and more innovative than has been suspected.[2] The chief innovation, it seems to me, is Aelfric's notion that one might arrange coherent collections of vernacular, exegetical homilies for the liturgical year. Continental canons and preaching

practice seem to have had in mind as "preaching" primarily
cathechetical discourses on such basic topics as the *Pater noster* and
Credo. Consistent efforts to adapt the exegetical sermons of the
Fathers on the pericopes for use among the people seem to have
been uncommon. Even the Blickling homilies, which are arranged
by the chronology of the liturgical year, are limited to major Dominical Sundays, to Lent (a classical season for teaching), and to a
few saints' days, in addition to material adaptable to general use
and assembled for the Rogation Days. The materials assembled for
devotional reading in the Vercelli Book seem to have been drawn
from collections similar in scope to Blickling.[3] It is open to question
whether Aelfric and his sermon-writing colleagues had the reading
of their works in a liturgical setting exclusively or even primarily
in mind. Assuming some such intention, however, it is likely that
even sermons on the pericope were read in a primarily catechetical
context. That context is a vernacular office, often apparently inter-
posed between the reading of the Gospel and the Offertory of the
mass, in which one might translate the pericope and perhaps explain
it, teach the meaning of the Lord's Prayer and Creed, and bid the
prayers of the faithful. What is unusual about Aelfric is that he
attempted to provide for this setting a set of expositions on the
Gospels for the Temporale.[4] Most other early medieval English
and Latin writers of sermons for the laity contented themselves with
general, catechetical addresses. Only occasionally—and then usually
for a very restricted group of days—did they treat the appointed
lections or pericopes exegetically.

In the present paper I want to address another aspect of the
larger picture: the language in which homilies were prepared in
several areas of Europe in order to fulfill the canonical injunctions
to preach to and to teach the laity. What is the place of the Old
English homilies in the history of European vernacular literatures
or (to be narrower and more precise) in the recorded, literary history of vernacular preaching? Few can pretend to the linguistic
expertise requisite to a definitive treatment of this problem. With
the aid of secondary guides, however, it may be possible to trace the
contours of the problem and to open the way to more detailed and
more expert consideration of the issues. Most of my space will be
devoted to examination of evidence for the writing of homilies and

other addresses to the people for oral delivery or devotional reading in European languages other than English before the mid-eleventh century. These findings will be compared with the English achievement. By way of conclusion some observations will be hazarded on the proliferation of vernacular preaching texts in the twelfth century and on possible English influences on this development.

It may be well, before turning to the main task, to define several terms which are crucial to distinctions to be made below, for one of the chief implications of this essay is that the modern commentators on medieval vernacular preaching have been too relaxed in their definitions of basic terms and have, therefore, blurred important distinctions. We must in the first place reinstate the distinction between *sermo,* a general address on a religious theme, and *homilia,* an exegetical address on a passage of Scripture. Benjamin Thorpe helped create our present confusion when he translated Aelfric's own title, *Sermones Catholici* (or *Liber sermonum Catholicorum*) as *Catholic Homilies* in his edition of 1844–46. There is some reason to think of Aelfric's work as a collection of homilies since so much of it is exegetical, but the abbot himself shunned the term in reference to his own writing because it had a special meaning which, however applicable to his sources, was not appropriate to his own adaptations. This confusion is further compounded by our tendency to categorize all religious discourses in Old English as "homilies" and their authors as "homilists." We ought to distinguish between sermons (in the broadest sense) and nonsermons. What makes a religious discourse in prose a sermon, at least for our present purposes, is that it is formally equipped to be read aloud to a congregation. Thus a sermon or homily will often begin and end with appropriate formulas of address (e.g., "Dearly beloved"; "In the Gospel which has just been read . . .") and closure (e.g., ". . . world without end. Amen.") or will in some other way betray the fact that it is addressed to a congregation. This will be the case even though the sermons may appear in a collection put together primarily or even exclusively for private devotional reading. Another distinction which is crucial is that between catechetical preaching and exegetical preaching. The latter takes for its text the Scripture lessons (usually the Gospel) appointed for a given day. Exegetical sermons for liturgical use are inappropriate on days of the year other than those for which they were written. Catechetical preaching is useful whenever one wants to use it (*quando volueris* is Aelfric's rubric). It usually addresses such basic matters as the Creed, the Lord's Prayer "and all other things which a Christian ought to know and believe to his soul's health," to quote the much later description of catechetical instruction in the baptismal office of the Book of Common Prayer.[5] In what follows we shall be looking for preaching texts in several languages. Where we find such texts, we shall attempt to classify them in order to be able to compare them the more accurately with the Old English preachers' materials.

It is a fact which is too easily forgotten that Greek and Latin, the major vehicles of Christian preaching texts before and during our period (and, indeed, throughout the rest of the Middle Ages), were the vernacular languages of the Mediterranean basin. The eastern churches were receptive to the notion that the use of vernaculars was a necessary tool of missionary effort.[6] The Latin church, however, tended to be more cautious in adapting native languages to liturgical and literary ends. As late as the fourth century Rome had not yet completed the transition in its own liturgy from Greek to the Latin vernacular.[7] In later centuries Latin became essentially a learned and hieratic language, as its dialects became more widely separated and as non-Latin languages became more and more important in areas related politically or ecclesiastically with the Latin church. Nevertheless little consideration was apparently given to possible adaptation of the new languages to catechetical, literary, or liturgical use. In this realm, as in many others, Gregory the Great is the major figure who might have made an exception, in the light of his tolerance for diversity of ecclesiastical custom, but this issue was apparently neither put to, nor raised, by him.[8] Latin survived as the liturgical language of western Catholicism into the present century, and it may have something to do with the history of language that the Reformation succeeded in German-language areas and the Latin church prevailed in the Romance-speaking countries.

It is, of course, certain that missionary preaching or catechesis was delivered on the frontiers of Europe in the appropriate vernacular languages. But apart from such possible exceptions as Caesarius of Arles, the matter of regular Sunday preaching in the dialect intelligible to the people seems not to have been considered a normal *desideratum* until the Carolingian era.[9] In the eighth and ninth centuries ecclesiastical teachers of the laity confronted not only the problem of newly converted peoples but also a tendency, resulting from the encouragement of higher norms of latinity in the schools, to increase the dichotomy between the learned language and the romance dialects. Liturgical Latin did remain in some sense a living, popularly rooted language. Nevertheless the dichotomy between Latin and the vernaculars must have been superable only when the native tongues were adopted for catechetical and homiletical purposes.[10] Of this activity, however, little trace survives, probably because such addresses *ad populum* were not reduced to writing. It is, therefore, striking to modern observers that the only theoretical treatise on preaching of the Carolingian period —the second book of Hrabanus Maurus's *De institutione clericorum ad Heistulphum archiepiscopum* (c. 819)—is basically a restatement of Augustine's *De doctrina Christiana* and Gregory's *Regula pastoralis* and ignores the issue of language as it must have existed in Hrabanus's Germany.[11]

Section 82 of the *Admonitio generalis,* issued by Charlemagne in 789, is often cited as a central text of the Carolingian effort to revive the teaching office of the clergy.[12] The duty of preaching to the people is enjoined upon pastors and rectors in this last and longest portion of the *Admonitio,* and there is a long discussion of the contents of such preaching. Those who address the people are, first of all, to stress basic doctrine as outlined in the creeds but with particular emphasis on eschatological matters, which provide the sanctions for moral teaching. Next comes preaching on the nature of sin and the virtues. Thus matters in the catechetical and penitential areas were to be the preoccupation of preachers or teachers to the apparent exclusion of any systematic exposition of the scriptures in general or the pericopes in particular.[13] There was no reference to the language of such preaching, let alone to writing out the sermons.

The language problem was specifically addressed in a series of councils held in 813 at Arles, Rheims, Mainz, Chalons-sur-Saône, and Tours, and in a *Concordia episcoporum,* which summarized and harmonized the conclusions of the local sessions.[14] Canon XVII of the Council of Tours states that bishops are to have homiliaries containing admonitions on the faith, morality, and the eschatological sanctions for Christian behavior; one should, the canon concludes, know how to translate this material clearly into Romance or German.[15] This canon, which was favorably cited in canon X of the *Concordia,* seems to contemplate both general or catechetical instruction and adaptations of the Fathers' sermons, like those of Caesarius, in the vernacular. The canon does not, however, seem to expect that homiliaries will be *written* in Romance or German. In fact we know of no homiliary that seems clearly to have been written to meet the needs created by the councils of 813.[16] There is no hint in the Carolingian legislation that preachers were expected either to write down sermons in the vernacular languages or to prepare cycles of homilies in Latin or other languages on the pericopes for the liturgical year.

There are two quite distinct periods of vernacular prose writing in German before the twelfth century. The first seems to have been encouraged by Charlemagne and his ecclesiastical advisers, a number of whom were Anglo-Saxons. This period of literary productivity was cut short in the tenth century, perhaps because of political unrest or a policy of downgrading the vernacular as a literary vehicle. It was only in the eleventh century that Notker Labeo or Teutonicus (d. 1022), a monk of St. Gall, revived the writing of prose in German.[17] In the first period those few items which might be classified as preaching materials in the broadest sense fall into two subcategories, catechetical and homiletic, of which the first is by far the larger group. This fact ought not, I think, to surprise the careful reader of the capitularies and canons, for it was clearly such basic matters as the teaching and explication of the Creed and Lord's Prayer that concerned the Carolingian rulers and ecclesiastical legislators.[18] A number of these texts are obviously intended for the instruction of newly converted peoples and are catechetical in the strict sense by virtue of their close relationship to the sacrament of baptism.[19] Only insofar as they intersect with such Old English instructional preachers' texts as Aelfric assembled at Rogationtide in the two series of *Sermones catholicae,* under the rubric *quando volueris,* or as general, prefatory items to his collections, do these catechetical materials in Old German represent a parallel to the achievement of the Old English sermon writers. The provision of true homilies on the Gospel pericopes in more-or-less ordered series seems not to have been attempted in Old German.

Indeed there is very little prose from Germany in the ninth century which is comparable in any way with the Old English products of the late tenth and early eleventh centuries. The chief witness is among a group of fragments, the so-called Monsee-Vienna Fragments, from a now-dismembered manuscript associated with the Bavarian monastery at Monsee, whence also comes one of the few Latin pastoral homiliaries of the ninth century.[20] This manuscript was a miscellany containing Old High German translations of Isidore's *De fide catholica contra Judaeos,* parts of the Matthew Gospel, an unknown Latin tract entitled *De vocatione gentium,* an Augustinian sermon on Matthew 14:24ff., and the end of a piece which may be either catechetical or homiletic.[21] The Augustinian homily, the earliest surviving in German, is part of a florilegium of pieces the nature of which does not allow us to posit a consistent effort to provide catechetical or exegetical preaching texts in the vernacular.[22] Other than glosses, such as those on the homilies of Gregory the Great, there are no other attempts to adapt homilies to the German dialects.[23] Despite the seeming purport of the Carolingian ecclesiastical legislation, one is forced to conclude that in the ninth century German efforts at translation went to what may have been considered more basic texts for the evangelical tasks of the church: biblical translation, capped by the translation of the *Tatian Harmony,* liturgical formulas connected with the rites of initiation and penance, and catechetical explanations of the fundamentals of the faith. Such interlinear translations of monastic texts as the *Benediktiner Regel* and *Murbach Hymns* may have been intended to acquaint laymen with the customs of monks or may have been school exercises. Otfrid's poetic *Evangelienbuch,* which some have thought to rest on pericope selections, was directed to a monastic audience and was not designed for homiletic exploitation, although it drew on the exegetical traditions of the Latin preachers. Otfrid speaks in his Latin preface of the fact that German writers almost invariably elected *in alienae linguae gloriam transferre et usum scripturae in propria lingua non habere.*[24]

Whether or not Otfrid was reflecting the general attitude of learned German clergy towards literary exploitation of the vernacular, there is little or no German prose from the tenth century before the time of Notker Labeo. Many bishops of the time were renowned as preachers. Their sermons, which (as I have already noted) are likely to have been catechetical or general rather than exegetical, must have been delivered *ad libitum,* like those of the missionary preachers of the two preceding centuries. Hence the age which historians of preaching have rightly called the *Blütezeit des Episkopats* has left only small traces of the sermons themselves— and those in Latin.[25]

Notker, the greatest German prose-writer of the tenth and eleventh centuries, did not himself produce homilies. A contemporary of Aelfric, he seems to have devoted himself almost exclusively to translation of works useful to his students at St. Gall.[26] One of the important manuscripts of his translation-*cum*-commentary of the Psalter (Vienna Hofbibliothek HS. 2681), however, contains some of the so-called Wessobrun homilies. It is to the Bavarian monastery of Wessobrun that one looks for the first evidence of sustained efforts at homiletic composition or translation in Germany.[27] Unfortunately, however, recent German scholarship has not lavished attention on these fragments—and they are that: three groups of remains in various locations. The homilies of the "A" group of Wessobrun fragments seem to be general or catechetical. They draw on Caesarius of Arles for teaching on such subjects as widowhood, penitence, purgatorial fire.[28] The "B" group begins with an adaptation of Gregory's Homily XVII on Luke 10:1-9, which appears only very rarely in homiliaries.[29] It continues with a run of homilies on the pericopes for Septuagesima, Sexagesima, and Quinquagesima, all based on sermons of Gregory the Great (XIX, XV, II) which were included in the Homiliary of Paul the Deacon.[30] The third, or "C," group begins with a run of homilies for the first three Sundays of Lent based on items which appear in the Homiliary. Two other items in the group seem to be general, and another homily is perhaps to be associated with the third or fourth Sunday after the Epiphany.[31] In other words the Wessobrun homilies present a mixed picture. Some are catechetical. Others are exegetical or homiletic in the strict sense and seem to have been presented in the proper order of the liturgical calendar. But the runs of the exegetical-liturgical homilies are short and restricted to the pre-Lenten and Lenten season, when preaching on the pericopes to the people seems to have been more common than, say, on Sundays after Pentecost. It would thus be wrong to hazard that Wessobrun possessed a set or sets of homilies comparable with those of Aelfric or even the Blickling book, and in their present form it is unclear that these translated sermons were to be read to a congregation at mass on Sunday.[32]

Two conclusions may be drawn from this rapid survey of written vernacular preaching material from the German-speaking areas of Europe before the twelfth century. The first is that nothing invites us to presume that Aelfric's efforts to provide a cycle of exegetical homiletical texts in the vernacular had German precursors or were inspired by contacts with the continent. The second is that, whatever the Wessobrun relics signify, they give no evidence that vernacular projects comparable to those undertaken by the writers of preachers' materials in England between c. 970 and 1020 were ever contemplated or begun in the German-speaking territories. It is possible, of course, that such projects were pursued; but if so, it is surprising, given such monuments as the *Tatian* and the work of Otfrid and Notker, that they have left such very fragmentary traces.[33]

The Irish church in the early Middle Ages, especially in matters relating to its influence on England, presents very great difficulties for historical scholarship.[34] Much recent work has enhanced our understanding of the importance of the Hibernian church for the history of the continental churches, its extremely interesting contributions in the realm of biblical exegesis, the influence of its visionary and apocalyptic literature, and the nature of its contribution to English vernacular writing.[35] In the area of homiletics, however, the Irish church does not seem to have offered much in Latin or in the Celtic dialects to the movement to collect the preaching of the Fathers in homiliaries, to the movement for ecclesiastical reform by means of better teaching or catechesis, or to what is emerging as the peculiarly English effort to assemble useful cycles of preaching materials in the native tongue. Indeed the chief homiletic document from the Celtic areas is neither in the vernacular nor, probably, from Ireland. The tenth-century Latin *Catéchèses celtiques,* probably from such a continental Celtic area as Brittany, is thought to have been collected under the influence of the Carolingian legislation.[36] Marked by imaginative, often apocryphally based approaches to the tasks of instruction and exegesis, the *Catéchèses* contain some materials which were also used by English and other vernacular writers. The Irish canonical and penitential literature betrays far less interest in the matter of preaching than do continental and English texts.[37]

The impression that there is a homiletic literature in Old Irish probably rests on a loose definition which would admit almost any prose discourse on religious or moral themes other than a saint's life to the homiletic realm. The situation is complicated, however, by the fact that Irish vernacular saints' lives were probably read aloud in church and elsewhere.[38] In our search for parallels to the Anglo-Saxon achievement, nevertheless, we must keep constantly in mind the distinctions not only between sermon and homily, or catechesis and exegesis, but also between pieces that bear evidence of the intention to read them orally before an audience or congregation and those that do not. When these distinctions are borne in mind, the liturgical-homiletic nature of many of the writings in Old Irish usually so designated is difficult to maintan. Thus, for example, the fragment embedded in a continental Latin manuscript and usually called "The Cambrai Homily" lacks both a homiletic opening and close.[39] The fragment, which discusses types of martrydom, could originally have been simply a short tract or an excerpt anthologized in a florilegium. Moreover a "homily" on the deadly sins based on the eighth-century Old Irish Penitential is purely catechetical.[40] Another Irish homiletic text of presumably early date appears in the fifteenth-century manuscript known as the "Yellow Book of Lecan." [41] It was recently the subject of the first "analysis of Celtic preaching," in which it is imagined that the preacher, working from an outline, amplified his subject (the need for thankfulness on the part of Christians) with a number of quotations of

Scripture, no exegetical development, and an indulgence of his imaginative powers of description.[42] The closing of the piece is, indeed, homiletic: "May we arrive at the Kingdom of that king, may we merit it, may we inhabit it in *saecula saeculorum.* Amen." But the sermon is a general one, suitable for moral exhortation on any occasion, and not related to a specific occasion of the Christian year or to the appointed pericopes. As an example of parenesis or moral exhortation, it is reminiscent of, say, some of the homilies based on Caesarius of Arles in the Blickling and Vercelli Books.

The best-known Irish homiletic collection is the famous *Leabhar Breac,* or "Speckled Book," which was possibly written by the same scribe as the "Yellow Book of Lecan." [43] This miscellany contains biblical paraphrase, verse, saints' lives, history, and homiletic matter. The manuscript itself dates from the late fourteenth or early fifteenth century. The texts which are of interest here, despite the fact they have sometimes been treated as earlier, are specimens of Middle Irish from the twelfth century.[44] As one might expect from the lapse of time between the presumed date of the composition of its sermons and the date of the assembling of the Speckled Book, the arrangement of the manuscript shows that the scribe drew upon a number of collections. Thus, for example, there seem to have been some pieces for the Temporale and also general sermons on such topics as charity, alms, repentance, the Decalogue, and the like. There are as well a few pieces having to do with the duties of the clergy and their own spiritual disciplines. A number of these items are distinctly catechetical.[45] Some of them end with prayers, and several refer to the reading of the Gospel.[46] Thus there is the possibility that some of these pieces were at one time intended for liturgical use. But in the *Leabhar Breac* we are dealing with a variety of kinds of discourse. There are catechetical sermons and exegetical homilies on the pericopes, as well as a number of pieces which may have been devised originally for private devotional reading and others which had such special purposes as the instruction of the clergy. In the manuscript as it stands, however, the liturgical character (if any) of the homiletic pieces has been obscured. Before there has been a critical edition with collations to other copies of some of the texts, analysis of the possible forebears of the manuscript, and study of its sources, nothing can be said about the history of vernacular preaching in Ireland on the basis of this florilegium. Given the date Celticists have determined for the language of the homilies in the manuscript, this preaching material cannot be regarded as precursory to the Old English homilies. Rather the homiletic pieces of *Leabhar Breac* postdate the creative period of English sermon-writing and may be more closely related to the introduction of reformed monasticism in Ireland in the late eleventh century and to the great surge of vernacular preaching texts in Scandinavia and elsewhere in Europe in the twelfth century than to the English writings of the tenth and early eleventh.

In Ireland, then, there is presently in print no evidence from before the mid-eleventh century of a tradition of recording in written form exegetical homilies on the pericopes designed to be read to the people. There is sufficient evidence to establish that catechetical or general instructional teaching for Christians was at least on occasion reduced to written form. One must stress, however, that there is less remaining in this category from Ireland than from England or Germany. It seems unlikely, given the evidence of considerable vernacular literary activity of other kinds in Ireland, that a corpus of earlier Old Irish vernacular preaching texts has vanished almost without trace.

When one turns from comparison of the vernacular homiletic literature of England before the end of the eleventh century with that in other European languages in the same period to a comparison of the Old English preaching materials with the products of the other vernaculars in the twelfth century, the results are rather different. In the earlier period, as I have argued, we can discover no true analogues to the liturgically arranged collections for the Temporale of Aelfric, and far less more general or catechetical material survives in other vernaculars than in Old English. In the later period we find a number of collections which are strongly reminiscent of such Old English sermon materials as are collected in the Blickling and Vercelli anthologies, but still nothing which matches either Aelfric's scheme or his achievement.

One may look first to Scandinavia, where two manuscripts, the

Old Norwegian and the Old Icelandic homily books, provide evidence from the end of the twelfth century of considerable homiletic activity.[47] There is reason to believe that in both Norway and Iceland there was direct English influence on the development of the vernacular literary tradition. It may have something to do with English influence that a preaching literature began to be produced, perhaps as early as the late-eleventh century, in those countries.[48] That the first preaching in Scandinavian dialects may have taken place in the Danelaw area of the archdiocese of York in the tenth and eleventh centuries is not beyond the bounds of reasonable speculation; and it may also be the case that Sweden and Denmark, unlike Norway and Iceland, did not produce early vernacular sermon texts because their conversion was undertaken by Germans rather than Anglo-Saxons.[49] In Iceland there are important records of the preaching tradition of the northern diocese of Holar in the twelfth century—traditions which for the first time seem to show a pastor reading from a vernacular homiliary to the laity on Sunday. So, for example, one hears of Gisli Finsson, who, under Jon Ogmundarson, bishop of Holar from 1106 to 1121,

> used to preach on feast-days. When he did so, he did not
> speak *ex tempore,* nor did he rely on his memory, for he was
> both young and humble, and he knew that the congregation
> would take his words more seriously if they could see that he
> was reading from a book, which lay before him on the lec-
> tern. . . . This book [of homilies] can only have been written
> in the vernacular, for Gisli could not have preached in Latin
> to the hundreds who flocked to the cathedral on feast-days.[50]

At the end of the century Páll Jónsson, bishop of Skalaholt (1195–1211), seems to have been disturbed by the great frequency of preaching in Iceland and to have discouraged it except at festivals, feeling that sermons would be more valued if less common.[51] His alarm perhaps mirrors an awareness that very frequent vernacular preaching had not, in fact, been common in other European churches theretofore.

The surviving manuscripts of early Norse preaching give evidence that the writing of sermons in the vernacular began early rather than late in the twelfth century, if not in the eleventh. One manuscript of homilies containing the famous Dedication Homily, which is also found in both the Norwegian and Icelandic collections, is dated c. 1150 and itself seems to have been copied from earlier exemplars.[52] An early thirteenth-century fragmentary translation into Icelandic of the homilies of Gregory the Great also overlaps the Norse homily book and seems to descend from a complete translation of the Gregorian sermons into Norwegian from before 1150.[53] The existence of a twelfth-century translation of the *Elucidarium,* a theological handbook associated with Honorius "Augustodunensis," a pupil of Anselm, shows that Icelandic theologians were acquainted with up-to-date currents in theological literature as well as with the rather more conservative kinds of sources one presupposes for the homilies.[54]

Much remains to be learned about the sources of the Scandinavian homilies, and we must content ourselves here with generalizations based on what work has already been done and on the shape of the collections preserved in the Norse and Icelandic homily books.[55] The homilies on pericopes for days of the liturgical calendar are based largely on the Fathers, notably Gregory and Bede; no study of their possible relationship with the homiliaries has been published. The more general, catechetical addresses present greater difficulties. Recent studies by Joan Turville-Petre and others have shown that some of these sermons are closely related to sources (not all of which are still extant) which were also drawn upon by the Old English writers and by the Irish and twelfth-century Middle High German writers.[56]

As for the organization of these two Scandinavian sermon collections, which have eleven items in common, they are quite different kinds of collections. The Norse is the better organized and is in some ways reminiscent of the Blickling book, for it provides homilies and sermons for major feasts from Christmas through Pentecost and a collection of pieces for a number of major saints' days. The first item of the collection, a translation of Alcuin's *De virtutibus et vitiis,* is not a sermon but a tract. It puts one in mind of Aelfric's occasional practice of opening his collections with general, introductory pieces. At the end there appear a *Visio sancti Pauli apostoli* and a piece on the Lord's Prayer. Some care seems to have been exercised in the employment of the terms *omelia, sermo* (*sermo ad populum, sermo necessaria*), *admonitio*. Thus we have a mixture of items which compositely are reminiscent not only of the Blickling collection but also of Latin collections of catechetical matter which provided pieces for the Dominical feasts, for catechetical instruction, and (perhaps) for the feasts of major saints. The Icelandic book is a less coherent assemblage, one which "looks as though it had come into being gradually, through constantly renewed work of the copiers." [57] Its pieces for the Temporale are approximately analogous to those of the Norwegian book, but they are not in order. There are a number of *sermones* for catechetical use. The inclusion of prayers and the obvious concern with catechesis may well point to the kinds of devotions associated with the Prone. One commentator has implied that the books may also have been for private reading as "books of devotion," [58] but in at least some of their opening and closing formulas, which seem to imply that they were to be read to a congregation, the Norse homilies are more reminiscent of the Old English than of the other vernacular traditions.[59]

There are connections between these texts and the works of Aelfric—or at least certain of Aelfric's sources.[60] It would probably be rash on the basis of the evidence now available, however, to state with Knudsen that the Scandinavian homiletic literature "shows considerable affinity, both in its composition and spirit" with Aelfric's *Catholic Homilies*.[61] On the basis of our present knowledge there is greater affinity to the traditions of Blickling and Vercelli and to the kinds of sermon collections (often with much Aelfrician material) which were put together in Worcester in the eleventh century. Such collections reverted from Aelfric's usual effort to provide homiletic or exegetical pieces on the pericopes *per circulum anni* to the earlier, more catechetical custom of providing general teaching, sermons for major saints' days, and sermons for major dominical feasts. In a sense, then, if one allows for a fairly strong influence of the English on early Scandinavian preaching, the famous Norwegian and Icelandic books provide further evidence that the achievement of Aelfric was unusual (not to say unique) and that his effort to compile a complete set of pieces for the Temporale was not often emulated by those who used his work. At the same time, however, the Scandinavian evidence enhances the importance of the anonymous homilists and even of Wulfstan, who seems to have had some influence on the form of English sermon collections emanating from Worcester.

The state of the texts and of research will not permit even as superficial a survey of the state of preaching texts in the vernacular in Middle High German and Old French as has been attempted above for earlier German, Irish, and the Scandinavian dialects. This will not matter for our present purposes, as enough has already been said to demonstrate that, in European perspective, the achievement of the Old English writers in general and of Aelfric in particular is remarkable. Nevertheless a few suggestions for further study may be set down.

The first involves a twelfth-century theologian of some importance, to whom allusion has already been made: Honorius "Augustodunensis," whose collection of Latin sermons, the *Speculum ecclesiae,* like his *Elucidarium,* was translated by a number of vernacular writers.[62] A shadowy figure, Honorius was probably an Irishman by birth and, despite his name, had no connection with Autun.[63] A disciple of Anselm at Canterbury, he ended his life in the Irish monastery at Regensburg.[64] The *Speculum ecclesiae* was a compilation of Latin preaching material for translation (*ad libitum,* apparently) into the vernacular. It is prefaced with an *instructio loquendi* which advises its users on the techniques of preaching:

> The text is to be given first in Latin, then in the vernacular.
> The speaker must speak humbly, without exaggerated
> gestures, but with due regard to the principles of rhetoric,
> suiting his voice to the subject "so that your hearers will think
> they actually see the events instead of hearing you." The
> length of the sermon must be adjusted to the season. . . .
> Sermons should not be delivered too often, lest they become
> tedious and commonplace. The preacher must adapt his
> discourse to the congregation ; the sermons in the *Speculum*

were suited to an urban group . . . ; for the "vulgus" a
simple exposition of the Gospel or Epistle was preferable.[65]

This Latin preaching manual is of interest here for two reasons.
First, it may, if it is ever studied closely and edited critically, provide further evidence that England was a major center for the dissemination of preachers' materials. It was written, apparently, at
the request of the *fratres Cantuarenses,* and it has been suggested
that Honorius was not ignorant of the works of the English
vernacular preachers.[66] Second, the work had a great influence on
a number of vernacular preachers' texts. The best known is a
Benediktbeuern manuscript of the mid-twelfth century which, in
modern times and rather misleadingly, has been given the same
title as Honorius' work.[67] Like the Scandinavian collections with
which it has something in common, it contains comparatively few
exegetical pieces and a large number of more general, or catechetical, sermons.[68] From both Honorius' *Speculum* and the
vernacular collections it influenced, then, there may be things to
learn about England as a disseminating center for Latin sermon
collections, about Old English preaching practices as an example
to other Europeans and perhaps as a spur to the practice of circu-
lating preaching materials in vernacular languages, and about the
kinds of Latin sources used by the Anglo-Saxons.

There remains, finally, the possibility of English influence on
French preaching in the twelfth century.[69] I know of no reason
to connect England with the work of Maurice de Sully (d. 1196),
whose Latin collection and its Old French translations are comparable to the *Speculum* of Honorius.[70] Unfortunately the homiletic
texts, which may be Anglo-Norman, have not been the subjects of
recent study. One versified epistolary "sermon" addressed to a
lady, the *Sermon* or *Romaunz de Temtacion de Secle* of Guischart
de Beaulieu, was thought some years ago to have drawn upon
Aelfric.[71] In view of the fact that there is now some evidence of
Anglo-Norman glossing of Old English manuscripts, the possibility of cross-fertilization in the area of preaching texts must be
left open.[72] Indeed all of the preaching materials in the early
medieval tradition antedating the new theories of the *artes prae-*

dicandi in the early thirteenth century ought to be studied comparatively.[73]

It is hardly my intention in this paper to have drawn firm conclusions or even to have stated hypotheses with mild confidence. Nevertheless there seem to me to be several hypotheses which could at least serve as testing-points for further research: 1) There is no evidence which allows one to suppose that preaching texts in the vernacular—whether homilies or sermons—were produced in any language in a volume comparable to that in Old English before the end of the eleventh century. 2) The few works now available in printed editions that were produced outside England—namely, in Germany in the ninth and eleventh centuries and in Ireland at various times, but most especially in the latter part of the eleventh century—seem to have been mainly catechetical sermons. The items that were exegetical tended to be limited to feasts of the Temporale between the pre-Lenten Sundays and Easter. Even so, it is difficult on the evidence presently available to sustain the thesis that the anonymous Old English Sermons, which seem to belong in the main to this kind of tradition, had any true analogues in other vernacular languages in terms of scope, persistence in time, or dissemination. 3) No one before Aelfric or in the century after him produced or attempted to assemble in the vernaculars a coherent set of exegetical commentaries on the pericopes for the Christian year. Thus Aelfric seems to be *sui generis,* without precursors or followers in his effort to provide a cycle of exegetical addresses *ad populum* for the Temporale. I have argued elsewhere that his intention was to turn the homilies of the Fathers that he found in the monastic homiliaries to use in a catechetical office known in later years as the Prone. It is, I believe, because he had this catechetical setting in mind that he thought of his exegetical writings as *sermones* rather than *homiliae*. What he did remains most unusual even though he tailored it to the prevailing tendency to stress catechesis in fashioning his addresses *ad populum*. His uniqueness in this respect and his lack of a following in this respect seem to me further evidence for rejecting the suggestion that the period be dubbed the "Age of Aelfric." [74] Even though Aelfric will continue to dominate the literary history of England in the late

tenth and eleventh centuries and though further comparative study
of vernacular preaching in the period may enhance his position in
the history of preaching, he stands apart from the other writers of
Old English sermons just as the entire company of English
sermon-writers before Aelfric and slightly beyond his time stand
apart from other Europeans because of their persistent effort to
record useful materials for preachers in the vernacular tongue.[75]

NOTES

1. Some indication of the scope of the corpus of OE homilies can
be had from an examination of the indices and MS descriptions in Ker, *Catalogue.* For recent summaries of research,
see Peter Clemoes, "Aelfric," and Dorothy Bethurum,
"Wulfstan," in *Continuations and Beginnings: Studies in
Old English Literature,* ed. Eric G. Stanley (London,
1966), pp. 176–209 and 210–46. On Aelfric, see also John
C. Pope, SS I. Throughout this paper I have virtually
eliminated specific citation of OE sources and criticism
in order to be able to present fuller notes on the non-
English sermon materials. For further bibliography see
my "Beginnings Continued: A Decade of Studies of Old
English Prose," *Anglo-Saxon England* 5 (1976): 225–
43.

2. *Preaching and Theology in Anglo-Saxon England* (Toronto,
1977). Although I have attempted to make the present
essay stand on its own, I cannot avoid a certain amount
of presupposition based on the conclusions of Part II of
this book, "The Uses of Old English Sermons."

3. The best study of the antecedents of Vercelli is D.G. Scragg,
"The Compilation of the Vercelli Book," *Anglo-Saxon
England* 2 (1973): 189–207.

4. On the growth of the Aelfric canon, see Peter Clemoes, "The
Chronology of Aelfric's Works," in *The Anglo-Saxons:
Studies . . . presented to Bruce Dickins,* ed. Clemoes
(London, 1959), pp. 212–47. M.R. Godden, "The Develop-
ment of Aelfric's Second Series of Catholic Homilies,"

English Studies 54 (1973) : 209–16, make observations on
subtle differences of emphasis between the two series.
Many scribes who later copied Aelfric's sermons did not
want sets of exegetical pieces for the entire year.

5. On the definition of technical terms for preaching, see Christine
   Mohrmann, "Praedicare-Tractare-Sermo : Essai sur la
   Termonologie de la Prédication paléochrétienne," *La
   Maison-Dieu* 39 (1954) : 97–109, and the theological
   dictionaries. On catechesis, consult H.W. Surkau, *s. vv.*
   "Katechetik," "Katechismus," in *Der Religion in Geschichte
   und Gegenwart* 3rd ed. (1959) ; the standard history of
   catechesis is Peter Göbl, *Geschichte der Katechese im
   Abendlande vom Verfalle des Katechumenats bis zum
   Ende des Mittelalters* (Kempten, 1880).

6. A key characteristic of the ninth-century mission of SS. Cyril
   and Methodius to the Slavs—and one which was severely
   criticized by Carolingians—was the systematic translation
   of both the Scriptures and the liturgy. See Nicholas Zernov,
   *Eastern Christendom: A Study of the Origin and Develop-
   ment of the Eastern Orthodox Church* (New York, 1961),
   pp. 91–93.

7. Christine Mohrmann, *Liturgical Latin: Its Origins and Character* (London, 1959), pp. 14, 27ff. Mohrmann believes the
   lessons and sermon and perhaps also the Psalter had been
   in Latin from an earlier date (p. 47).

8. See Paul Meyvaert, "Diversity within Unity: A Gregorian
   Theme," *Heythrop Journal* 4 (1963) : 141–62.

9. "Non hic aut eloquentia aut grandis memoria quaeritur, ubi
   simplex et pedestri sermone admonitio necessaria esse
   cognoscitur" (Caesarius, *Sermo* 1, ed. Morin; CCL, 103,
   p. 10). See also Henry G.J. Beck, *The Pastoral Care of
   Souls in Southeast France During the Sixth Century,*
   Analecta Gregoriana 51 (Rome, 1950), pp. 269–70.

10. See Christine Mohrmann, "Le Dualisme de la Latinité médié-
    vale," rpt. in *Latine Vulgaire, Latin des Chrétiens, Latin
    Medieval* (Paris, 1955), pp. 37–54.

11. *De inst. cler., PL,* 107, 293–420. See also M.L.W. Laistner,
    Thought and Letters in Western Europe, A.D. 500–900,
    2nd ed. (Ithaca, N.Y., 1957), pp. 306–08.

12. *Monumenta Germaniae Historica, Legum* II, *Capitularia Regum Francorum* 1 (1883), pp. 52–62.

13. "... et non sinatis nova vel non canonica aliquos ex suo sensu et non secundum scripturas sacras fingere et praedicare populo" (*Adm. gen.* 82).

14. *Monumenta Germaniae Historica, Legum* III, *Concilia* 2 (1906), pp. 245–306.

15. "Visum est unanimitati nostrae, ut quilibet episcopus habeat omelias continentes necessarias ammonitiones, quibus subjecti erudiantur, id est de fide catholica, prout capere possint, de perpetua retributione bonorum et aeterna damnatione malorum, de resurrectione quoque futura et ultimo iudicio et quibus operibus possit promereri beata vita quibusve excludi. Et ut easdem omelias quisque aperte transferre studeat in rusticam Romanam linguam aut Thiotiscam, quo facilius cuncti possint intellegere quae dicuntur."

16. For inventories and analyses of Carolingian homiliaries, see Reginald Grégoire *Les Homélaires du Moyen Âge,* Rerum Ecclesiasticarum Documenta, Series Maior: Fontes 6 (Rome, 1966); Henry Barré, *Les Homéliares Carolingiens de l'École d'Auxerre,* Studi e Testi 225 (Vatican, 1962); and Barré, "Homéliaires," *Dictionnaire de Spiritualité* (Paris, 1969), cols. 597–606. The most important homiliary, that of Paul the Deacon, is inventoried by Grégoire and by Cyril L. Smetana, "Aelfric and the Early Medieval Homiliary," *Traditio* 15 (1959): 163–204. Among the homiliaries which may possibly have been written in response to the 813 councils, see that of Hrabanus Maurus for Haistulf (*PL,* 110) and the not completely published work of Abbo of Saint-Germain-des-Prés (Jean Leclercq, "Le Florilège d'Abbon de Saint-Germain," *Revue du Moyen Âge Latin* 3 [1947]: 113–40).

17. For brief accounts of early German literary history, see M.O'C. Walshe, *Medieval German Literature* (Cambridge, Mass., 1962), pp. 7–33; J. Knight Bostock, *A Handbook on Old High German Literature* (Oxford, 1955). For histories of German preaching, see Anton Linsenmayer, *Geschichte der Predigt in Deutschland von Karl dem Grossen bis zum Aus-*

gange des vierzehnten Jahrhunderts (1886; rpt. Frankfurt,
1969) ; R. Cruel, *Geschichte der deutschen Predigt im
Mittelalter* (Detmold, 1897).

18. See Gustav Ehrismann, *Geschichte der deutschen Literatur bis
zum Ausgang des Mittelalters,* 1, 2nd ed. (Munich, 1932),
pp. 290–95 ; Helmut deBoor, *Die Deutsche Literatur von
Karl dem Grossen bis zum Beginn der höfischen Dichtung:
770–1170,* vol. 1 of *Gesch. der deutschen Literatur,* ed. de
Boor and Richard Newald, 5th ed. (Munich, 1962),
pp. 25–30. For collections of texts (cited below by editor and
text number), see K. Müllenhoff and W. Scherer, eds.,
*Denkmäler deutscher Poesie und Prosa aus dem VIII–XII
Jahrhundert,* 3rd ed., rev. E. Steinmeyer (Berlin, 1892) ;
Elias von Steinmeyer, ed., *Die kleineren althochdeutschen
Sprachdenkmäler,* 12th ed. rpt. (Berlin, 1963).

19. See Bostock, *Handbook,* pp. 99, 101, on *Exhortatio ad plebem
christianum* and Weissenburg Catechism.

20. On the MS and its contents, see Ehrismann, *Geschichte der
Deutschen Literatur* pp. 280–86 ; de Boor, *Die Deutsche
Literatur,* pp. 31–36 ; Bostock, *Handbook,* pp. 107–13 ;
texts: Mühlenhoff-Scherer lix–lx, and esp. George Allison
Hench, *The Monsee Fragments* (Strassburg, 1890). On
the Latin homiliary from Monsee by Abbot Lantperthus,
see Barré, *Les Homéliares,* p. 25.

21. Another copy of *De fide* is said to have been made at Tours or
Orléans, perhaps under the influence of Alcuin (de Boor,
Die Deutsche Literatur, p. 31 ; Ehrismann, *Geschichte der
Deutschen Literatur,* pp. 273–80; but see also Bostock,
Handbook, pp. 108–10). The fragment of a translation of
Bede's homily for All Saints' (Müllenhoff-Scherer 1) is
so brief that it is impossible to know whether it was made for
preaching or other uses. The MS was an elegantly written
one with Latin texts and German translations on facing
pages—a phenomenon without parallel in the OE homiletic
literature.

22. The text for Augustine's homily (Matthew 14:22–33) is not
a Sunday pericope; the pericope is not treated in Paul the
Deacon, and in the homiliaries surveyed by Barré is used

only once, on the Octave of Apostles, by Hrabanus Maurus in his nonliturgical homiliary for the Emperor Lothair (on the two collections, see Barré, *Les Homéliaires,* pp. 13–17). Thus the homily may well have been intended as a nonliturgical reading piece, despite the fact that it retains Augustine's homiletic opening: "Euangelium quod recentissime recitatum . . .": "Diz gotspel daz nu niuuuost hear galesan."

23. deBoor, *Die Deutsche Literature,* pp. 30–31, 109; Ehrismann, *Geschichte der Deutschen Literatur,* pp. 260–61. On OHG glosses of texts of Caesarius' sermons which may have come to Germany via the English missionaries, see Ingeborg Schröbler, "AHD Glossen zu Caesarius von Arles," *Beiträge zur Geschichte der deutschen Sprache und Literatur* 63 (1939): 287–94.

24. Quoted from the art. with translation by Francis P. Magoun, Jr., "Otfrid's *Ad Liutbertum,*" *Publications of the Modern Language Association* 58 (1943): 869–90. On the pericope issue, see Hilda Swinburne, "The Selection of Narrative Passages in Otfrid's 'Evangelienbuch'," *Modern Language Review* 53 (1958): 92–97; on his purposes, Donald A. McKenzie, *Otfrid von Weissenburg: Narrator or Commentator?,* Stanford University Publications, Language and Literature, vol. 6, no. 3 (1946), or (among numerous recent studies stressing numerological and allegorical matters) Wulfgang Haubrichs, *Ordo als Form: Strukturstudien zum Zahlenkomposition bei Otfrid Weissenburg und in karolingischer Literatur* (Tübingen, 1969).

25. Cruel, *Geschichte der Deutschen Predigt,* pp. 80–96; Ehrismann, *Geschichte der Deutschen Literatur,* p. 346.

26. Ehrismann, *Geschichte der Deutschen Literatur,* pp. 416–58; de Boor, *Die Deutschen Literatur,* pp. 109–19; Bostock, *Handbook,* pp. 245–57.

27. de Boor, *Die Deutschen Literatur,* pp. 108–18; Ehrismann, *Geschichte der Deutschen Literatur,* pp. 348–52; Bostock, *Handbook,* p. 254; for texts, Steinmeyer, xxx, xxxii, xxxiii (and comments in apparatus of xxvii); Mühlenhoff-Scherer, lxxxvi.

28. Ingeborg Schröbler, "Zu der Vorlage der Althochdeutschen
    Predigtsammlung A," *Beiträge* 63 (1939) : 271–87. On
    sources for "B" and "C," I rely on the commentary on
    texts in Mühlenhoff-Scherer, pp. 417–30, except as noted.

29. It is found with the rubric "in natale omnium apostolorum vel
    in conventu episcoporum" in an eighth-century version of
    an Italian homiliary at Vienne (Grégoire, p. 141). The
    pericope is treated (but with a different homily) in only
    one other of the homiliaries which have been inventoried:
    Barré's I, an Italian collection of the Carolingian type.

30. According to the inventories of Grégoire, pp. 71–114, and
    Smetana, *Traditio* 15 (1959) : 165–80.

31. A conclusion I draw from its apparent use of Matthew 8:5–13.

32. Ehrismann, p. 347, states that "C" was "eine nach dem
    Kirchenjahr geordnete Predigtsammlung" but does not
    stress the existence of a run in "B." De Boor, pp. 118–19,
    feels that the Notker Psalter, with which "A" and "B"
    are associated, was a basic text of the monastic reform
    movement and that in the Vienna MS we see an appropria-
    tion of Notker's work—originally a schoolbook or lecture
    notes—"im Dienst der reformerischen Laienwerbung
    verwendet." In other words it has become a catechetical
    document. Some further hint on the purposes of the Vienna
    Notker may be gleaned from the fact that the homilies
    evidently appeared in three groups in the MS interspersed
    among the Psalms; "A" came before the group of Psalms
    i–l (Schröbler, *Beiträge* 63 [1939] : 287n).

33. The German and English situations were hardly identical, of
    course, but it is worth recalling the conclusion of
    R.M. Wilson that "it is unlikely that the survival of complete
    manuscripts of which [only fragmentary evidence is pro-
    vided by documents comparable to the Monsee-Vienna and
    Wessobrun MSS] would have led to any appreciable
    difference in the general picture of Old English prose"
    (*The Lost Literature of Medieval England* 2nd ed.
    [London, 1970], p. 65).

34. Two invaluable recent introductions are Kathleen Hughes,

The Church in Early Irish Society (London, 1966) and
Early Christian Ireland: Introduction to the Sources
(London, 1972). The basic guide to sources remains
James F. Kenney, *The Sources for the Early History of
Ireland: Ecclesiastical* (1929; rpt. with some new material
by Ludwig Bieler, New York, 1966). It needs to be
stressed that the following discussion is based only on
documents available in print. Many Celticists assume that
among the unprinted and undescribed Old Irish materials
a homiletic literature remains to be examined. The conclusions offered here may, thus, have to be altered radically,
although I personally doubt (on the basis of the sample
now available) that this will be the case.

35. For a general survey, see Ludwig Bieler, *Ireland: Harbinger
of the Middle Ages* (London, 1963), esp. pp. 65–136. On
Irish exegesis, see Bernhard Bischoff, "Wendepunkte in
der Geschichte der lateinischen Exegese im Frühmit-
telalter," *Sacris Erudiri* 6 (1954) : 189–279; Robert E.
McNally, "The Imagination and Early Irish Biblical
Exegesis," *Annuale Mediaevale* 10 (1969) : 5–27; Martin
McNamara, "Psalter Text and Psalter Study in the Early
Irish Church (A.D. 600–1200)," *Proceedings of the Royal
Irish Academy* 75C (1973) : 201–98. On Irish apocrypha,
see D.N. Dumville, "Biblical Apocrypha and the Early
Irish: A Preliminary Investigation," *Proc. Roy. Irish
Acad.* 73C (1973) : 299–338. The most recent study of
Celtic-OE literary relations is P.L. Henry, *The Early
English and Celtic Lyric* (London, 1966); for influences
on homilies, see Rudolph Willard, *Two Apocrypha in Old
English Homilies,* Beiträge zur englischen Philologie 30
(Leipzig, 1935), and a recent series of articles by J.E. Cross
in *Anglia* 90 (1972) : 132–40; *Proc. Roy. Irish Acad.* 71C
(1971) : 247–54; and *Anglo-Saxon England* 2 (1973) :
209–20.

36. Ed. André Wilmart, *Analecta Reginensa: Extraits des
Manuscrits latins de la Reine Christine conservés au
Vatican,* Studi e Testi 59 (Vatican, 1933), pp. 29–112. On

the Anglo-Saxon connection, see the articles of Cross cited
note 35. Not all the items printed by Wilmart have rubrics
indicating their calendrical connections.

37. In Ludwig Bieler, ed., *The Irish Penitentials,* with appendix
by D.A. Binchy, Scriptores Latini Hiberniae 5 (Dublin,
1963), the only reference to preaching (though *praedicare*
is used also of the confessor's admonition to a layman,
Paenitentiale S. Columbani 24) is in a monastic context:
monks are to be in church on the Lord's Day "Ante
praedicationem" (*ibid.*, 29; see also p. 5). On the Old
Irish Penitential, see below. Hughes, *Church in Early Irish
Society,* cites several references to the importance of
preaching or catechetical instruction (pp. 195, 181, 277),
but she does not discuss the homiletic genres in *Early
Christian Ireland.*

38. I owe this observation to Kathleen Hughes. But the martyrology, which elsewhere (as in England, see *Regularis Concordia,* 21, ed. Thomas Symons [London, 1953], p. 17)
became a paraliturgical book which was read in meetings
of the chapter, had very little narrative matter in Ireland.
See J. Hennig, "Studies in the Latin Texts of the Martyrology of Tallaght, of *Félire Oengusso,* and *Félire Húi
Gormain," Proc. Roy. Irish Acad.* 69C (1970): 45–112
at 47–48. Hagiography, a highly developed genre, is treated
by Hughes, Kennedy, Bieler in the works already cited.

39. Ed. with trans. Whitley Stokes and John Strachan, *Thesaurus
Palaeohibernicus* 2 (Cambridge, 1903): 244–47. The
"homily" is dated in the second half of the eleventh century
by McNally, *Annuale Medievale* 10 (1969): 24; but
Hughes (*Church in Early Irish Society,* p. 145) accepts it
as later seventh or eighth century.

40. See Binchy in Bieler, *Old Irish Penitentials,* pp. 258–59.

41. Text printed by J. Strachan, "An Old-Irish Homily," *Eriu* 3
(1907): 1–10.

42. Leslie Hardinge, *The Celtic Church in Britain* (London, 1972),
pp. 44–47.

43. The only complete publication is the facsimile, *Leabhar Breac,*

The Speckled Book (Dublin, 1876). The best description is by Kathleen Mulchrone and Elizabeth Fitzpatrick in *Catalogue of Irish Manuscripts in the Royal Irish Academy* (Dublin, 1943), fasc. 27, pp. 3379–3404 [the MS is numbered 1230] ; see also, Kenney, *Sources,* pp. 739–40. There is no critical edition of all the "homiletic" matter, but see (in addition to other editions noted by Kenney) Robert Atkinson, ed., *The Passions and the Homilies from Leabhar Breac,* Roy. Irish Acad. Todd Lecture Series 2 (Dublin, 1887), and Edmund Hogan, ed., *The Irish Nennius . . . ,* and *Homilies and Legends from L. Breac* [*sic*], Roy. Irish Acad. Todd Lecture Series 6 (1895). On the scribe, see Thomas Ó Concheanainn, "The Scribe of the Leabhar Breac," *Eriu* 24 (1973) : 64–79.

44. See Myles Dillon, "Nominal Predicates in Irish," *Zeitschrift für Celtische Philologie* 16 (1927) : 313–56 at pp. 318, 321. Dillon's dating of c. 1150 is confirmed (except for Atkinson's XIX and XXIV which are dated c. 1200 and thirteenth century, respectively) by Gerard Murphy in *Duanaire Finn,* III, Irish Texts Society 43 (Dublin, 1953), at p. cviii. I owe these references to the kindness of David N. Dumville.

45. Kenney, *Sources,* pp. 739–40. See esp. Hogan's pieces on the sacraments and the Creed at pp. 17–37.

46. Atkinson's V on St. George and XII (p. 442) for Pentecost; Atkinson's X (p. 426) on the Temptation of Christ (for Quadragesima?) : "This holy lesson, telling of the noble and venerable deed that is preached on this day." Hogan prints (beginning at p. 38) a collection of infancy narratives beginning, "For they are three Gospels that are read and sung in Christian churches on Christmas night."

47. *Gamalnorsk Homiliebok etter AM 619 QV* [facsimile], with intro. by Trygve Knudsen, Corpus Codicum Norvegicorum Medii Aevi, Quarto Series 1 (Oslo, 1952) ; ed. George T. Flom, *Codex AM 619 Quarto . . . ,* University of Illinois Studies in Language and Literature 14, no. 4 (1929) ; and Gustav Indrebø *Gamal Norsk Homiliebok* (Oslo, 1931). Fredrik Paasche, ed. *Homiliu-Bók (Icelandic Sermons)* :

Perg 4to *No. 15 in the Royal Library, Stockholm*
[facsimile], Corpus Codicum Islandicorum Medii Aevi 8
(Copenhagen, 1935) ; Theodor Wisen, ed., *Homiliu-Bok:
Isländska Homilier* . . . (Lund, 1872). For general studies,
in addition to the indispensible work of E.O.G. Turville-
Petre cited below, see Hans Bekker-Nielsen *et al.*, *Norrøn
Fortaellekunst: Kapitler af den norsk-islandske middelal-
derlitteraturs Historie* (Copenhagen, 1965), at pp. 11–12,
19–23, 149–51 ; Trygve Knudsen, "Homiliebøker," in
*Kulturhistorik Lexicon for nordisk middelalder fra
vikingetid til reformationstid* 6 (Copenhagen, 1961) : pp.
657–66. There is no record of Swedish preaching in the
period ; on Danish sermon writing (none of which survives
from the twelfth or thirteenth century), see Anne Riising,
"Danmarks Middelalderlige Praediken," (Diss. Odense
1969), and an important critique of her work by E. Lade-
wig Petersen, "Preaching in Medieval Denmark," *Mediaeval Scandinavia* 3 (1970) : 142–71.
48. Turville-Petre, *Origins of Icelandic Literature* (Oxford, 1953),
pp. 71–87, esp. at p. 75. See also his essays on the homilies
for the dedication of a church and the Assumption of the
Virgin in *Nine Norse Studies,* Viking Society for Northern
Research, Text Series 5 (London, 1972), pp. 79–101 and
102–17. For discussion of Anglo-Scandinavian relations and
references to the historian Adam of Bremen, see Frank
Barlow, *The English Church, 1000–1066: A Constitutional
History* (London, 1963), p. 233.
49. I owe these suggestions to Ursula Dronke.
50. Turville-Petre, *Origins,* p. 113, summarizing *Jons Saga Helga.*
In the light of the German canonical evidence, it cannot be
absolutely certain that Gisli did not translate from Latin
ad libitum. Alternatively the book may, Turville-Petre
notes (p. 114), have been written in Norwegian rather
than Icelandic. Paasche (p. 22) thinks this record of the
reading of homilies may indicate the practice was uncommon.
51. Paasche in intro. to *Homiliu-Bók,* p. 11.
52. Stockholm, Arna-Magnaean MS 237. See Paasche, in intro. to

Homiliu-Bók p. 13; Turville-Petre, *Origins,* pp. 116–17;
Norse Studies, pp. 79–80.

53. *The Arna-Magnaean Manuscript 677, 4to* [facsimile], ed.
Didrik Arup Seip, Corpus Codicum Islandicorum Medii
Aevi 18 (Copenhagen, 1947), pp. 23–33.

54. Turville-Petre, *Origins,* pp. 137–39. On Honorius, see further
below; the *Elucidarium* was probably written at Canterbury
as a popularization of the teaching of Anselm.

55. In addition to the works already cited, see Joan Turville-Petre,
"Sources of the Vernacular Homily in England, Norway,
and Iceland," *Arkiv förNordisk Filologi* 75 (1960) : 168–82.

56. "Translations of a Lost Penitential Homily," *Traditio* 19
(1963) : 51–78, and the article cited in note 54. The English
aspects of Mrs. Turville-Petre's study has recently been
refined by M.R. Godden, "An Old English Penitential
Motif," *Anglo-Saxon England* 2 (1973) : 221–39. See also
Mattias Tveitane, "Irish Apocrypha in Norse Tradition?
On the Sources of some Medieval Homilies," *Arv: Tid-
skrift för Nördisk Folkminnesforskning* 22 (1966) : pp. 111–
35. Tveitane shows that there are connections between the
homily on observance of Sunday in the Norwegian books
and the Old English homilies of the sort which may be
called heterodox, Irish texts, the *Catéchèses Celtiques,* the
MHG sermon-collection *Speculum ecclesiae,* etc.

57. Paasche, in intro. to *Homiliu-Bók,* p. 21.

58. Ibid., pp. 21–22.

59. See, for examples, Tveitane, "Irish Apocrypha in Norse Tradition?" p. 116; J. Turville-Petre, "Sources for the Vernacular Homily," pp. 172, 180.

60. J. Turville-Petre, "Sources for the Vernacular Homily," pp.
181–82.

61. *Gamalnorsk Homiliebok,* p. 36.

62. Ed. in *PL* 172, 607–1108.

63. So R.W. Southern, *Saint Anselm and his Biographer: A Study
of Monastic Life and Thought, 1059–c. 1130* (Cambridge,
1963), pp. 209–17.

64. On details of the biography, see Eva Matthews Sanford,
"Honorius, *Presbyter* and *Scholasticus,*" *Speculum* 23

(1948) : 397–425, and Hermann Menhardt, "Der Nachlass des Honorius Augustodunensis," *Zeitschrift für deutsches Altertum und deutsche Literatur* 69 (1958/59) : 23–69. The latter believes Honorius was at Canterbury by 1097, wrote the *Elucidarium* there before 1108 and departed for Germany before 1115, and wrote the *Speculum* c. 1120. He may have gone to Regensburg in 1126, about a decade before his death.

65. Sanford, "Honorius," p. 412, summarizing in part a passage from several MSS which is not included in the ed. in *PL* but is edited by Johann von Kelle, "Untersuchungen über das *Speculm ecclesiae*," *Sitzungsberichte der Philoso-phisch-Historischen Classe der Akademie der Wissen-schaften* (Wien) 145 (1902), viii, pp. 18–19.

66. See works cited by Menhardt, "Der Nachlass des Honorius Augustodunensis," p. 68.

67. The best and most recent edition is that of Gert Mellbourn, *Speculum Ecclesiae: Eine frühmittelhochdeutsche Pre-digtsammlung,* Lunder Germanistische Forschungen 12 (Lund, 1944).

68. Tveitane, "Irish Apocrypha in Norse Tradition," pp. 111–35.

69. The standard study is l'Abbé L. Bourgain, *La Chaire française au XIIᵉ Siècle* (Paris, 1879) ; see also Paul leCoy, *La Chaire française du Moyen Âge* (Paris, 1868). For general reference, see Urban Tigner Holmes, Jr., *A History of Old French Literature from the Origins to 1300* (New York, 1937), esp. pp. 42–43 ; Paul Zumthor, *Histoire littéraire de la France médiévale* (Paris, 1954). On Anglo-Norman literature, see M. Dominica Legge, *Anglo-Norman Literature and its Background* (Oxford, 1963) ; *Anglo-Norman in the Cloisters* (Edinburgh, 1950) ; and K.V. Sinclair, "Anglo-Norman Studies: The Last Twenty Years," *Australian Journal of French Studies* 2 (1965) : 113–55 and 225–78 ; esp. 141–49. The rise of preaching in the Romance dialects is so sudden in the twelfth century and the literature is so sophisticated that allowance must be made for earlier written sermons that have not survived. Whether literary forms must evolve is a vexed question to

which I am inclined to answer in the negative, assuming that the written vernacular sermon appeared only in Romance at about the date of the earliest extant texts.

70. On Maurice, see C.A. Robson, *Maurice de Sully and the Medieval Vernacular Homily* (Oxford, 1951).

71. Ed. Arvid Gabrielson, *Le Sermon de Guischart de Beaulieu,* Skrifter utgifna af K. Humanistiska Vetenskaps-Samfundet i Uppsala, XXIV.5 (1909). Sources discussed by Gabrielson, "Guischart de Beaulieu's Debt to Religious Learning and Literature in England," *Archiv für das Studium der neueren Sprachen* 128 (1912) : 309–328, and (more skeptically) by Legge, *Anglo-Norman in the Cloisters,* pp. 31–35.

72. Professor Angus Cameron informs me privately of the existence of fairly extensive Anglo-Norman glosses of OE texts.

73. See Thomas M. Charland, *Artes praedicandi: Contribution à l'Histoire de la Rhétorique au Moyen Âge,* Publ. de l'Institut d'Études médiévales d'Ottawa 7 (Ottawa, 1936) ; and, for further bibliography, James J. Murphy, *Mediaeval Rhetoric: A Select Bibliography,* Toronto Mediaeval Bibliographies (Toronto, 1972).

74. This sentiment is also expressed by John C. Pope, review of James Hurt, *Aelfric,* in *Speculum* 49 (1974) : 344–47.

75. This paper was completed in 1975, and it has not been possible to update its bibliography as it goes to press. One basic reference work, however, may be cited : Karin Morvay and Dagmar Gruke, *Bibliographie der Deutschen Predigt des Mittelalters,* Münchener Texte und Untersuchungen zur deutschen Literatur des Mittelalters (Munich, 1974).

CYRIL L. SMETANA & PAUL THE DEACON'S PATRISTIC ANTHOLOGY

Although contemporaries of Paul the Deacon [1] knew him as a grammarian and poet, and later centuries have known him mainly through his third and last historical work, the *Historia Langobardorum,* perhaps his most significant contribution to the Carolingian renaissance and his greatest influence on western civilization was in the area of liturgy.[2] At the end of the eighth century he compiled a selection of readings from the Fathers for Sunday and feast days of the church year, which became standard for the western church for eleven hundred years. There were, of course, significant changes in successive versions of the homiliary, but these were occasioned more by the addition of new feasts and by an increased number of readings (e.g., for all the ferial days of Lent) than by radical substitution. Catholic in the wide range of patristic readings as well as in its widespread use, the homiliary served for centuries as a source of continuing education and inspiration in the church. Yet this compilation has remained relatively unknown and unappreciated.

More than two hundred years ago J. Mabillon pointed out that the early printed editions under Paul's name, filled with numerous authors who postdated the compiler, could hardly be the form of his original homiliary. He suggested the original homiliary was much more like the ninth-century manuscripts from the Reichenau collection.[3] One hundred years later Ernest Ranke found these manuscripts in Karlsruhe and enthusiastically but prematurely promised a critical edition.[4] Some forty years later Frederich Wiegand was able to reconstruct the original schedule of homilies.[5] Drawing on the earlier Reichenau manuscripts, he was able to fill the lacunae from the later and fuller Benediktbeuren versions of the homiliary which he discovered in Munich.[6] Wiegand, cognizant of the massive proportions of editing these early manuscripts, contented himself with an inventory of the contents. He printed Paul's dedicatory verses, Charlemagne's prefatory letter, Paul's

votive verses to Charlemagne, and the short prose conspectus;
of the homiliary proper he quoted the full Gospel pericope, the
incipit of each patristic selection, and a source-citation to Migne
or other patristic compilations. The thirty-nine pieces Wiegand
was unable to identify were supplied in the following year by Dom
Germain Morin.[7]

Wiegand's inventory together with the additional sources discovered by Morin was published twice with citations to more recent
editions of the Fathers, but without further critical work on the
sources until Dom Réginald Grégoire published his important
study of medieval homiliaries.[8] Drawing on Dekker's *Clavis
Patrum* and other patristic studies, Grégoire considerably enlarged
and refined our understanding of the contents of the homiliary
and the authenticity of its contents. Until a definitive edition appears, Grégoire's work will serve as a most helpful guide to Paul's
original homiliary. An inventory of an homiliary, however, can
substitute for the text no more than an outline can replace a novel
or play. The following attempt to flesh out the skeleton schedule
of homilies is not offered by way of *Ersatz;* it may, however,
convey a sense of the homiliary's vast richness and variety.

Charlemagne commissioned Paul the Deacon to compile a series
of readings from the works of the Fathers for use at the night
office of the church. The king found the homiliaries then in vogue
unsuitable for divine service because of the dubious origin of many
of their lections and because of the numerous errors in transcription, but a more important reason, which he speaks of in his prefatory letter, was his desire to institute Roman usage in the liturgical functions of the kingdom.[9] Paul, a monk of Monte Cassino,
was admirably suited for the task. Whether he compiled these two
volumes while still at court or after his return to Monte Cassino
cannot be easily decided, but at any rate Charlemagne was satisfied
with Paul's work and promulgated it by royal letter as the official
homiliary of the kingdom.[10]

Within a short time Paul's homiliary (henceforth PD) was preferred to other collections. Manuscript evidence shows that the
earlier compilation by Alan of Farfa continued to be copied, but
not with the same frequency as PD.[11] The fact that PD was the
official homiliary of the kingdom accounts, no doubt, for its wide-

spread use, but its completeness of coverage and the quality of the readings certainly made it a most useful service book in churches and monasteries even beyond Frankish confines. Comparison with Alan's work immediately indicates that they are compilations of a fundamentally different order. Though Alan's work in plan and content reflects an ancient Roman lectionary, its scope is much narrower than PD. There is, for instance, no provision at all for the Sundays of the year. The 203 entries in its two volumes cover the greater feasts and fasts of the year and a number of saints' days. It certainly was never envisioned as an homiliary in any sense of the word, for it has only nine homilies, properly so-called, in the entire collection. It is simply a collection of sermons, and thus it was called by its first analyst.[12]

PD is also unlike the *catena*-collections of the later Carolinians, such as that of Haymo or Smaragdus, whose sermons were made up of brief excerpts from various patristic sources.[13] Paul's homilies and sermons consist of complete selections from the Fathers and thus comprise a fair representation of patristic exegesis, for much of the Fathers' exegesis is contained in their commentaries on sacred scripture.

The homiliary of Paul the Deacon was, however, no innovation in liturgical usage. The commentaries of the Fathers had long been used as readings in the offices of the church, as reading at table, and, as recent scholarship has demonstrated, for private devotional purposes.[14] Paul's work was designed specifically for the liturgy, and its merit lies in the completeness of its coverage and in its careful selection and transcription of patristic texts. Paul's mandate, as Charlemagne's letter clearly states, was to fashion a new homiliary, not to touch up and correct the old ones. At any rate Paul's debt to the extant homiliaries is not great: of Alan's 195 sermons, only 32 are found in Paul's collection, of the nine homilies, only three. A further eleven texts, nine homilies, and two sermons, are common to Paul and Agimund, who, in the eighth century compiled a lectionary for use in Rome.[15] Correspondences with other homiliaries are almost negligible.

Paul's homiliary, then, is an independent collection of 244 homilies and sermons distributed over the whole liturgical year. Volume I begins with the fifth Sunday before Christmas and ends with Holy Saturday; volume II provides readings from Easter to the end of November.[16] Interspersed with the temporal cycle, which includes the Sundays, the commemorations of the mysteries in Christ's life, and the seasons of fasting (i.e. the winter and autumn Ember days), there are entries for the feasts of Mary and other great saints of the church calendar. PD also has thirty-five selections under the rubric *Commune Sanctorum*. This forms a section of the second volume and includes lections for saints besides those who have proper readings and are included in the temporal cycle. The lections are arranged in groups and according to rank: apostles, martyrs, confessors, virgins. There are finally, a further ten lections for such occasions as the dedication of a church, for Rogation days, and for the commemoration of the dead. This latter section of the common of the saints lends considerable flexibility for use of the homiliary in the cult of local saints and for other celebrations.

Of the 244 readings thus assigned to the temporal and sanctoral cycles, 151 are given under the term *sermo*, 91 under *omelia*. This preponderance of sermons over homilies may cast doubt on the propriety of the name *liber omeliarum*, or it may suggest that there was no distinction between the two terms. Scholars have generally inclined to the latter opinion.[17] Early versions of Paul's homiliary show, however, that Paul distinguished between the two. Though this point cannot be made without a short excursus, I think the point is worth making, especially since it is neither readily apparent, nor is it possible to show it from the modern inventories.[18]

A homiliary may include both sermons and homilies, but strictly speaking a homily is a discourse that expounds or comments on a text of sacred scripture for the instruction and edification of the listeners, while a sermon to the same purpose is an address on a dogmatic or moral theme. I contend that Paul is not blurring the distinction, even though twenty-eight of the readings he calls *sermones* function as *homiliae*.[19] A review of these twenty-eight functional homilies shows that twenty-six of them are drawn from sources other than the homilies of the Fathers. Of these, twenty-four are drawn from commentaries, books, letters, or *sermones* properly so-called.[20] Only two, both drawn from Bede's authentic homilies, present a problem. One is clearly an oversight, since it appears immediately under the title, *Incipit omelia* . . . ; the other is anomalous.[21] Among the ninety-one selections designated *omeliae* there are only four that seem to be misnamed. Though none of them has a preceding pericope, two are expositions of a scriptural text, though not a Gospel text, while two others are clearly sermons.[22] The four anomalies among 244 readings could possibly be the errors of the editors, his scribe, or of the scribe who copied the manuscript. It seems obvious from this that Paul did not confuse his terms any more than Aelfric did when he entitled his two volumes *Sermones Catholici*. Since the distinction is an ancient one, and since both Paul and Aelfric were careful to honor it, we may well question the advisability of perpetuating titles like Thorpe's arbitrary *Homilies of the Anglo-Saxon Church* and of calling "sermons" of Wulfstan, the Vercelli, or Blickling collections, "homilies." [23]

Paul's commission to compile lections for the year's liturgical cycle was generously fulfilled in the two volumes which provide for the Sundays and the major feasts of the year. The great festal days are provided with a pericope, a homily, and several sermons.[24] Ordinary Sundays have only a pericope and a homily, but two Sundays in Advent and the Sundays from Septuagesima to Palm Sunday have a sermon besides the homily. Why these Sundays, the one Sunday after Peter and Paul and two Sundays *Post Sancti Angeli,* have sermons is not clear. In all, Paul has made provision for fifty Sundays of the year.

According to the time-honored metaphor of Charlemagne's letter Paul was asked to collect certain flowers from the wide-flung fields of the Catholic Fathers.[25] The homiliary is proof positive that he took his mandate seriously. It indeed covers a wide field and includes representatives of both eastern and western theology, though naturally the homilists of the west predominate. Of these the Venerable Bede's homilies and commentaries furnished the greatest number of readings in Paul's homiliary.

Though not a Father of the church himself, Bede is unquestionably patristic in both inspiration and articulation. Of the fifty-seven lections from Bede, thirty-six are designated as homilies, eighteen as sermons, and one simply as *commentum*. A final two, though not

attributed to Bede in the early manuscripts, are from his commentaries on Luke and Mark respectively. Of the thirty-six designated as homilies by Paul, thirty-four have been verified by modern
scholarship as authentic homilies. Evidently Paul's sources differed
from the garbled and confused manuscripts of the later Middle
Ages. Bede's works are used for twenty-three of some thirty-five
pericopes from the Gospel of Luke and for seventeen of the twenty-
eight selections from the Gospel of John. This preference for Bede
over Augustine as a Johannine commentator is somewhat surprising. Paul knew and used Augustine's *Tractatus in Johannem*
several times in the homiliary. It may be that he preferred the more
tightly knit and plain comments of Bede to the brilliant but
rambling exposition by Augustine. Bede's homilies serve for readings on St. Matthew in eight instances and for Mark in only one
case. In all, Bede's contribution forms almost one-quarter of the two
volumes.

The exegetical work of Bede is only one facet of this Anglo-Saxon
Benedictine, but it shows at every turn his in-depth knowledge of
sacred scripture and intimate acquaintance with the Fathers. His
work, is of course, not innovative or creative. His commentaries
are heavily indebted both to the doctrine of the Fathers and to
their very mode of expression,[26] and his homilies are, for the most
part, a mosaic of biblical and patristic sources. He quotes five or
six patristic sources for each homily and quotes from Scripture
(other than that on which he is commenting) on the average of
twenty-five times in each homily.[27]

We cannot know whether Paul was acquainted with fifty authentic homilies of Bede as separate readings or in the form of a
homiliary,[28] but we do know that he drew freely on both homilies
and commentaries. He could not have found more admirable instruction and inspiration for the monks and clerics who attended
the night offices. Bede's work was wholesomely orthodox and
stylistically correct, but cloistered and scholarly compared to the
sermons of Maximus.

Of the fifty sermons under the name of Maximus in the homiliary
only fourteen are today considered authentic.[29] Scholars, however, have been unwilling to discredit Paul in this case, since he is
generally reliable in assigning readings to their rightful authors.

It has been suggested that Paul may have been drawing on a collection of sermons by a bishop of the same name in the latter part of the seventh century.[30] The fourteen authentic sermons show that Maximus was a popular preacher in every sense of the word. There is an extraordinary robustness and energy as well as a welcome brevity in most of Maximus's sermons. He seizes upon natural happenings: light, darkness, lightning, youth and age, and makes them the vehicle for spiritual analogies and moral lessons. Eagles, camels, worms, millstones, grapes, and manna are all part of his sacramental universe, and Maximus sees each image as a symbol of man's spiritual life. Though the authentic sermons are far richer in this approach, the spurious works do not entirely lack these themes or other favorite themes of Maximus: baptism, fasting, fear of wars, idol worship. Generally, however, the authentic sermons are much more concrete in both content and form. Paul deserves some indulgence for failing to recognize the disparity between the true and false sermons, for it is only in the present century that scholarship has been confident enough to establish definitively the Maximian canon.

The sermons of Leo the Great add a further dimension to Paul's homiliary. Like the works of Maximus they are brief, even to the point of severity, but there is no fantasy or allegorizing in them. Leo had a precise and ordered mind, fond of formulas expressed in simple, unequivocal language. There is neither metaphysical subtlety nor theorizing; his sermons are doctrinal, but avoid the mystifying nuances and distinctions of the eastern theologians of his time. He was a man of action whose sermons exude the very simple but majestic eloquence that is said to have turned Attila from Rome. Of St. Leo's ninety-six sermons Paul chose thirty-five.[31] All authentic, they present variations on the great themes of redemption and sanctification of man, stressing the part played by Adam, Christ, and the church. They usually occur in series for the great feasts of the year along with Maximus's sermons.

It is hardly strange that Paul included thirty-two of Pope Gregory's forty homilies.[32] It would be interesting to speculate why Paul did not use the other eight homilies, particularly since most of them appear in later versions of the homiliary. Priests in the early

Middle Ages were expected to be acquainted with these homilies, and bishops were enjoined to examine clerics on them during canonical visitation. Gregory's homilies are truly popular expositions of Gospel texts that contrast markedly with the careful and scholarly expositions of Bede. Gregory's themes are those that animated theology and art during the Middle Ages: the end of the world, death, heaven, hell—but without the patina of morbid brooding of a later age. Christ's resurrection, glorification, and ascension have a prominent place in his preaching.

Gregory's approach to scripture is practical and existential. Like Maximus he uses scriptural metaphors: fire, dove, thorns, talents, and banquets. These metaphors, however, play an important part in his allegories. With all his allegorizing the homilies are still pastoral in character, and like his stories, they clearly appealed to audiences in his later days.

Paul uses Gregory the Great for all the highest feasts of the year: Christmas, Epiphany, Easter, Ascension, Pentecost, and the three Sundays before the beginning of Lent. After the Third Sunday of Pentecost (II 39) there are no Gregorian homilies until the Sunday after the Ember days in September.[33] Paul shows particular deference to Gregory by drawing on his homilies for at least one homily for every class of saint in the *Commune Sanctorum*.

Compared to contemporary and later homiliaries, Paul's collection is curiously spartan in its use of homilies and sermons from Augustine. There are only eight selections from the *Tractatus in Johannem*. From some 500 authentic sermons only three appear in the homiliary of Paul.[34] A further seven readings are drawn from four different works of Augustine.[35] In only four instances sermons attributed to Augustine are certainly spurious, an index of Paul's scholarship.[36] "Augustine" was virtually a "brand name" during the Middle Ages. His name on a sermon was considered a guarantee of orthodoxy and high theology. Otherwise astute men became quite vulnerable when dealing with a piece that bore Augustine's name, if not his characteristic impress. Alan of Farfa, for instance, has eighty-six sermons under the name of Augustine, of which only twenty-three are authentic. Much the same ratio holds for later versions of Paul's homiliary, which were less critical than Paul in admitting doubtful or spurious Augustinian material.

Though small in number, the lections from Augustine give a representative picture of his works. The *Tractatus in Johannem,* from which the greatest number of homilies are drawn, shows Augustine as teacher and preacher. They are not, and were never intended to be, scientific exegesis. Augustine's *Quaestiones evangeliorum* and the *De sermone Domini in monte,* however, are more in the traditional method of exegesis. The *Enchiridion* and *De diversis quaestionibus* are considered, after Augustine's *De trinitate,* his most important dogmatic contributions. The *De civitate Dei* contains Augustine's philosophy of history and treats the larger historical perspectives of faith. It must be confessed, however, that the readings which Paul chose from *De civitate Dei* are hardly representative of the book's grand sweep.

Paul's critical acumen is not so apparent in his choice of lections from John Chrysostom as it was in the case of Augustine. Of nineteen selections only one is unquestionably authentic, namely, homily 3, *De laudibus Pauli* (II 53). Peter Chrysologus is the author of two sermons, while the *Opus imperfectum in Matthaeum* furnished two more.[37] This Latin series of sermons from which Paul drew fourteen readings was possibly inspired by Chrysostom's homilies, but was certainly not a translation of any of his known works.[38] Stylistically they hardly reflect the practical, direct manner of Chrysostom. They are heavy with rhetoric and strained with allegory and symbolism foreign to the literal and objective approach of the Antioch school of exegesis to which Chrysostom belonged. Of course Paul can hardly be blamed for being unaware of facts that have been discovered a thousand years later.

Of the eight selections from Jerome, on the other hand, all are authentic. Six sermons are from Jerome's commentary on Matthew, composed for a friend who wished to have some spiritual reading on a long sea journey.[39] It was written in a matter of a few weeks and owes a heavy debt to Origen's commentary. It is really little more than a brief series of notes loosely strung together. The interpretation is literal, at times heavy, but lightened with rare touches of wry, dry humor. In quite a different vein are two other sermons drawn from letters by Jerome, one a commentary on Matthew, the other on Luke.[40] The question-and-answer method employed in these letters is admirably suited to the exposition of a text, though questions are often proposed without any attempt to answer them. It is regrettable that Paul did not use some of the lively homilies preached by Jerome to the monks in Bethlehem (AD 393–400). That three of the eight pieces he chose remained constants in the church's breviary for over a thousand years, however, speaks well of his choice.[41]

Jerome was an admirer and translator of Origen, but he was also highly critical of his theological opinions. The fact that Paul includes any of Origen's works is quite remarkable. Alan of Farfa does not have a single homily. In light of the Council of Constantinople's anathemas against Origen, it seems a rather bold move on the part of Paul to include him among the orthodox Fathers. Yet modern scholarship has taught us how to read his exegesis and has vindicated Paul's choice of him as a homilist. Unlike John Chrysostom, preacher and moralist, Origen was essentially a speculative theologian. Keenly aware of the maze of symbols in the Scriptures, he became the first great typologist. In fact it was he who made the first methodical digest of biblical typology. He deepened and complicated scriptural exegesis by attributing a threefold meaning to scripture—adding a moral and an allegorical meaning. Few though they are, the six homilies enrich the quality and enhance the scope of the homiliary. They also posed a problem.

The excerpt for the vigil of Christmas is a case in point.[42] Compared to the work as it came down to us in the Latin version, Paul's selection is unduly brief. No doubt the bold speculation that both Mary and Christ were in need of purification, since no human being is free from stain, was offensive to Paul and thus eliminated. For the Sunday after Christmas the homily is not radically cut, but certain elements which Grégoire describes as *trop osées* have been excised.[43] Paul does not avoid this perennially controversial exegete, but he does exercise editorial prerogative when there is a question of the orthodoxy of his homiliary.

Considering the wholesale destruction of Origen's works after his condemnation and the untrustworthiness of the Latin versions generally, it is impressive that of the six readings from Origen five are genuine. Of the five homilies two are from St. Jerome's translation of Origen's commentary on Luke, while three more are based on a faithful exposition in Latin of Origen's Matthew commentary.[44] Only the first homily (I 15) is now considered to be spurious.

St. Ambrose of Milan was so heavily indebted to Origen in his exegesis that Jerome uncharitably suggested that Ambrose's commentary on St. Luke's Gospel was a mere translation of Origen into Latin. We do not know whether Paul was aware of this judgment, but he draws very little from Ambrose. Of the five readings from Ambrose, four are from his commentary on Luke, one of which serves as a homily for a pericope from Matthew![45] The fifth selection is from the *De virginibus*.[46] Like Alan, Paul draws upon Ambrose for the Circumcision and Purification. Paul also uses his sermons for the feast of St. Agnes, the Nativity of Mary, and *plurimorum martyrum,* in the common of saints, which are all New Testament themes.[47] Ironically Ambrose's most impressive exegesis is generally considered to be found in his commentaries on the Old Testament and particularly in his *Hexaemeron libri sex*. With Philo and Origen as his model, he inquired into the allegorical and tropological meanings of the events recorded in sacred Scripture. We know that it was precisely his treatment of the Old Testament that so moved Augustine.[48] Paul's compilation, however, had little need for Old Testament exegesis, and for what was needed he preferred Chrysostom.

Of Fulgentius's eight topical sermons, Paul uses the first four. Sermon I is found in the *Commune sanctorum*. There are also sermons on Christmas, on St. Stephen, and on Epiphany.[49] These sermons are characterized by an excessive rhetorical balance, by contrast, apostrophes, and questions. Fulgentius, an ardent admirer of Augustine's teaching, imitated the master's style but did so without the master's sensitivity.

Isidore of Seville is represented by only two readings: Chapter 26 of his *De ecclesiae officiis* is used for a short doctrinal introduction to Christmas; Chapter 72 of *De ortu et obitu patrum,* a nutshell biography of John the Evangelist, is used on the saint's feast.[50] The entire contribution is very small: some seventy-one lines in Migne's edition. Isidore's work, neither original nor creative, is an erudite product of an industrious compiler. The *De ortu* is a compilation of lives of saints of the Old and New Testaments and in this sense a work of exegesis, while the *De ecclesiasticis officiis* is important for an understanding of the liturgy in Spain in the seventh century.

There are, finally, two more entries. One is a sermon on the Feast of the Innocents by Peter Chrysologus, attributed to Severianus by Paul.[51] The other, an excerpt from Eusebius's *Ecclesiastical History* in Rufinus's translation, details the picaresque career of one of St. John's disciples.[52] It follows Isidore's biography as a second reading for the feast of St. John the Evangelist.

Contemporaries were not slow to recognize the richness of this homiliary, for there is evidence that it was used far beyond the kingdom of Charlemagne. Only a few ninth-century manuscripts are still extant on the continent and, given the attrition of time and the wholesale destruction in England during the Danish raids and after the dissolution of the monasteries in the sixteenth century, it is surprising that we still have some manuscripts from the tenth and eleventh centuries in England. We know that in the late tenth century Aelfric used Paul's homiliary, though we do not know the version he used.[53] I have suggested elsewhere that he perhaps had a shortened form adapted for monastic use.[54] It may be worthwhile to list here homiliaries extant in English libraries that can be called versions of Paul the Deacon's homiliary and that are roughly from the time of Aelfric and Wulfstan.[55]

At the beginning of this century Carlo Cipolla recorded six homiliaries related to Paul the Deacon's work in English libraries.[56] Only three manuscripts of these are versions of Paul's original work. Durham Cathedral MS B II.2, an eleventh-century work, though imperfect at both beginning and end, contains 78 of the 110 selections in the *Pars hiemalis* of Paul with only one additional homily. Since the manuscript begins with I 16 and ends with I 105, there was little change in the contents. Bodley MS 276 (twelfth century) is an abbreviated form of the *Pars aestiva*. Though there are variations and additions, the sequence is similar, and twenty-nine of the forty-five homilies are the same as in Paul's homiliary. Lincoln Cathedral MS 158 (C.2.2.) is a lectionary-homiliary of the eleventh century. Though defective at the beginning (it begins with Septuagesima), it follows through the liturgical year and includes the greater part of the *Commune sanctorum* with 100 lections, 54 of which are found in Paul's work. The other three manuscripts mentioned by Cipolla—Hereford Cathedral o. 7. 4. (twelfth century), Bodley Meerman MS T. 2. 23 (tenth century), and Bodley 473 (twelfth century),—have some lessons in common with Paul's collection, but the divergencies in content and order are too great to consider them versions.

There are, however, other manuscripts in English libraries that are not too distant cousins to Paul's homiliary. Durham Cathedral A III.29 (an eleventh-century manuscript curiously passed over by Cipolla) is one.[57] Though it is divided into two sections, a temporal and sanctoral cycle, and though it does not follow the order of homilies in Paul strictly, ninety-four of its components are identical with those in the earlier homiliary. H. Schenkl long ago pointed out the resemblance between this manuscript and the two volumes (also eleventh century) originally from Bury St. Edmunds and now in Pembroke College, Cambridge.[58] Pembroke MSS 23 and 24 contain 172 sermons and homilies; 121 of these are the same as those in PD. There are 17 new items in the *Temporale* and 34 new feasts in the *Sanctorale*. Finally B.L. Royal 2 c iii (late eleventh century), with readings from Septuagesima to Easter and a sanctoral series, has 121 lections in all. Of these, 72 correspond with those in PD. This homiliary is most probably the one mentioned in the Rochester library catalogue in the early thirteenth century.[59] The manuscripts we have mentioned may have been made and used in England. None of them, however, has any overt indication that it is a version of PD. As far as I know there is only one homiliary that has the letter of Charlemagne and the dedicatory verses of Paul, a twelfth-century homiliary, Cambridge, Magdalene College MS CII. It has 103 of the 110 lections in the *Pars hiemalis* of PD with 37 additional sermons, almost half of which are from St. Augustine. There is also a fragment in Corpus Christi College (Oxford) MS 255. It consists of three folios and contains the dedicatory verses of Paul, Charlemagne's letter, the votive verses, and a table of contents. There is no positive evidence that these folios were part of a homiliary, but there is some evidence that they are castoffs.[60]

The homiliary published by Migne under the name of Paul the Deacon has Charlemagne's letter and the verses but is vastly different from the original homiliary.[61] It is a reprint of a 1539 Cologne edition and is representative, in an exaggerated form, of the changes

and variations in successive versions of PD. The most obvious difference between the Migne edition and the original homiliary is that
it has 300 readings as compared with the original 244 in PD.[62]
These additions would not, of themselves, destroy the shape or alter
the structure of the original. The addition of sermons for each of
the ferial days of the five weeks of Lent and of a second of two
sermons before the homily for most Sundays of the year considerably increases the number of readings. New feasts for the saints
are few, but each feast has two or more sermons. In fact there are
only eleven new feasts, while four saints provided for in the original
PD have been dropped.[63]

The homiliary printed by Migne subsumes both the dominical
and ferial offices of winter and summer under a *proprium de
tempore,* while the proper offices of the saints and the common of
saints are brought together under the rubric *proprium sanctorum.*
This division, which is already found in the eleventh-century Durham MS A III 29, and the fact that it has only 119 of the original
244 readings indicate how little similarity there is between this
late form and the original PD. The character of the homiliary in
Migne will appear clearer by a brief resumé of the 181 additional
lections.

The largest single addition is from the works (authentic and
spurious) of St. Augustine, fifty-three as opposed to the thirty-two
in PD: of these only twelve are in PD. Of the fifty sermons by
Maximus only eleven are found in this later homiliary and of these
two belong to Maximus's authentic works. St. Leo is represented by
nineteen sermons as against the thirty-five in PD, and seven of
these are new. All except one of Gregory's homilies are given
(thirty-nine to the thirty-two in PD). Only Gregory's Homily 11,
In Natali Virginum, is missing. There are fifty-two readings from
Bede as compared to the fifty-six in PD, fifteen new works among
them. Of the five sermons by Ambrose three are new. Origen is
used for four, Jerome only for two lections. There are also writers
later than Paul: Hericus (eleven sermons) Haymo (five sermons),
and Anselm (one sermon). For the most part the Lenten sermons
and the first sermon for the Sundays are given anonymously (forty-
three in all).

Neither the truncated form of the manuscripts of earlier centuries nor the overblown version in the Migne editions can compare with the breadth and riches of the original form of the homiliary as compiled by Paul the Deacon in the late eighth century. Dogma and morality, hagiography and liturgy, symbol and allegory, preaching in a classic vein and in a popular mode, narrative, dramatic and expository forms all find their place in it. Here indeed is God's plenty. One has no yardstick to measure the influence on the minds and hearts of the monks and clerics who listened to or read these lessons for over a period of a thousand years. We do know that they had influence in the cloister and the pulpit. I have demonstrated elsewhere how extensively Aelfric made use of PD in his *Sermones catholici*, and Professor Pope has shown that though he used this same source less consistently in his later homilies, he still uses it "for at least some passages of thirteen of the twenty-one full homilies." [64] Professor Cross has been able to point out some new debts of Aelfric to PD.[65]

It has long been recognized that the Anglo-Saxon poets were influenced by the liturgy and that hymns, homilies, and antiphons inspired some of the best poetry.[66] Max Förster, before the turn of the century, had demonstrated the influence of patristic thought on Aelfric and others.[67] Once we are aware of what the versions of PD in England and the numerous other homiliaries have to offer, we will be in a position to assess more closely what English preachers and poets owe to such sources.[68] It is necessary to recall, however, that the homiliary is only one source. Besides the homiliaries, there are antiphonaries, lectionaries, sacramentaries, and pontificals all waiting to be explored.

APPENDIX

Pericopes with homilies in PD

Matthew	PD	Mark	PD	John	PD
1:18	I 15	12:28	II 90	1:1–3	I 26
2:1–2	48	16:1–2	5	1:19	I 8
2:13	36	16:15–16	28	1:26–31	49

NOTES

1. Known also as Paulus Warnefrid, Paulus Casinensis, Paulus Levita. The dates of his birth and death, like his name, are variously given: c. 720–24, c.797–800. The facts of his life are gleaned from remarks in his own works. The pioneer biography, L. Bethmann, "Paulus Diaconus Leben und Schriften," *Archiv der Gesellschaft für ältere deutsche Geschichtskunde* 10 (1851): 247–334, is still valuable. A brief but informative account of his life and works is "Paulus Diaconus" in Wattenbach-Levison, *Deutschlands Geschichtsquellen in Mittelalter,* 2nd ed. W. Levinson and H. Loewe (Weimar, 1953), pp. 203–24.

2. For his connection with the sacramentary, see K. Gamber, "Il sacramentario di Paolo Deacono: La rendazione del Gelasiano s.viii in Pavia," *Revista di storia della chiesa in Italia* 16 (1962): 412–38.

3. J. Mabillon, *Annales O.S.B.* (Paris, 1704), II, p. 239. The late printed edition of the homiliary in Migne (PL 95, 1159–1566) is still attributed to Paul in the *New Catholic Encyclopedia* (1967) s.v. Paul the Deacon. The citation is also wrongly given as *PL* 95, 1159–66.

4. E. Ranke, "Zur Geschichte des Homiliariums Karls des Grossen, Eine literarische Notiz," *Theologische Studien und Kritiken* 28 (1855): 382–96.

5. F. Wiegand, *Das Homiliarium Karls des Grossen,* Studien zur Geschichte der Theologie und der Kirche I.2 (Leipzig, 1897). See also his important, but seldom-cited article where he makes some corrections on the manuscript list he offered in the earlier work: "Ein Vorläufer des Paulushomiliars," *Theologische Studien und Kritiken* 75 (1902): 188–205.

6. Clm. 4533/4534 of the tenth century. Wiegand also used three ninth-century Reichenau manuscripts: Aug. xxix, xix, and xv. The New York Public Library has facsimiles of Aug. xix, xxix, and the Clm. manuscripts.

7. G. Morin, "Les sources non identifiées de l'homéliaire de Paul Diacre," *Revue Bénédictine* 15 (1898): 400–03.

8. J. Leclercq, "Tables pour l'inventaire des homiliaires manuscrits,

Scriptorium 2 (1948) : 205–14 and Cyril L. Smetana, "Aelfric and the Early Medieval Homiliary," *Traditio* 15 (1959) : 165–80; Réginald Grégoire, *Les homéliaires du Moyen Âge,* Rerum Ecclesiasticarum Documenta, Series Major : Fontes 6 (Rome, 1966), pp. 71–114.

9. "Accensi praeterea venerandae memoriae Pippini genitoris nostri exemplis, qui totas Galliarum ecclesias Romanae traditionis suo studio cantibus decoravit, nos nihilominus sollerti easdem curamus intuitu praecipuarum insignire serie lectionum," Wiegand, *Homiliar,* p. 15. For the liturgical reform under Charlemagne, see Cyrille Vogel, "La réforme liturgique sous Charlemagne," *Karl der Grosse* Vol. II, ed. W. Braunfels (Düsseldorf, 1965), pp. 217–232.

10. " . . . nostra eadem volumina auctoritate constabilimus vestraeque religioni in Christi ecclesiis tradimus ad legendum," Wiegand, *Homiliar,* p. 16.

11. Alan of Farfa compiled two volumes of sermons at the request of Fulcoad, his abbot. See Grégoire, *Homéliaires,* pp. 17–70.

12. Ed. Hosp, "Il sermonario di Alan di Farfa," *Ephemerides Liturgicae* 50 (1936) : 375–83 ; 51 (1937) : 210–24. Grégoire, *Homéliaires,* pp. 23–70, gives an inventory of Alan's work.

13. Haymo, *PL* 118, 11–816; Smaragdus, *PL* 102, 13–552.

14. St. Benedict, writing about A.D. 529, prescribes : "Codices autem legantur in uigiliis diuinae auctoritatis tam ueteris testamenti quam nobi (sic) ; sed et expositiones earum, quae a nominatis et orthodoxis catholicis patribus factae sunt," *Benedicti Regula* 9 :8, CSEL 75, p. 55. Alcuin's often-quoted letter to Higbald, bishop of Lindisfarne is pertinent : "Verba dei legantur in sacerdotali convivio. Ibi decet lectorem audiri, non citharistam ; sermones patrum, non carmina gentilium, *Monumenta Germaniae Historica Epistolae Karolini Aevi* IV, 24, p. 183. Also the appendix : "Le lectionnaire utilisé au réféctoire," in R. Etaix, "L'homiliaire cartusien," *Sacris Erudiri* 13 (1962) : 103. H. Barré, *Les homéliaires Carolingiens de l'École d'Auxerre, Studi e Testi* 225 (Vatican, 1962), has analyzed collections made *ad legendum vel ad praedicandum,* p. 5.

15. G. Loew, "Ein stadtrömisches Lektionar des VIII. Jahrhun-

derts," *Römische Quartalschrift* 37 (1929) : 15–39 (*Cod.
Vat. lat.* 3835–3836).

16. For the more ancient usage of five rather than four Sundays
of Advent, see A. Chavasse, "L'Avent romain, du vi^e au viii^e
siècle," *Ephemerides Liturgicae* 67 (1953) : 300–04.

17. B. De Gaiffier, "Lhomiliaire-légendier de Valére," *Analecta
Bollandiana* 73 (1955) : 126–28, concludes that the terms
are generally synonymous. He says, however, of Paul :
". . . les premiers textes de chaque solennité sont appelés
sermo; celui qui suit la péricope évangelique : *homilia*,"
note 5, pp. 127–28.

18. Grégoire, *Homéliaires,* pp. 77–116, is of no help on this matter,
since he does not give the manuscript titles consistently ;
Wiegand does.

19. I 30 refers to the homiliary of Paul the Deacon, *Pars hiemalis,*
sermo 30; II refers to the *Pars aestiva* together with the
Commune sanctorum, since they are numbered consecutively.
All references are to Grégoire; *Homéliaires.* I 30, 60, 90, II
2, 37, 57, 58, 63, 64, 74, 75, 76, 80, 82, 84, 87, 88, 89, 90, 92,
94, 95, 96, 110, 111, 114, 115, 129. A complete list of the pericopes used in PD is given in an appendix.

20. Commentaries : Bede I 40, II 7, 57, 64, 74, 75, 76, 80, 82, 84, 87,
95, 96, 114, 129, all of which appear in Bede's homiliary with
little change; Jerome I 30, II 92, 94, 110, 111 and II 62
(from a letter) ; Augustine II 58; Ambrose II 115 ; Ps.
Chrysostom II 90. Two are given as *sermones:* Maximus II
88, Ps. Chrysostom II 89 (by Peter Chrysologus.)

21. I 60 and II 2.

22. I 28, II 59, I 101, II 106.

23. Volker Mertens, *Das Predigtbuch des Priesters Konrad,*
Münchener Texte und Untersuchungen zur Deutschen
Literatur des Mittelalters 33 (Munich, 1971), p. 79, distinguishes between homilies "die den Text der Perikope
erläutern," and sermons "die an einen gewählten Textspruch
frei anknüpfen. . . ." When he remarks in a footnote that
the distinction is late, he overlooks the fact that Origen had
already distinguished between them. See the *New Catholic
Encyclopedia* s.v. homily.

24. e.g., Christmas I 15–26; Epiphany I 42–58 (with the octave);
Easter II 2–15 (with the octave).

25. ". . . ut, studiose catholicorum patrum dicta percurrens, veluti
e latissimis eorum pratis certos flosculos legeret, et in unum
quaeque essent utilia quasi sertum aptaret," Wiegand,
Homiliar, p. 16.

26. The reading for the feast of St. Bede in the Roman Breviary
puts the case well: "sanctorum Patrum doctrinis adeo in-
haesit, ut nihil proferret nisi illorum judicio comprobatum,
eorundem etiam fere verbis usus" (Lection iv, Nocturn ii,
Breviarium Romanum Pii V jussu editum).

27. *Bedae Venerabilis Homeliarum Evangelii Libri II* ed. D. Hurst,
CCL 122.

28. Ibid., p. vii and G. Morin, "Le recueil primitif des homélies de
Bede sur l'évangile," *Revue Bénédictine* 9 (1892) : 316–26.

29. There are actually fifty-three sermons: I 45 and 46 are under
Leo's name; II 89 is under the name of John Chrysostom.
All three are Pseudo-Maximus. Grégoire, *Homéliaires,*
under II 46 fails to mention that it also appears under the
name of Leo.

30. A. Mützenbecher, "Zur Ueberlieferung des Maximus Taurinensis," *Sacris Erudiri* 6 (1954), Anhang 3, "Die Lebenszeit des
Maximus," 370–72; also "Bestimmung der echten Sermones
des Maximus Taurinensis," ibid. 12 (1961) : 201–02 and
note 18. See also his edition of Maximus's sermons CCL 23,
xv–xvi.

31. *PL* 54, 141–468.

32. *PL* 76, 1075–1314.

33. There are no homilies for mid-summer among the forty homilies
of Gregory. The reason for this is no doubt that given in the
incipit of II 39: "Aestivum tempus quod corpori meo valde
contrarium est loqui."

34. I 1, II 14, 23, 25, 68, 100, 102, 103 (*Tractatus*); I 65 (*Sermo*
370), II 93 (*Sermo* 80), II 113 (*Sermo* 31).

35. I 7 (*Quaestiones evangeliorum*); I 29, II 55 (*De civitate Dei*);
II 58 (*De sermone Domini in monte*); II 121 (*De diversis
quaestionibus LXXXIII*); I 131 and 132 (*Enchiridion*).

36. I 9, 10, II 127, 128.

37. II 71, 89. The *Opus imperfectum in Matthaeum* (*PG* 56, 611–946) consists of fifty-four homilies long attributed to John Chrysostom. It was thought by earlier scholars to be the work of an Arian; but Dom G. Morin, "Les homélies latines sur S. Matthieu attribuées à Origène," *Revue Bénédictine* 54 (1942) : 3–11, suggests that it was rather by an anti-Arian, a translator of Origen's commentary on Matthew. PD uses it for two lections: I 2 and II 90.

38. I 35, 68, 70, 72, 85, 88, 89, 91, 93, II 56, 72, 91, 120, 130.

39. I 30, II 54, 92, 94, 110, 111.

40. II 1 (letter 120) ; II 62 (letter 121).

41. I 30, II 54, 94.

42. I 15.

43. Grégoire, *Homéliaires,* p. 83 (I 41).

44. I 38, 41, I 61, 64, II 61.

45. I 39, 66, II 77, 115.

46. I 63.

47. I 39 (Circumcision), 66 (Purification), 63 (St. Agnes), II 77 Nativity of Mary), 115 (Martyrs).

48. *Confessions* VI. iv. 6.

49. II 108, I 19, 27, 47 respectively.

50. I 16, 31.

51. I 34.

52. I 32.

53. Smetana, "Aelfric and the Early Medieval Homiliary," pp. 163–204.

54. J. E. Cross, "Aelfric and the Early Medieval Homiliary—Objection and Contribution," *Scripta Minora Regiae Societatis Humaniorum Litterarum Lundensis* 4 (1961–62) : 4–7, has pointed out that Aelfric did "echo or translate parts of a sermon by Maximus" (II, 106), a point that had escaped my attention.

55. With the aid of two grants from the Canada Council I have been able to verify the received lists of version of PD in England and on the continent. I hope to publish a list of all the extant manuscripts of homiliaries that belong to the family of PD.

56. Carlo Cipolla, "Note bibliograffice circa l'odierna condizione delli studi critici sul testo delle opere di Paolo Diacono,"

Reale deputazione di storia patria per le Venezie, Ser. 4, Miscellanea II (1901), pp. 10–12.

57. T. Rud, *Codicum manuscriptorum ecclesiae Cathedralis Dunelmensis, catalogus classicus* (Durham, 1825) 46, suggested that it might possibly be the companion volume to B II 2, since it has lections for *Pars aestiva.*

58. H. Schenkl, *Bibliotheca Patrum Latinorum Brittanica* X, Die Bibliotheken der englischen Kathedralen (Vienna, 1891–1905) No. 4380.

59. Sir George P. Warner and Julius P. Gilson, *Catalogue of Western Manuscripts in the Old Royal and Kings Collections,* 4 vols. (London, 1921) vol. I Royal Manuscripts IAI to II, and XI, p. 51.

60. H.O. Coxe, *Catalogus Codicum MSS.,* Pars II *Collegii Corporis Christi* (Oxford, 1852), p. 105; "Titulus libri Homiliarum sub iussu Caroli Magni a Paulo Diacono compilati, paeviis [sic] eiusdem Pauli ad Carolum versibus et Caroli ipsius praefatione." The twenty-two lines of the dedicatory verses are followed on f. 2 by the same verses, abandoned halfway through because the scribe has failed to follow the verse divisions. Charlemagne's letter begins bravely in column 1 of f. 2^r, but continues in script half as large in column 2. The votive verses and the conspectus follow in large Roman letters, with an omission at the bottom of column 1, f. 3^r. The text ends with the introduction to the first pericope (I 1 in PD).

61. *PL* 95, 1159–1566.

62. According to the numeration there are 298, but numbers 97 and 176 have two sermons each.

63. Conversion of St. Paul (two sermons), Chair of St. Peter (two sermons), Annunciation (three), Finding of the Cross (two), Bartholomew (one), Luke (one), All Saints' (four), All Souls' (three), Mary Magdalene (two), Chains of St. Peter (two), St. James (one); Sts. Cyprian, Hilary, Eusebius, and Martin are left out.

64. Smetana, "Aelfric and the Early Medieval Homiliary," pp. 163–204; SS I, p. 159.

65. See note 54 and J.E. Cross, "More Sources for two of Aelfric's

Catholic Homilies," *Anglia* 8 (1968) : 59–78; "Aelfric— Mainly on Memory and Creative Method in two Catholic Homilies," *Studia Neophilologica* 41 (1969) : 135–55; "On the Blickling Homily for Ascension Day *XI,"* *Neuphilologische Mitteilungen* 70 (1969) : 228–40; "Source and Analysis of some Aelfrician Passages," ibid. 72 (1971) : 446–53.

66. Ed. Dietrich, "Cynewulf's Christ," *Zeitschrift für deutsches Altertum* 9 (1853) : 193–214 (esp. 204); A.S. Cook, ed., *The Christ of Cynewulf* (Boston, 1900); Samuel Moore, "Sources of the Old English *Exodus,"* *Modern Philology* 9 (1911) : 83–108; "The Source of Christ 416," *Modern Language Notes* 29 (1914) : 226–27; James Bright, "The Relation of the Caedmonian *Exodus* to the Liturgy," *Modern Language Notes* 27 (1912) : 97–103; E. Burgert, *The Dependence of Part I of Cynewulf's Christ upon the Antiphonary* (Washington, 1921).

67. M. Förster, "Über die Quellen von Aelfrics exegetischen Homiliae Catholicae," *Anglia* 16 (1894) : 1–61; "Altenglische Predigtquellen," *Archiv für das Studium der neueren Sprachen* I, 116 (1905) : 301–14; II, 122 (1909) : 246–62.

68. See J.D.A. Ogilvy, *Books Known to the English 567–1066* (Cambridge, Mass., 1967), pp. 160–61.

MALCOLM GODDEN ❧ AELFRIC & THE VERNACULAR PROSE TRADITION

In studies of Anglo-Saxon literature it has been customary to view Aelfric in the context of vernacular prose writings generally, to see him as in some sense following on from earlier prose writers and occupying a major place in the tradition. I want here to explore this aspect a little more deeply in relation to Aelfric's own time: to see how he actually responded to earlier prose, and what kind of mark his work made. It is, as it were, an attempt to see Aelfric's place in Anglo-Saxon literary history at the period when he wrote, rather than from our present viewpoint.[1]

First, then, Aelfric's relationship to earlier writings in English prose: which ones did he know, how well did he know them, and how did he react to them? His most important remarks on the subject are the familiar sentences from the preface to his very first work, the First Series of *Catholic Homilies:*

> Þa bearn me on mode, ic truwige þurh Godes gife, þæt ic ðas
> boc of Ledenum gereorde to Engliscre spræce awende; na þurh
> gebylde mycelre lare, ac forþan þe ic geseah and gehyrde my-
> cel gedwyld on manegum Engliscum bocum, þe ungelærede
> menn þurh heora bilewitnysse to micclum wisdome tealdon;
> and me ofhreow þaet hi ne cuþon ne næfdon þa godspellican
> lare on heora gewritum, buton þam mannum anum ðe þæt
> Leden cuðon, and buton þam bocum ðe Ælfred cyning
> snoterlice awende of Ledene on Englisc, þa synd to hæbbenne.
> (CH I, p. 2)

What, one immediately asks, *were* these "many English books" containing "much *gedwyld*" (a word which in Aelfric's usage includes both heresy and folly), and what was wrong with them? Is this merely a *topos,* or did Aelfric really know of such books? Caroline White has suggested that the reference was to writings, now lost and otherwise unknown, in defense of clerical practices (such as the marriage of priests) that Aelfric opposed.[2] R.M.

Wilson also concludes that the reference was to writings now lost to us; in his view the only eligible text now extant was the Blickling collection of homilies, but in these, he thinks, "there is little if anything to deserve Aelfric's blame." [3] He does note, too, the possibility that Old English religious poetry was meant. But the most natural interpretation of the passage is that it refers to earlier homilies, and it is possible to show that the early homilies still extant in the Blickling and Vercelli collections may well have been known to Aelfric and that they do contain material to which he objected.

There is first a neutral reference by Aelfric to existing accounts of St. Peter and St. Paul:

We wyllað æfter ðisum godspelle eow gereccan ðæra apostola drohtnunga and geendunge, mid scortre race; forðan ðe heora ðrowung is gehwær on Engliscum gereorde fullice geendebyrd.
(CH I, p. 370)

A long account of the passion and martyrdom of the two saints, similar to Aelfric's version, occurs in one of the Blickling homilies.[4] The only other account extant in Old English is the brief one in the *Old English Martyrology*.[5] Then there is a more severe reference to works in English in Aelfric's second homily for the Assumption of the Virgin. In his first homily he gives a careful and hesitant summary of the evidence for the Assumption, based on a source which he thinks has the authority of Jerome, and refers scathingly to apocryphal accounts of the event.[6] In his second homily he gives a commentary on the Gospel passage for the occasion (admitting that it has no reference to the Virgin), then adds one brief sentence recording the bare fact of the Virgin's Assumption, and goes on:

Gif we mare secgað be ðisum symbeldæge þonne we on ðam halgum bocum rædað, þe ðurh Godes dihte gesette wæron, þonne beo we ðam dwolmannum gelice, þe be heora agenum dihte, oððe be swefnum, fela lease gesetnyssa awriton; ac ða geleaffullan lareowas, Augustinus, Hieronimus, Gregorius, and gehwilce oðre, þurh heora wisdom, hi towurpon. Sind swaðeah

gyt ða dwollican bec, aegðer ge on Leden ge on Englisc, and
hi rædað ungerade menn. (CH II, p. 444)

Aelfric clearly has in mind here English versions of the apocryphal
legend of the Assumption. There *is* such a version in the Blickling
collection of homilies, and another copy of it in an eleventh-century
manuscript, Corpus Christi College Cambridge 198; another
English version occurs amongst some homilies in Corpus Christi
College Cambridge 41, an Exeter manuscript of the later eleventh
century.[7]

Two other remarks in the *Catholic Homilies* indicate Aelfric's
objections to material present in the earlier Old English homilies
known to us, though the remarks do not themselves refer to
English books. In one of his homilies for Rogationtide Aelfric
quotes St. Paul's story of a man who was led up to the third
heaven and heard secrets that no man can tell. He goes on:

Humeta rædað sume men ða leasan gesetnysse ðe hi hatað
Paulus gesihðe, nu he sylfe sæde þæt he ða digelan word gehyrde,
þe nan eorðlic mann sprecan ne mot? (CH II, p. 332)

The "false composition" is, of course, the popular apocryphal
description of Heaven and Hell known as the *Visio Pauli*. Aelfric's
objections to it closely follow those of St. Augustine, but Aelfric
clearly expected at least some of his readers or hearers to be
familiar with it.[8] There are short descriptions of Hell taken from
the *Visio* in two of the Blickling homilies, both specifically connected with St. Paul. There is also a fuller rendering of part of
the *Visio* in a collection of Old English homilies in a later,
eleventh-century, manuscript, Junius 85.[9]

In his homily in commemoration of Holy Virgins Aelfric refers
to another heresy, this time connected with the Last Judgment:

Sume gedwolmen cwædon þæt seo halige Maria, Cristes mo-
dor, and sume oðre halgan, sceolon hergian, æfter ðam dome,
ða synfullan of ðam deofle, ælc his dæl; ac þis gedwyld
asprang of ðam mannum þe on heora flæsclicum lustum symle
licgan woldon, and noldon mid earfoðnyssum þæt ece lif
geearnian. (CH II, p. 572)

This seems to have been an uncommon idea, but it does occur in an Old English homily in the tenth-century Vercelli collection: we are given a long and graphic account of the Last Judgment, at which first the Virgin, then St. Michael, and then St. Peter rise to intercede successfully for a third of the damned each.[10] Aelfric must have been referring to just such a description.

These references taken together suggest that Aelfric was referring to homilies like those in the Blickling and Vercelli collection when he wrote his preface and that he knew their contents fairly well. We cannot conclude from this that he knew the Blickling or Vercelli manuscripts themselves, or even the specific collections now preserved in these manuscripts, but the Blickling book in particular matches up surprisingly well to his references to other English works and to current *gedwyld*. To judge from the passages quoted, what Aelfric objected to in these earlier homilies was not primarily their theological ideas or their views on religious practices, but rather their use of sensational narratives which were clearly fictitious and in some cases of dubious morality. One may compare Aelfric's comment on the Passion of St. Thomas: it has already been translated, he says, into English verse and is all perfectly credible except for one particularly lurid and unpleasant incident which, in St. Augustine's view, it is not permitted to believe.[11] Possibly he objected on similar grounds to another story in the Blickling collection, the rather implausible legend of St. Andrew among the cannibals (well known from *Andreas*), which is never mentioned by Aelfric, although he gives the Scriptural account of the saint and an account of his martyrdom and elsewhere mentions his mission to Achaia.[12] Aelfric does refer from time to time to heretical beliefs too of course, but he does not suggest that these are to be found in English writings and tends to present them as belonging to the past.[13]

Aelfric's preface also refers, approvingly, to the books "which King Alfred wisely turned from Latin to English, which are available." Which of these did he know, and how well did he know them? He certainly knew of the Old English version of Bede's *Ecclesiastical History,* for he refers to it in his opening remarks on St. Gregory:

Manega halige bec cyðað his drohtnunge and his halige lif,
and eac 'Historia Anglorum,' ða ðe Ælfred cyning of Ledene
on Englisc awende. Seo boc sprecð genoh swutelice be ðisum
halgan were. Nu wylle we sum ðing scortlice eow be him
gereccan, forðan ðe seo foresaede boc nis eow eallum cuð,
þeah ðe heo on Englisc awend sy. (CH II, p. 116–18)

The translation is not now thought to be by Alfred, of course, but
Aelfric is not alone in attributing it to him and the work may have
been connected with Alfred's program of translation.[14] The Old
English version is in fact used by Aelfric in this homily on St.
Gregory in his account of Gregory's meeting with the Anglian
slave-boys in the marketplace.[15] The debt is odd, because otherwise
in this homily Aelfric seems to use the original Latin text and
nowhere else in all his borrowings from the *Ecclesiastical History*
does Aelfric show any signs of having used the Old English version. Possibly this one passage, for one reason or another, stuck
in Aelfric's memory or was copied down in a commonplace book.
He can hardly have followed it for its style, for Aelfric extensively
rewrites it.

Aelfric also knew King Alfred's translation of the *Pastoral Care*
or *Cura Pastoralis* of Gregory the Great. There are no explicit
references to it, but one sentence in a homily by Aelfric is quite
clearly taken from it:

Hu ne is ðis sio micle Babilon ðe ic self atimbrede to
kynestole and to ðrymme, me silfum to wlite and wuldre mid
mine agne mægene and strengo?[16]
Hu ne is þis seo miccle Babilon ðe ic sylf getimbrode to
cynestole and to ðrymme me sylfum, to wlite and to wuldre,
mid minum agenum mægene and strengðe? (CH II, p. 432)

Again there seems no reason to use the Alfredian text here. Aelfric
is summarizing the biblical story of Nebuchadnezzar at this point,
as an example of the punishment of pride, but not following
Alfred, and this particular sentence, spoken by Nebuchadnezzar,
comes originally from the Old Testament too. It must have stuck
in Aelfric's memory, perhaps because of its rhythmical phrasing,

since this time there is no recasting, Alfred too had used Nebuchadnezzar as an example of pride.

Borrowings of this kind show that Aelfric also knew King Alfred's translation of Boethius's *Consolation of Philosophy*. W.F. Bolton has shown that Aelfric's discussion of the nature of the soul in the Christmas homily in his *Lives of Saints* collection is indebted to the discussion at the very end of Alfred's *Boethius* and that the discussion of the nature of God in the same homily may have been influenced by an earlier passage in the *Boethius*.[17] Whether Aelfric also knew the Latin text of Boethius but preferred to use the Old English is uncertain, since he is not otherwise known to have used Boethius at all. At any rate before composing this homily he must have been very familiar with Alfred's *Boethius,* if he was able either to remember these passages or to recall their existence and look them up. The *Consolation of Philosophy* is not the most obvious source to consult for a sermon on the Nativity.

The other Alfredian text which Aelfric definitely knew is the translation of Gregory the Great's *Dialogues* by Bishop Wærferð, undertaken for King Alfred.[18] Aelfric refers to it at the end of his brief sermon on the efficacy of the mass:

> Eac se halga papa Gregorius awrat on ðære bec Dialogorum hu micclum   seo halige mæsse manegum fremode. Seo boc is on Englisc awend, on ðære mæg gehwa be ðison genihtsumlice gehyran, seðe hi oferrædan wile. (CH II, p. 358)

He does not refer to it specifically as an Alfredian work, but if he had seen the preface he would have known of its association with King Alfred. Aelfric occasionally uses the *Dialogues* as a source, but probably not the Old English version, since there are no verbal reminiscences.[19]

There is no positive evidence that Aelfric knew the other two Alfredian works, the *Soliloquies* and the translation of Orosius's history of the world, but he may have. There was no particular occasion to recommend these two to his readers, as he recommended the *Old English Bede* and the *Dialogues,* and it is only because of the identification of chance borrowings that we are aware of his familiarity with the *Pastoral Care* and the *Boethius*. We can say, then, that Aelfric knew at least four of the Alfredian works and seems to have been so familiar with them that he could recall particular sentences and passages and even quote them unconsciously. Possibly these were texts on which Aelfric had been trained in his youth.[20]

The other main writings in vernacular prose extant from the period before Aelfric's time are not mentioned or quoted by him, so far as I know, and he does not refer to any other works. He must have known—or at least known about—some of the translations made as part of the monastic revival, such as the *Rule of St. Benedict* and the *Pseudo-Egbert Penitential,* but these were rather technical works of interest only to the clergy.[21] The only other important religious prose text left out is the *Old English Martyrology.* This work was certainly known at Winchester (though at the New Minster) a little after Aelfric's time, but I know of no evidence of his attitude to it, or even whether he knew it.[22] In the field of nonreligious prose the major omission is the *Anglo-Saxon Chronicle.* The Parker version was present at Winchester when Aelfric was there, but there was perhaps no occasion for him to use it or refer to it in his own writings. Generally, then, Aelfric was familiar with two main groups of writings in vernacular prose: on the one hand, homilies full of apocryphal legends and unorthodox ideas, which he knew well and generally disapproved of; on the other, the sound Alfredian works of a hundred years before his time, which he knew intimately and respected highly.

The next stage is to consider what relationship, if any, existed between Aelfric's work and these earlier writings. Unlike many other writers of the late Old English period, Aelfric did not use vernacular prose works as sources. Wulfstan based several of his homilies on homilies by Aelfric. Byrhtferth borrowed from Aelfric's *De Temporibus Anni* for his manual. Numerous anonymous homilies of the eleventh century borrowed from both Wulfstan and Aelfric. And Aethelweard, writing in Latin, drew on the *Anglo-Saxon Chronicle* and the *Old English Bede.* But Aelfric seems to have borrowed nothing apart from the very brief reminiscences already noted. Where the content of an Old English work was useful to him, as with the Old English versions of Bede's *Ecclesiastical History* and Gregory's *Dialogues,* he seems to have preferred to use the Latin originals. The earlier vernacular writ-

ings were important to him, if at all, not as sources but as models
or precedents, consciously or unconsciously influencing his own
work.

In one major respect Aelfric must have been influenced by the
homiletic tradition in English. The very concept of writing homilies in the vernacular, in a fixed form, was an unusual one in the
period. There are no recorded instances from the continent, so far
as I know: preaching was in the vernacular of course, but was
presumably improvised on the basis of Latin sermons or notes.[23]
It must have been the existence of written collections of homilies
in the vernacular in England that prompted Aelfric to devote his
major literary efforts to this form rather than to translating major
texts like Alfred or to writing in Latin. The vernacular collections
may also have suggested to him the idea of including saints' legends
amongst his homilies. These do not figure largely in the Latin
homiliaries on which Aelfric drew, and the wording of the preface
to his First Series suggests that he thought of them as an extra
element:

> Nec solum Evangeliorum tractatus in isto libello exposuimus,
> verum etiam Sanctorum passiones vel vitas, ad utilitatem
> idiotarum istius gentis. (CH I, p. 1)

But Aelfric reacted against the actual content of these earlier
vernacular homilies, as we have seen. In this respect the Alfredian
tradition was a more likely model, since Aelfric approved of it. At
first sight there is little connection between Aelfric's work and the
Alfredian corpus. Alfred and his circle were translating solid,
lengthy works of ancient and ecclesiastical history, philosophy,
theology, and doctrine; Aelfric was composing short homilies and
saints' lives. Alfred was trying to restore learning by making the
scholarship of the Latin tradition available to readers who knew
no Latin; Aelfric, to judge from his first preface, thought of himself as offering elementary instruction to the simple and ignorant
laity. But one can see how in various ways Aelfric tried to infuse
the more scholarly and intellectual traditions of the Alfredian
works into the genre of the homily.

There is first of all his choice of authorities. As Förster has
shown, Aelfric's three main sources for the *Catholic Homilies*

were Gregory, Bede, and Augustine; the same three figure largely
in the Alfredian corpus—Gregory as the original author of the
Pastoral Care and the *Dialogues* and as a source for part of the
Soliloquies: Bede as the author of the *Ecclesiastical History,* translated into Old English; and Augustine as the main source for the
Soliloquies.[24] The other Alfredian sources, Orosius and Boethius,
demonstrate a similar preference for scholarly writers from the
patristic or late antique period, as does Aelfric's use of Jerome as
another major source. Of these authorities Gregory at least was
also used by pre-Aelfrician homilists in English, but they, and
particularly the Vercelli homilists, tended to rely more on the
homilies now attributed to Caesarius of Arles and various anonymous and apocryphal sources.[25] They certainly do not show the
same interest as Aelfric and the Alfredian writers in citing their
authorities by name.

Aelfric followed the Alfredian precedent too in using vernacular
prose as a medium for theology and the more intellectual aspects of
religious doctrine. In his very first homily in his First Series of
Catholic Homilies, he discusses free will, original sin, the origin of
the devil, and the origin of evil. In later homilies he takes up such
knotty issues as the doctrine of the Trinity and the mass, the
nature of the soul, and the reasons for the existence of suffering.[26]
The early vernacular homilists seem to have avoided such problems,
preferring to concentrate on the simpler issues of man's duties in
this world and his fate in the next, but Alfred, like Aelfric, was
apparently happy to deal with theological and philosophical issues
in the vernacular.

History had a very important place in the Alfredian corpus, with
the translation of Orosius, the *Old English Bede,* and the *Anglo-
Saxon Chronicle* (if Aelfric thought of this as Alfredian), as well
as the explanations of historical and classical allusions in the
Boethius. Aelfric never wrote any historical works himself, but his
writings are infused with an enthusiasm for historical information
and historical accuracy. In composing his homily on St. Gregory
Aelfric filled out his hagiographical source, Paul the Deacon's
Life of St. Gregory, with historical details drawn from Bede's
Ecclesiastical History.[27] For his account of the finding of the True
Cross he did not use the traditional legend, which was used in the

poem *Elene* and in an Old English prose version and was probably
known to Aelfric, but carefully pieced the story together from
separate incidents in a sound historical work, the *Ecclesiastical
History,* which Aelfric thought of as the work of St. Jerome but
which is in fact a translation and continuation by Rufinus of the
Greek text of Eusebius.[28] He used the same source for his account
of St. James and the fall of Jerusalem.[29] In his homily on St. Cuthbert his main sources were the two lives (prose and verse) by
Bede, but he checked these with Bede's *Ecclesiastical History* and
imported a few details from there.[30] Bede's *Ecclesiastical History*
was also used for Aelfric's *Life of St. Oswald* and other works.
One notes too the way in which Aelfric prides himself in his preface to the *Lives of Saints* on his historical sense in not citing two
emperors as ruling at the same time, as did the legends he used as
sources.[31] Even his choice of saints in the *Lives of Saints* collection
reflects an interest in history. He is not interested in solitaries and
desert saints, such as Antony and Guthlac, or the more legendary
saints who had no historical setting, such as Christopher and Mary
of Egypt. Instead he shows a fondness for saints whose lives could
be seen as having a place in ecclesiastical or secular history, such
as Martin, Dionysius, Edmund, and Oswald, and the victims of
imperial persecution in the early Christian church.[32] The same
collection includes stories from Old Testament history. Indirectly
Aelfric's work must have communicated considerable information
about earlier history.

There is a scholarly element too in Aelfric's use of the Bible.
Many of his homilies are virtually biblical commentaries that
explore the allegorical senses of a particular passage. Indeed the
biblical commentaries of Augustine and Bede were often his
sources; where he used instead the exegetical sermons of Gregory
and others, he often kept closer to the biblical text than they did.
He drew extensively on the Bible for moral exempla and illustrations. He would also weave together related texts drawn from all
over the Bible: there is a splendid example in one homily where
the original texts on good trees bringing forth good fruit leads on
to an argument illustrated by a series of biblical texts using tree
and planting images, culminating in a discussion of avarice
prompted by St. Paul's "avarice is the *root* of all evil." [33] Biblical

exegesis figures little in other Old English homilies: there is a little in the Blickling collection but virtually none in the Vercelli Book (except for XVI and XVII) or other anonymous homilies. Alfred, though, had given a precedent in the *Pastoral Care,* where the Bible in both its literal and its allegorical senses is an important source of authority, illustration, and imagery.

What is particularly important about Aelfric's use of this theological, historical, and biblical learning is the form in which it was communicated. Alfred and his circle dealt with these subjects in separate, lengthy works. Aelfric created a more approachable synthesis of all this material. Within each Series, and again in the *Lives of Saints,* there is theological discussion, Old Testament story and commentary, lives of saints and other stories of events in the history of the church, as well as moral and exegetical homilies. In this variety he moved away from the Latin homiliaries of Paul the Deacon, Haymo of Auxerre, and Smaragdus, and the forty homilies on the Gospels by Gregory the Great, which were probably his main models.

The one major aspect of Aelfric's relationship to earlier vernacular prose that remains to be considered is the difficult question of style and technique. It is never possible to explain the sheer quality of a writer as the product of earlier influences, but it should be possible to indicate which models or traditions were followed or which of them prompted the use of particular features. With Aelfric even this is a vexed issue. For his characteristic use of the regular two-stress rhythm, reinforced by alliteration, the influence of both Latin prose and Old English verse has been canvassed.[34] But the use of a two-stress phrase with alliteration is also to be seen in earlier homiletic prose, as Otto Funke has shown.[35] It can be found too in Alfredian prose: the quotation from the *Pastoral Care* given above is a good example and suggests that Aelfric had noticed this feature in Alfred's work. And if, as seems likely, Aelfric's homily on St. Cuthbert was his first attempt at a regular use of this style, one should perhaps add the influence of Latin verse as a stimulus to a more ornate kind of writing, since the Cuthbert homily was the first work by Aelfric in which he used a poem as a major source.[36] In his early, non-alliterative prose it is difficult to find links with either branch of the vernacular prose tradition. Aelfric clearly shunned the rich, poetic style and the effusive, piled-up clauses of many of the early homilies. As any comparison of his work with earlier homiletic renderings of the same material would show, he preferred a more restrained, elegant style, understated rather than overstated, using a precise syntax to create an appearance of simple matter-of-fact statement. He also avoided, though, the word-pairing technique which marks much of Alfredian prose, especially the *Bede* and the *Dialogues*. Alfred's predilection for explanatory images, perceptible especially in the *Boethius,* does not seem to have been taken up by Aelfric either, except for isolated examples. Alfred's own works must have helped Aelfric to confront the problems of rendering difficult arguments and difficult concepts in a vernacular idiom, but it seems impossible to demonstrate that Aelfric's solutions owe much to Alfred.

In general, then, we can see Aelfric as following an existing tradition of vernacular homilies and saint's legends, written in a fairly formal, literary style, and transforming this tradition by developing the learned and scholarly concerns introduced to the vernacular by the translations of Alfred and his circle. In doing so he acquired a high reputation during his lifetime. His writings were apparently praised by Sigeric, archbishop of Canterbury, and used by Wulfstan, archbishop of York. Some of them were written at the request of Wulfstan and other bishops, others at the request of Aethelweard and other influential laymen. But it would be useful to consider what actually happened to his writings: how widely they were read, and in what ways they were used and copied.

His homilies had an extensive circulation. There are twenty-four major manuscripts drawing on the *Catholic Homilies,* nine fragments probably from large collections and six manuscripts containing just one or two items from the collection.[37] Reconstruction of the manuscript relationships reveals that many more copies must formerly have existed. The manuscripts extend right through the eleventh century and, in smaller numbers, up to the end of the twelfth. The geographical spread is wide too: there are copies from Canterbury, Durham, Exeter, Rochester, Winchester, and Worcester and, if one includes the main manuscript of the *Lives of Saints,* from Bury St. Edmunds.[38] Many of the manuscripts are still unplaced though, and could well come from other centers. Further evidence of the extensive knowledge of Aelfric's work is the occurrence of passages lifted from his homilies in other works. An anonymous account of the finding of the True Cross in an eleventh-century manuscript, possibly from Glastonbury, includes two sentences interpolated from Aelfric's rather different account of the subject.[39] A short address for the use of a confessor in a Canterbury manuscript of the middle of the eleventh century includes a passage on the meaning of Lent taken from an Aelfric homily.[40] The twelfth-century copy of Aethelwold's account of the revival of the monasteries has marginal additions on the conversion of the English based on Aelfric's homily on St. Gregory.[41]

Aelfric's text was generally treated with respect. The scribes made mistakes, but they did not write as if one phrase was as good as another. It is not generally until the twelfth century that we find radical rewriting of the text and then only to bring it up to date linguistically. Many deliberate alterations of detail were made, but mainly out of a zeal (often unnecessary) for clarity, not in order to change the meaning or the manner of expression. Sometimes, though, more radical changes were made. One reviser apparently found Aelfric's treatment of the doctrine of the mass unacceptable and amended it to make it perfectly clear that the bread was truly Christ's body.[42] Another, probably at Canterbury, utterly destroyed Aelfric's concise, selective account of the Passion and commentary on it. He made scores of small additions, some for style and some for extra detail; St. Peter has to be identified as *se halga apostol* and Moses as *se maera heretoga*. He added details of the Scriptural accounts of the Passion, sometimes taken not directly from the Bible but from an earlier homily on the Passion, a variant version of Vercelli homily I.[43] Another reviser, whose work appears in an Exeter manuscript, excised large portions of Aelfric's homily for the dedication of a church, especially the sections on the Old Testament story of Solomon and the queen of Sheba and its meaning, and filled the gaps with strings of excerpts from other homilies, including some not by Aelfric. The general effect is to remove all the more learned and informative material and provide a mundane series of injunctions about the proper treatment of churches.[44] Wulfstan's rewriting of homilies

by Aelfric was a more independent activity, producing original
work though inspired by Aelfric's works, but a comparison suggests that Wulfstan too was less interested in theological discussion, biblical story, and commentary than Aelfric and preferred
moral discussion.[45]

Aelfric's homilies and saints' lives were originally issued in sets
of about forty, covering a wide variety of topics and approaches.
These sets did not survive long after leaving Aelfric's hands. Only
three copies of the First Series survive (and one other with inter-
polations), and only one of the Second Series. The only complete
copy of the *Lives of Saints* that survives has several items not by
Aelfric interpolated into it. Instead we find homiliaries formed by
selecting freely from Aelfric's collections and adding other homilies
not by him.[46] The additional items would not generally have met
with Aelfric's approval. They are mainly penitential homilies for
Lent and Rogationtide, the sort that Aelfric seldom wrote himself
but which dominate the earlier Vercelli collection. They also include homilies for the three days before Easter, when, in Aelfric's
view, no homilies should be preached, and in one manuscript some
earlier saints' legends of the sort that Aelfric disliked—the Blickling homily on the Assumption and the Blickling story of Andrew
among the cannibals.[47] In other manuscripts the homilies are used
in collections not related to the church year and in some cases not
designed for use in preaching. There are, for instance, collections
of saints' lives and legends, drawn from the *Catholic Homilies*
and the *Lives of Saints* and other sources, generally omitting the
Gospel expositions which Aelfric had often combined with his
account of a saint's life.[48] There are collections of homilies on
general subjects, selected on the grounds that nothing tied them to
a particular occasion.[49] There is the curious collection in the
British Museum MS Cotton Vespasian D. xiv, perhaps intended
as a compendium of religious instruction and drawing heavily on
Aelfric but having little resemblance to his own collections.[50]
Sometimes one homily is picked out for its usefulness in other
collections. A Lenten homily which contains a section on the Last
Judgment is included in a collection of anonymous homilies and
tracts mainly on the fate of the soul after death and the Last
Judgment (the collection also includes a version of the objection-

able *Visio Pauli*).[51] A homily by Aelfric which happens to deal
with the role of the clergy is included in an Exeter collection of
ecclesiastical laws and pieces on the duties of the clergy.[52]

Often extracts were made from Aelfric's homilies. The Vespasian manuscript excerpts a single sentence from Aelfric's homily on Job:

> Godes gecorene synd on gewinne on þyssere wurlde. and þa
> arlease on hire blissigeð. ac þære rihtwisera manna gewinn.
> awænt to blisse. and þære arleasra blisse awænt to bitere
> sarnysse. (f. 74ᵛ)

It also includes a definition of the Trinity extracted from another
Aelfric homily. The brief but dramatic passage on avarice which
Aelfric had skillfully linked into an exegetical homily through the
use of tree and plant imagery, as described earlier, was taken out
again and appears as a separate excerpt in two manuscripts.[53] One
of these manuscripts also includes, as an independent extract,
Aelfric's brief discussion of the false belief in the intercession of
the saints for the damned at the Last Judgment, quoted above.[54]
Several times the brief discussion of the origin and meaning of a
particular festival, which Aelfric tended to include in his homilies,
is excerpted.[55] Occasionally extracts from Aelfric were linked
together, along with extracts from other writers, to form new,
composite homilies. Clearly his writings were becoming a quarry
for useful information and authoritative statements.

In some respects, then, Aelfric's aims were not honored by
contemporaries or posterity. His zeal for orthodoxy, accuracy, and
good taste was foiled by compilers who mingled or interpolated
his work with the writings of others, often writings of which
Aelfric disapproved, and by revisers who rewrote his homilies.
His careful synthesis of many different kinds of material, within
individual homilies and within collections, was often broken up by
revisers and compilers who made extracts or omitted the more
learned material or made selections for use in more homogeneous
collections (though it is only fair to add that Aelfric himself began
this process by issuing collections made up entirely of homilies on
the Gospels). On the other hand, the homilies were widely read,
copied and collected during the two centuries and more that

followed their composition, and highly respected as a source of information and explanation. They may not have been used and transmitted in quite the way Aelfric had intended, but all the different kinds of material that he had included were passed on to the eleventh and twelfth centuries, separately if not together. In one form or another, the original achievement made its mark.

The first really scholarly study of Aelfric's work (by Dietrich) rightly emphasized Aelfric's contribution to learning and the range and detail of his knowledge and writings.[56] Since then the elegant simplicity of Aelfric's style and the increasing recognition of his debt to Latin sources has encouraged a tendency to present him as essentially a popularizer, or at best as primarily a stylist. Looking at Aelfric's relation to earlier (particularly Alfredian) prose and at the response to his work in the eleventh and twelfth centuries helps us to realize again his role in fostering learning.

NOTES

1. This paper has developed out of a talk given to the Medieval Society of the University of Sheffield in 1974, and I would like to express my debt to the members of that society for their suggestions and criticisms.
2. Caroline L. White, *Aelfric: a New Study of his Life and Writings* (New York, 1898), p. 51.
3. R.M. Wilson, *The Lost Literature of Medieval England,* 2nd ed. (London, 1970), p. 71.
4. BH, pp. 170–93.
5. *An Old English Martyrology,* ed. G. Herzfeld, EETS OS 116 (1900), p. 108.
6. CH I, pp. 436–54.
7. BH, pp. 136–59; CCCC 41, pp. 280–87. For the provenance of CCCC 41, see Ker, *Catalogue,* p. 45 (it was probably not actually written at Exeter).
8. See *PL* 35, 1885.
9. BH, pp. 43–45 and 209–11; Bodleian Library, MS Junius 85, ff. 3–11.

10. See the facsimile, *The Vercelli Book* EEMF 19, ed. Celia Sisam (Copenhagen, 1976), f. 84. The same belief is more briefly mentioned in another Old English homily, printed by W.H. Hulme in *Modern Philology,* 1 (1903–04): 32–36.

11. CH II, p. 520.

12. BH, pp. 229–49.

13. See, for example, CH II, p. 46.

14. See D. Whitelock, "The Old English Bede," *Proceedings of the British Academy* 48 (1962): 57–90.

15. As was shown by Professor Whitelock, *ibid.* p. 58 and note 10. See further my article, "The sources for Aelfric's homily on St. Gregory," *Anglia* 86 (1968): 79–88.

16. *King Alfred's West Saxon Version of Gregory's Pastoral Care,* EETS 45, 50 (1871; repr. 1958) ed. H. Sweet, p. 39.

17. LS 1, pp. 10–24; W.F. Bolton, "The Alfredian Boethius in Aelfric's Lives of Saints I," *Notes and Queries* N.S. xix (November 1972): 406–07.

18. *Bischofs Wærferth Übersetzung der Dialoge Gregors des Grossen,* ed. H. Hecht, *Bibliothek der angelsächsischen Prosa* 5 (Leipzig, 1900).

19. See M. Förster, Über die Quellen von Aelfrics exegetischen *Homiliae Catholicae,"* *Anglia* 16 (1894): 17.

20. A possibility suggested by Peter Clemoes in a paper given in 1971. Professor Clemoes generously gave me a copy of the relevant part of the paper, which is to be published shortly.

21. On Aelfric's possible knowledge of the latter, see J. Raith, *Die altenglische Version des Halitgarischen Bussbuches* (rpr. Darmstadt, 1964), p. xi.

22. See my article in *Anglo-Saxon England* 4 (1975): 57–65.

23. See the Gatch article in this volume.

24. Förster, "Über die Quellen . . ."

25. See R. Willard, "The Blickling-Junius tithing homily and Caesarius of Arles," in *Philologica: the Malone Anniversary Studies,* ed. T.A. Kirby and H.B. Woolf (Baltimore, 1949), pp. 65–78; Paul E. Szarmach, "Caesarius of Arles and the Vercelli Homilies," *Traditio* 26 (1970): 315–23; Joseph B. Traherne, Jr., "Caesarius of Arles and Old English Literature," *Anglo-Saxon England* 5 (1976): 105–19.

26. See CH I, pp. 276–92; CH II, pp. 262–82; LS 1, pp. 14–24;
    CH I, pp. 470–76.
27. See my "The sources for Aelfric's homily on St. Gregory."
28. The Old English prose version of the legend is edited by
    R. Morris in *Legends of the Holy Rood,* EETS OS 46
    (1871), pp. 3–17. The passages of the *Ecclesiastical History*
    used by Aelfric are in Book IX, c. ix and Book X, c. x. It
    is the shape which Aelfric gives to this material, and a few
    changes of detail, which lead me to believe that Aelfric
    knew the traditional legend as well.
29. See Max Förster, *Über die Quellen von Aelfric's Homiliae
    Catholicae, I, Legenden* (Berlin, 1892), p. 23.
30. Ibid., pp. 35–36.
31. LS 1, pp. 2–4.
32. The same point does not apply to the *Catholic Homilies,* where
    Aelfric's choice was dictated by the need to deal with all the
    saints celebrated by the laity nationally.
33. CH II, pp. 404–12.
34. G.H. Gerould, "Abbot Aelfric's rhythmic prose," *Modern
    Philology* 22 (1924–5) : 353–66, and Dorothy Bethurum,
    "The Form of Aelfric's *Lives of Saints,*" *Studies in
    Philology* 29 (1932) : 515–33.
35. "Studien zur alliterierenden und rhythmischen Prosa in der
    älteren altenglischen Homiletik," *Anglia* 80 (1962) : 9–36.
36. The alliterative style first appears in the Second Series, and the
    Cuthbert homily (the tenth) is the first in the present order
    of the Series in which the style is used. It is also more
    "poetic" in its rhythm and vocabulary than Aelfric's later
    attempts at an alliterative style. As already noted, Bede's
    verse Life of St. Cuthbert was one of Aelfric's sources for
    the homily.
37. See Ker, *Catalogue,* pp. 511–15.
38. Viz. Ker, *Catalogue,* nos. 86, 186 and possibly 38; 15 and 74;
    69 and 283; 309 and probably 209; 21; 41, 48 and 331; and
    162.
39. The Old English text is edited by Morris (see note 28).
    Morris, p. 3, lines 5–7, 12–13, and 25—p. 4, line 3 cor-
    respond to CH II, 304/3–5, 7–9, 13–15 in Aelfric's homily.

For the possible connection with Glastonbury, see Ker, *Catalogue,* p. 355.

40. The address is printed by H.S. Logeman, "Anglo-Saxonica Minora," *Anglia* 12 (1889) : 513–15. Logeman, p. 513/30–514/7 and 514/16–21 correspond to CH II, pp. 98/23–31 and 100/19–22. The manuscript is British Library Cotton Tiberius A iii.
41. See Ker, *Catalogue,* p. 196.
42. His work appears on pp. 387–89 of CCCC 162.
43. The result is the text on ff. 77–83 of British Library MS Cotton Tiberius A iii.
44. See Lambeth Palace Library MS 489 ff. 38–44.
45. See homilies VI, XII, and XVIII in *The Homilies of Wulfstan,* ed. Dorothy Bethurum (Oxford, 1957).
46. See especially CCCC 162, 198, 302, 303, Bodley MSS 340/342 and parts of 343, and Hatton 113–114, and British Library MS Cotton Faustina A ix.
47. See CCCC 198.
48. Cambridge University Library MS Ii.1.33 and British Library MSS Cotton Otho B x. and Vitellius D xvii.
49. Bodleian MS Hatton 115, and parts of CCCC 178, 419 and 421.
50. See Rima Handley, "British Museum MS Cotton Vespasian D. xiv," *Notes and Queries* N.S. xxi (July 1974) : 242–50.
51. Bodleian MS Junius 85/86.
52. CCCC 190.
53. CCCC 178 pp. 141–42 and Bodley MS 343 f. 166ʳ.
54. CCCC 178 pp. 140–41.
55. Cambridge University Library MS Ii.4.6 f. 238, British Library MS Cotton Tiberius A iii ff. 51–3 (this is the text referred to above note 43) and Bodleian MS Hatton 114 f. 4ᵛ.
56. E. Dietrich, "Abt Aelfrik," *Zeitschrift für die Historische Theologie* 25 (1855) ; 26 (1856).

BERNARD F. HUPPÉ ❦ ALFRED & AELFRIC: A STUDY OF TWO PREFACES

That Aelfric was indebted to Alfred seems placed beyond doubt by Professor Godden. Although no further evidence need be educed to make the point, further study of the quality and depth of the indebtedness is called for, in particular of the influence of Alfred's *Preface* to the *Cura Pastoralis*. The *Preface* provides an example of the prototypical struggle to achieve a style and to transform Latin rhetoric into an English rhetoric equal in power and effectiveness to Old English poetic rhetoric. Alfred's *Preface* is all the more interesting because it would appear to mark a beginning, much as Cædmon's *Hymn* marks a beginning. To read the *Preface* is to perceive that Alfred is doing something new; that he is, in fact, struggling to create an English prose style responsive to intellectual demands. Aelfric read Alfred's translation of the *Cura;* unless he ignored the *Preface,* he would certainly not have missed the drama of its composition or have failed to respond to Alfred's problem and to his success.[1]

The *Preface,* for all its brevity, is a moving piece of literature. The image of one of the great men in history shines through it: Alfred's intelligence, his humanity, his patience in adversity, his compelling vision of a peaceful, literate society, his persuasive power and capacity to evoke the desire to make dreams come true. Such matters Aelfric would have noted as we should, but they are not the immediate concern of this study, which concentrates on the matter of style and stylistic example. What makes the *Preface* vital in any evaluation of Old English prose style is the fact that it is not a translation or development of an established style; but rather it appears to be the first piece of original English prose dealing not with narrative, but with intellectual concerns. It sets forth Alfred's own reflections, problems, ideas, and ideology, and it presents dramatically the picture of a man's mind at work, solving problems and presenting solutions. For what Alfred was doing he had no direct model, although it would appear that he was working with a

concept of effective and convincing presentation such as he would
have gained from classical rhetoric, and in particular from a study
of the rhetorical form of the epistle.[2]

The king's message, however, he writes by himself, and he himself creates the vehicle; he does not simply use the formulas of the
Latin epistle. Although the precedent of the Latin epistle is before
him, Alfred is writing in English, creating a style which is not
an imitation of Latin, but one suitable and responsive to Alfred's
own language. It appears also to be responsive to the modes of
Old English poetry because this poetry appears to influence his
style, particularly in its pattern of enlacement and progression, with
premises leading to a conclusion. The logical argument is in turn
supported by the persuasion of rhetoric: Alfred employs balanced
constructions, and he makes use of paranomasia, polyptoton,
antithesis, homeoteleuton, ethopopoeia. His conscious use of such
devices as these provides a rich embroidery upon which he has
woven his argument with care.

In its basic form the *Preface* appears to be like the early papal
epistle, which later developed into the standard form of the *ars
dictaminis:* 1) Protocol, or Salutation, 2) Arenga, or Proem,
(*Captatio Benevolentiae*); 3) Narration or Statement, 4) Disposition or Petition, 5) Final Clauses or Conclusion. Professor
Poole has described the form of the early papal letter. The opening
protocol gives the pope's name and title, then the name of the
addressee, followed by the salutation. The arenga enunciates "the
obligation of the Pope's duty or authority." The statement describes
"with greater or less detail the situation with which the Pope has
to deal." "When the statement is ended, the Pope makes his decision," the disposition.[3] In later practice the statement was in
syllogistic form leading to a conclusion, the petition. This pattern
is, in fact, what we find in Alfred's *Preface*. In the final part, the
Final Clauses, the pope provides for safeguards. Alfred's conclusion
includes such safeguards, but also has the form we find in model
epistles of later date, the conclusion, which is the decision or enactment.[4]

The detailed analysis of Alfred's epistolatory *Preface* must follow
a presentation of the text which reveals its rhetorical structure.
The text so presented gives the parts of the epistle by name and

indicates subordinate parts in the margin and by punctuation as follows: small Roman numerials (i,ii) and indentation indicate paragraphs; small arabic numbers (1,2) and pointing designate periods; small italicized letters (*a, b*) and semicolons designate clausules,[5] that is, sets of clauses grouped and ordered for rhetorical effect; the constituent clauses of the clausules are indicated by subscript (a_1, a_2) and commas. To illustrate, the proem in the schematic presentation consists of two paragraphs (i and ii), each with two periods. Paragraph i is introduced with the request for understanding and is developed in three clausules, *a* containing two clauses, *b* and *c*, each containing three. In period 2 the completion of the introductory *Swæ clæne hio wæs oðfeallenu on Angelcynne* is suspended until the end of the period, *ða ða ic to rice feng,* a clause which also serves to complete the three clausules (*a, b,* and *c*) which in turn develop the concept of decay presented in the introductory clause. Period 3 consists of a simple exclamatory statement.

I Salutation

Ælfred kyning hateð gretan Wærferð biscep his wordum luflice ond freondlice.

II Proem

i 1   Ond ðe cyðan hate ðæt me com swiðe oft on gemynd:

  a a_1 hwelce wiotan iu wæron giond Angelcynn ægðer ge

    a_2 godcundra hada ge woruldcundra, ond hu gesæliglica

  b b_1 tida ða wæron giond Angelcynn; ond hu ða kyningas ðe ðone onwald hæfdon ðæs folces on ðam dagum Gode

    b_2 ond his ærendwrecum hiersumedon, ond hie ægðer ge hiora sibbe ge hiora siodo ge hiora onweald innan-

    b_3 bordes gehioldon ond eac ut hiora eðel rymdon, ond hu him ða speow ge mid wige ge mid wisdome;

  c c_1 ond eac ða godcundan hadas hu giorne hie wæron ægðer ge ymb lare ge ymb liornunga ge ymb

    c_2 ealle ða ðiowotdomas ðe hie Gode scoldon, ond hu

        man utanbordes wisdom ond lare hieder on londe

c₃ sohte, ond hu we hie nu sceoldon ute begietan

2   gif we hie habban sceoldon. Swæ clæne hio

a   wæs oðfeallenu on Angelcynne ðæt swiðe feawa
wæron behionan Humbre ðe hiora ðeninga cuðen
understondan on Englisc oððe furðum an ærend-

b   gewrit of Lædene on Englisc areccean; ond ic
wene ðæt noht monige begiondan Humbre næren;

c   swæ feawa hiora wæron ðæt ic furðum anne anlepne
ne mæg geðencean be suðan Temese ða ða ic

3   to rice feng. Gode ælmihtegum sie ðonc ðætte we nu
ænigne onstal habbað lareowa!

ii 1 *a*   Ond for ðon ic ðe bebiode ðæt ðu do swæ ic geliefe ðæt

b b₁   ðu wille; ðæt ðu ðe ðissa woruldðinga to ðæm

    b₂ geæmetige swæ ðu oftost mæge, ðæt ðu ðone wisdom
ðe ðe God sealde ðær ðær ðu hiene befæstan mæge

2 *a*   befæste. Geðenc hwelc witu us becomon for ðisse
worulde ða ða we hit nohwæðer ne selfe ne lufodon

b   ne eac oðrum monnum ne lefdon; ðone naman ænne
we lufodon ðætte we Cristene wæron ond swiðe
feawa ða ðeawas.

III Narration

i 1 *a*   Ða ic ða ðis eall gemunde ða gemunde ic eac hu ic
eac geseah ær ðæm ðe hit eall forhergod wære ond

b b₁   forbærned; hu ða ciricean giond eal Angelcynn stodon
maðma ond boca gefylda ond eac micel mengeo

    b₂ Godes ðiowa, ond ða swiðe lytle fiorme ðara boca
wiston for ðæm ðe hie nanwuht ongiotan ne meahton
for ðæm ðe hie næron on hiora agen geðiode awritene.

2 *a*   Swelce hie cwæden: "Ure ieldran ða ða ðas stowa
ær hioldon hie lufodon wisdom ond ðurh ðone hie

b   begeaton welan ond us læfdon; her mon mæg giet
gesion hiora swæð ac we him ne cunnon æfter

c   spyrigean; ond for ðæm we habbað ægðer
forlæten ge ðone welan ge ðone wisdom for

ðæm ðe we noldon to ðæm spore mid ure mode
onlutan.

ii 1   Đa ic ðis eall gemunde ða wundrade ic swiðe swiðe
ðara godena wiotena ðe giu wæron giond Angelcynn
ond ða bec eallæ be fullan geliornod hæfdon ðæt hie
hiora ða nænne dæl noldon on hiora agen geðiode wendan.

2   Ac ic sona eft me selfum andwyrde ond cwæð:

a   "Hie ne wendon ðætte æfre menn sceoldon swæ recce-

b b₁ lease weorðan ond sio lare swæ oðfeallan; for ðære

  b₂ wilnunga hie hit forleton, ond woldon ðæt her ðy
mara wisdom on londe wære ðy we ma geðeoda
cuðon."

iii 1 *a*   Đa gemunde ic: hu sio æ wæs ærest on Ebriscgeðiode

b b₁ funden; ond eft ða hie Creacas geliornodon ða wendon

  b₂ hie hie on hiora agen geðiode ealle, ond eac ealle oðre

  b₃ bec, ond eft Lædenware swæ same siððan hie hie
geliornodon hie hie wendon ealla ðurh wise wealhstodas

c   on hiora agen geðiode; ond eac ealla oðra Cristna ðioda
sumne dæl hiora on hiora agen geðiode wendon.

2 *a*   For ðy me ðyncð betre gif iow swæ ðyncð: ðæt we eac
suma bec ða ðe niedbeðearfosta sien eallum monnum
to wiotonne ðæt we ða on ðæt geðiode wenden ðe we ealle

*bb*₁ gecnawan mægen; ond gedon swæ we eaðe magon mid
Godes fultume gif we ða stilnesse habbað ðætte eall sio
gioguð ðe nu is on Angelcynne friora monna ðara ðe
ða speda hæbben ðæt hie ðæm befeolan mægen sien to
liornunga oðfæste ða hwile ðe hie to nanre oðerre note
ne mægen oð ðone first ðe hie wel cunnen Englisc

  b₂ gewrit arædan, lære mon siððan furður on Læden-
geðiode ða ðe mon furðor læran wille ond to hieran
hade don wille.

IV Disposition

1 *a* a₁   Đa ic ða gemunde hu sio lar Lædengeðiodes ær ðissum

  a₂ afeallen wæs giond Angelcynn, ond ðeah monige cuðon

b   Englisc gewrit arædan; ða ongan ic ongemang oðrum

mislicum ond manigfealdum bisgum ðisses kynerices
ða boc wendan on Englisc ðe is genemned on Læden
"Pastoralis" ond on Englisc "Hierdeboc" hwilum
word be worde hwilum andgit of andgiete swæ swæ
ic hie geliornod æt Plegmunde minum ærcebiscepe
ond æt Assere minum biscepe ond æt Grimbolde
minum mæsseprioste ond æt Iohanne minum mæsse-
2 *a*   preoste. Siððan ic hie ða geliornod hæfde swæ swæ
ic hie forstod ond swæ ic hie andgitfullicost areccean
b b$_1$ meahte ic hie on Englisc awende ; ond to ælcum biscepstole
b$_2$ on minum rice wille ane onsendan, ond on ælcre bið an
æstel se bið on fiftegum mancessa.

V Conclusion

a   Ond ic bebiode on Godes naman ðæt nan mon ðone
æstel from ðære bec ne do, ne ða boc from ðæm mynstre ;
b b$_1$ uncuð hu longe ðær swæ gelærede biscepas sien swæ
b$_2$ swæ nu Gode ðonc welhwær siendon, forðy ic wolde
ðætte hie ealneg æt ðære stowe wæren buton se biscep
hie mid him habban wille oððe hio hwær to læne sie
oððe hwa oðre bi write.

ANALYSIS

Salutation: Alfred as king places his name first, the addressee
second, the verb of greeting being in the formal third person. This is
standard and unexceptional except possibly for the concluding
adverbial phrase, *luflice and freondlice,* which may just possibly
serve, in its warmth, to give a sense of the personal and humanizing
to the formal phrases of salutation.

Proem: The function of the proem is to persuade the bishop to
join him in his great design by showing vividly the problem that
they together face. Alfred creates an elaborate two-paragraph structure to serve this purpose. In effect the proem serves the purpose of

the later *captatio benevolentiae* in presenting his reflections on English history in such a way to make it follow (*for ðon*) that the bishop will wish to engage in friendship and love on the great work of restoring a Christian kingdom.

The rhetorical devices by which Alfred informs the elaborate structure of the proem consist largely in varieties of repetition, variation, balance, along with paranomasia to enforce the concluding exhortation. He links the proem to the salutation by variation, the formal, third person *hateð* of the latter becoming the first person *hate*, with the effect of a personal request to Wærferð to share his remembrance of time past and his grief over time present. In turn the conclusion of the proem (ii) is introduced by a variant on *hate*, viz., *bebiode*. Alfred, having asked the bishop to heed the problem, requires him in conclusion to join him in the works of wisdom by turning as often as possible from worldly to spiritual concerns. Clausule *a* of period i contains two simple clausules; *a*, introduced by *hwelce* establishes three basic considerations: wisdom (*wiotan*), the past (*iu*), the two estates, spiritual (*godcundra*) and temporal (*woruldcundra*). Against this clause is balanced a_2, introduced by *hu*, which in effect presents the blessedness of England as a consequence of the presence of wisemen then. The repeated phrase *geond Angelcynne* also provides a motif of repetition for the entire epistle, in effect emphasizing Alfred's claim of overlordship.

The ensuing two clausules develop in detail the picture of the former blessedness of England, which was the consequence of wisdom in the two estates; the repetition of *hu* which introduces each of the constituent clausules serves both the purpose of balance and of linkage. The *b* clausule, bound internally by verbal rhyme (homeoteleuton), reverses the order of the presentation of the two estates in a_1, describing first the actions of the *woruldcundra*, specifically the actions of past kings. In b_1 the basis of their power is given: it springs from their obedience to God and His messengers (*ærendwrecum*), the latter term seeming to define the role of the church as the expositor of God's word, and thus by implication reserving temporal rule to the king. Clause b_2 describes this temporal rule under spiritual direction in the two aspects of internal and external dominion. The aspect of internal dominion receives a tripartite definition, *sibbe, siodo, onwald,* "peace," "custom," "power." A definition of kingship appears involved which demands close investigation beyond the compass of this essay; it must suffice here to note the primary position given to peace, *sibbe*, the king's peace deriving from Christian purpose, or the *visio pacis*, as in Augustine's definition in the *City of God*. The king also governs through customary law, *siodo*; from these two flow the exercise of the king's justice or power, *onwald*. The description of external dominion in the same clause may appear to the modern reader incongruous with the primacy given to peace, since it speaks of conquest, not defense or diplomacy. But consideration of the key word *eðel*, native land, explains the apparent incongruity, for the word has heavy Christian connotations: man's native land (*patria*) is heaven, of which the Christian state ought to be an emblem. What Alfred is praising in his predecessors is conversion by conquest, the broadening of the Christian imperium, as with Oswald. Clause b_3 parallels a_2 as a summary statement of kingly prosperity in the extremes of war and wisdom, action and thought, a kingly prosperity which stems from the possession of *sapientia* and *fortitudo*.

Clausule c now describes, in parallel to b, the spiritual estate, introduced in a. In c_1 the activity of this estate is given tripartite definition as in b_2. The description is, as would be expected, governed by the monastic ideal of learning, teaching, and prayer, specifically in canonical services *ðiowotdomas*. Clauses c_2 and c_3 reflect the division between internal and external.

Period 2 of i makes the transition from past to present; it is introduced by a clause of comparision making a statement about the decay of learning *on angelcynne*, which is developed in the three, ensuing *ðæt* clausules (a, b, and c). In turn the introductory statement and the three clausules are completed by the concluding temporal clause which brings us to the time when Alfred began his reign. The singular subject, *hio*, of the introductory clause has as its antecedant the phrase *wisdom and lare* of $1c_2$, the learning once sought in England from abroad. The three clausules of development have *hie* of $1c_3$ as subject, the scholars who must now be sought in England from abroad. The three clausules develop "geographically," the first two with relation to the Humber, *behionan*, *begiondan*, the c clausule with relation to the Thames, *be suðan*; that is, the motion is from the north to Alfred's own domain "when he began to reign." There is a climactic effect in the structural use of incremental repetition and variation. Thus clausule *a* is introduced directly by *ðæt*, the subject being the *swiðe feawa* who could understand their *ðeninga* or could translate an *ærendgewrit* from the Latin. The two words refer back in inversion to *ðiowotdomas* of $1c_1$ and *ærendwrecum* of $1b_1$. Variation in clausule *b* consists of the *ðæt* clause being made dependent on *ic wene* and of the substitution of *noht manige* for *swiðe feawa*. In clausule *c* there is variation brought about by having the clausule introduced by the comparative *swa feawa* with the *ðæt* clause completing the comparison, its predicate being, *ic . . . ne mæg geðencean,* and the object, *anne anlepne,* climaxing the chain, *swiðe feawa, noht monige, swa feawa.* The incremental variation serves vividly to picture the dearth of scholars Alfred encountered when he became king and gives particular effectiveness to period 3 with its simple statement of thanksgiving for the present time when there is *ænigne onstal . . . lareowa.*

Paragraph ii consists of a request and an exhortation. The request, period 1, (*bebiode*) follows (*for ðon*) from Alfred's thinking about the past and present, for which he has asked Wærferð's sympathetic understanding: now particularly when learning has revived, Wærferð must not let concern with the world interfere too much with the pursuit and promotion of wisdom. Period 1 consists of a concatenation of *ðaet* clauses following the formula of request: *a, that* you do as I believe *that* you will; *b, that* you free yourself from worldly concern (so) *that* you may make firm the gift of God's wisdom. (Subjectively I feel Alfred stumbles here in this elaboration of structure in that he strives for a Latin rhetorical effect which doesn't quite come off, but this reaction may result simply from my early difficulties in translation.) [6] Period 2 consists of the exhortation to think of the consequences of worldly preoccupation, which is defined in an elaborately constructed clause involving word play on *lufodon, lefdon,* and contrast: *selfe—oðrum, naman—ðeawas.* If there is an echo here of Caesarius of Arles, "Non nobis sufficit, fratres, quod christianum nomen accepimus, si opera christiana non fecerimus," the complexity of the Alfredian structure is the more remarkable, in attempt at least. [7]

Narration: Having, as it were, prepared the foundation, Alfred moves in the narration, to a logical development of the problem, leading to his decision which he will give in IV, Disposition. Although Alfred adorns the first two paragraphs with imaginary dialogue and monologue (ethopoeia), essentially they set forth premises leading to a syllogistic conclusion. The first premise, drawn from Alfred's imaginary dialogue with monks living before their monasteries were destroyed, is that the destruction of the books was not as important as the fact that the books did no good because they were written in Latin, the learned language which the monks had lost. The second premise (ii), drawn from his imaginary monologue, is that the monks who had filled the monasteries with the treasure of books in Latin, a treasure now useless, must have done so with the purpose of encouraging learning, never dreaming that what they had amassed would ever be lost. It follows from these propositions that their educational purpose, however laudable, was proved invalid by the facts and that it would have been better for them to have left translations along with the originals. It would also follow that a program of translation is something which should begin now.

This point is, in fact, the conclusion stated in iii,2, but before reaching it Alfred, with considerable subtlety, introduces in iii,1 a further premise. This premise responds to an unstated but profound problem which is implicit in any theoretical discussion of translation, namely, the question of propriety. The question was a vexing one, and one that continued to be vexing, as we may observe in Aelfric's *Preface* to *Genesis*. Alfred did not avoid the question, but his response is basically pragmatic. He saw both a need and a means to satisfy it. By raising the large, theoretical problem peripherally, as it were, he was able to indicate his awareness of it and to forestall objection. By placing the problem in a noncentral, peripheral position in his syllogistic chain, he could avoid the need for theoretical argument and provide a purely pragmatic answer by citing earlier, approved translations of the Bible, but ignoring the thorny issue raised by such translations, an issue which Aelfric would later have to face. At any rate, some such reasoning must have been behind Alfred's introduction of the additional premise, found in iii,1, that the translation is authorized by the examples of the Greek translation of the Bible, of the Latin translation of the Bible and other books (of the Bible? of the Greek Fathers?), and of other vernacular translations. Clearly this premise responds to an implied theoretical problem. From the premise follows the implicit conclusion that translation is justified by authority. The conclusion, as has been observed, is pragmatic, the theoretical objection being answered simply by appeal to authority.

In iii,2 Alfred reaches his final conclusion. This twofold conclusion follows from Alfred's two sets of propositions. It takes as demonstrated, first (*a*) that a program of basic translation is required, second (*b*) that a program of education should be adopted in which free men with the opportunity would learn to read and write in English and that those with the aptitude might learn Latin. The clarity of argument by which this conclusion is reached is supported by clarity of structure, with the three paragraphs held together by the repetition of *Đa ic gemunde* and the periodic structure of question (1) and response (2) within each paragraph.

The logical development of the argument by which this conclusion is reached is not, however, what gives the narration its subtle and provocative distinction. Rather its persuasive force comes from Alfred's dramatic rhetoric, his use of ethopoeia and reinforcing imagery. Alfred shows himself here to be fully aware of the Christian function of rhetorical adornment. If one were looking for models, it would be Augustine's *Soliloquies,* or even more certainly, Boethius's *Consolation* that would come to mind. Their subtlety, clarity, and dramatic effectiveness would have provided inspiration to Alfred in his effort to express the problem which the plight of England presented to him when he came to the throne. Worthy of Boethius is his dramatic presentation of his problem by having a group of monks collectively lament their loss and their helplessness. In particular he vivifies their speech through having them employ hunting imagery, where they imagine themselves as hunters who have "lost the scent," who cannot follow the "traces." The subtle juxtaposition of wealth and treasure in the monks' speech is also effective in making the point that the one is empty without the other, as is the word play: *ongietan—begeaton; lufodon —læfdon; forlæten—onluton—forleton.* Alfred's "soliloquy" which follows is of equal note for the effective immediacy of its dramatization of the king's reflections as they had been described in the proem.

Disposition. The disposition serves its purpose of presenting the king's decision through a brief description of what Alfred had actually done in response to his reflections upon the fall of learning in England and what he planned to do to preclude its happening again. The disposition is linked to the narration by repetition, period 1, of the introductory *Ða gemunde* clause which frames the latter. The period introduced by the formula of remembrance gives the gist of his reflections. He remembers first (a_1) the decay of Latin learning *giond Angelcynne,* second (a_2) the continuing ability to read English. These two considerations lead him to his conclusion, as reported in the narration, to translate and to establish schools where English, at least, would be taught, but also Latin. They thus serve to introduce Alfred's description (1,b) of what he had, in fact, already initiated, *ða ongan ic ongemang oðrum.* The word play here serves perhaps to give special force to Alfred's understatement about the demands which his reign has made upon him. It also serves by implication as a reminder of Alfred's earlier injunction (II,ii,1,b) that Wærferð find time for the works of wisdom amidst the press of the world's work.

In the description 1,*b* of the beginning of his undertaking Alfred specifies only his turning to the translation of Gregory's *Pastoral Care.* In the particularization Alfred makes an important point about his translation, that it is faithful to the original, literal except where the literal would be unfaithful to the spirit, *andgite.*[8] Here again Alfred shows himself aware of the theoretical problems of translation. Like his description of kingship, the succinct statement he makes encapsulates the results of what must have been extended study of the problem. The fact of his long careful preparation is suggested by Alfred's thoughtful carefulness to name all those through whose training he was enabled to proceed on his own translation. His translation of Gregory was not a work undertaken without careful preparation and consideration of the whole problem of translation.

In the second period Alfred gives the results of his determination; he has translated the *Cura* and will send a copy to each cathedral along with the gift of an *æstel*(?) in each. Here, perhaps, in the determination to produce enough copies so that each cathedral school would have one may be an oblique allusion to what was omitted in the decision, that is, any reference to a start on his educational program. It would appear that the beginning of this program was still in the future, but that it would follow as a consequence of the provision of books in English to serve the educational plan. Thus supplying books would be to establish the base for Alfred's long-range educational plans.

Conclusion. In the formula *ic bebiode* which begins the conclusion, his "enacting clause," Alfred repeats in variation the introductory formula of the salutation, *hateð*, and the *hate—bebiode* formulas which serve to introduce both paragraphs of the proem. The *bebiode* of the conclusion differs from the others in that it is not addressed to Wærferð, but to all men, present or future, who will make use of the book. Alfred, in giving his specific instructions about his book, thus moves from a particular audience to a universal one. What he enjoins on everyone in the *a* clausule is that the *æstel* not be removed from the book and the book from the minister. In the *b* clausule he gives his reasons for this injunction. These reasons serve to remind his wider audience of the perilous state of England which he had described in the body of his letter. The implicit warning that such times could come again is sharpened by the detailed limitations he places upon the removal of the book.

To summarize, Alfred's *Preface* is both deceptively simple and stylistically refined. It is a remarkably successful first venture in the creation of an intellectual prose style in English which would be a match for Latin and which would employ the principles of Latin rhetoric, but in a thoroughly English manner, making use particularly of the devices of repetition, of word play, and of dramatization, the mainstays of the Old English poetic style.

These are matters which, as I have suggested, Aelfric would not have missed. But beyond this statement of the obvious there appears to me evidence in Aelfric's *Preface* to *Genesis* that he had given thought to the content and the manner of Alfred's *Preface*. First of all, Aelfric, in writing his *Preface,* adopts Alfred's epistolatory form. The *Preface* begins with the salutation, "Aelfric munuc gret Aeðelweard ealdorman eadmodlice" (line 1).[9] There follows the proem, in which Aelfric reveals to Aeðelweard the difficulties present in his apparently simple request that he translate *Genesis* (2–40). The problem as he presents it lies not in translation but in the necessity to understand that behind the letter is the spirit of the Bible. He summarizes the problem at the end of the proem (37–40) : "We secgað eac foran to þæt seo boc is swiðe deop gastlice to understandenne, and we writað na mare buton þa nacedan gerecednisse. Ðonne þincð þam ungelæredum þæt eall þat andgit beo belocen on þære anfealdan gerecednisse; ac hit ys swiðe feor þam." The narration consists in a masterful presentation of the principles of exegesis involved in the spiritual understanding of Genesis (40–98). As with Alfred's *Preface,* the proem and, in particular, the narration are fully developed; and the disposition (99–102) and conclusion (103–106) are brief. The disposition simply declares Aelfric's intention not to translate any other books of the Bible after he has complied with Aeðelweard's request. His epistolatory preface may serve, in short, to guard against abuse of this particular translation, but the problem of translation has convinced him of the unwisdom of opening up the whole of the Bible to the unlearned, whether clerics or laymen. The conclusion consists of a brief injunction that in the copying of the book great care be taken and a stern warning of the consequences of careless copying. As with Alfred in his conclusion, Aelfric appears to be addressing posterity.

It may be conjectured that Aelfric in part adopted Alfred's epistolatory form for his own *Preface* because like Alfred he was dealing with the thorny problem of translation. In particular he is concerned with the large question, which Alfred answers pragmatically, of the potential danger in translation, particularly when it comes to translation, as Alfred had felt free to do, according to the spirit (*andgite of andgite*). For in dealing with the Bible Aelfric is aware that his freedom of translation has severe limits : "heo (*Genesis*) is swa geendebyrd swa swa God sylf hi gedihte þam writere Moyse, and we durron na mare awritan on Englisc þonne ðæt Leden hæfð, ne þa endebyrdnesse awendan buton þam anum ðæt ðæt Leden and ðæt Englisc nabbað na ane wisan on ðære spræce fandunge." For this reason he will translate no further than he has already agreed to do—a curiously pragmatic solution in the Alfredian manner ! (81–100)

Aelfric, it seems to me, also responds to the spirit of Alfred's *Preface*. He uses the device of dramatic monologue, for example, in the first paragraph of his proem, where he pictures his former teacher as speaking of Jacob's wives and concubines but without understanding the difference between the old and new laws (10–20). Again in the second paragraph he employs monologue. There he first pictures unlearned priests who suppose that a little Latin learning is sufficient to justify their status, but who are ignorant of the typology of the Old Testament, which properly understood would teach them the truth about their calling. He pictures them as arguing for a married priesthood on the basis of a deadly literal reading of the New Testament (11–36).

In his narration Aelfric appears to adopt something of Alfred's manner of involving his reader in direct response, of teaching by example. Thus he begins by setting a question, a kind of trap for the unwary, a question which derives from word play: "Seo boc ys gehaten Genesis, þæt ys 'Gecyndboc' for þam þe heo ys firmest boca and spricð be ælcum gecinde, ac heo ne spricð na be þæra engla gesceapenisse" (40–42). He goes on without answering the obvious question: why doesn't it speak of the creation of the angels? The answer rests, of course, in the spiritual understanding that the "beginning" in the opening verse includes all eternal creation and thus, by implication, the angels. The function of the unanswered question is to force the reader into discovery for himself. It is similar to the device of the implied question which Alfred employed to address the deep question of the propriety of vernacular translation.

Aelfric goes on to the standard demonstration of the evidence of the Trinity to be found in the opening of Genesis, but subtly shifts in dealing with the Holy Ghost from the anagogical to the tropological level, "And se Halga Gast færþ geond manna heortan and sylð us synna forgyfnysse" (52–53). Through the shift Aelfric must have intended that the reader exercise his own intelligence in following what Aelfric leaves unstated, but clearly implied. The instructive transition the reader must supply, for Aelfric simply goes on to ensuing pieces of anagogical evidence of the Trinity in Genesis. He notes the grammatical evidences in the use of the plural-singular combination, "Uton wircean to ure anlicnesse," (58) and in Abraham's use of the singular in addressing the three

angels (60–61). Paralleling his earlier shift to the tropological
level, he reintroduces this level without explanation by tropological
exegesis of Abel's blood crying out to God (61–63).[10]

He pauses here to call attention to the difficulty involved in
understanding biblical *sententia,* with its depth of spiritual meaning, "hu deop seo boc is on gastilicum andgyte" (63–64). This
period of admonition to the unwary concludes the first paragraph
of the narration and provides a transition to the second paragraph,
where Aelfric introduces the reader, who is careful to follow him,
to the third level, the allegorical, which is concerned with Christ
and His Church. He does this by giving first the exegetical interpretation of Joseph in Egypt as prefiguring Christ (65–67), followed by exegesis of Moses' tent in the wilderness, where the tent
in its various details is interpreted as prefiguring the Church in its
various functions designed for the salvation of mankind (67–76).
He concludes with a tropological interpretation of the tail of the
sacrificial animal (76–80). His interpretation of the tail as indicating the constant need for good works completes the tropological
interpretation of the works of the Holy Spirit (52–53) as grace
operating in baptism and penance.

In the third and final paragraph of the narration (81–98) Aelfric
turns to a detailed examination of the problems in translation that
are posed by the depth and complexity of Scriptural *sententia* and
the close, fixed relation this has to its *litera.* Two problems derive
from the special quality of Scriptural *litera.* The first problem in
translation arises from the precision of the biblical lexicon, which
has direct and inviolate relation to the *sententia.* Obviously where
English has no direct equivalent for the Latin word, problems
arise. The second difficulty facing the translator rests in the divinely inspired ordering of sentence elements, syntax; since Latin
and English differ in their syntactic structures, how can the one be
effectively translated into the other language? These problems
imply that a translation of Scripture must be rigidly faithful to the
litera, to its precise wording and to sentence order. But more often
than not English does not have a literal equivalent word or syntactic structure. Here careful attention must be given to the differences between the two languages, so that the letter of the Latin
lexicon and syntax is not violated by too literal a translation into

English; an equivalent in the English idiom must be sought which is responsive to the letter of the Latin. A completely literal rending can lead to error.

In the concluding periods (89–98) of this paragraph, which deals with the difficulty of translation, Aelfric makes another of his startling shifts, introducing, without overt transition, mention of two heretical notions. There have been heretics, he says, who wished to reject the Old Testament, others, like the Jews, who reject the New. The reader is left puzzled by the sudden transition to the subject of the two heresies. Aelfric's purpose is only later revealed. These heresies, Aelfric continues, are revealed as such in two special ways. First, Christ and his apostles taught us that the old law was to be obeyed spiritually, the new truly in works. Second, God in his creation of man with two eyes, two ears etc. revealed that there are two testaments. One does not ask of the Creator "why two?" Similarly one does not ask "why are there two laws?" Therefore, Aelfric declares, man must live according to God's will, not according to his own. The statement concludes the paragraph dealing with the translation of scripture, but its relevance as conclusion is anything but obvious. Again Aelfric challenges the reader to discover the implicit chain of reasoning which connects subject and conclusion. God has created things and His word as revelation to man. Creation and Scripture exist as God willed them; man cannot deal with Creation according to his desires anymore than he can shape the Scriptural word according to his own rhetorical fancies or sense of decorum. Translation must be true to the letter and spirit of Scripture. The intrusion of an individual sense of the fitting can do violence to the depth of the Bible where words and their arrangement reflect divine meaning. In this *tour de force* of reader engagement, Aelfric's brilliant use of informing analogy teaches by its very method the manner in which Scripture must be approached and translated; bad translation violates the very essence of Creation. Here is a model of great teaching and reflection of the Alfredian spirit to which Aelfric has responded.

Even now, if a student wished a "short course" in exegetical method, he could find no better text than Aelfric's *Preface* in its clarity and its method of instruction through direct involvement. And if he wished to understand the roots of English prose style, he could do no better than to turn to Alfred's *Preface* for close and detailed study. These two statements serve almost to frame the history of the beginning, development, and culmination of intellectual Old English prose. Where we find Alfred attempting what had not been done, we find in Aelfric the assurance of the writer who has completely mastered a tradition, who can solve with assurance any stylistic problem with which he is faced. For example, the lucidity of his handling of the translation of patristic exegesis and his informed discussion of the theory of translation itself testify to the assurance of a master. What Alfred created, Aelfric completed. The art of persuasion and teaching can find few more splendidly successful practitioners. One would have to be sullenly obdurate not to respond to Alfred's call to learning, or not to respond to Aelfric's demand for informed, involved enlightened reading.

NOTES

1. In addition to Alfred's *Preface* I shall be making detailed reference to Aelfric's *Preface to Genesis*. Because both texts, soundly edited, are conveniently to be found in James W. Bright's *Anglo-Saxon Reader* 3rd ed., ed. Frederic G. Cassidy and Richard N. Ringler (New York, 1971), pp. 180–83, 251–59, they are the ones employed in this essay. I am not disregarding the *Chronicles,* including the superb historical narrative of Cynewulf and Cyneheard. It is not narrative prose with which I am concerned, but with a prose capable of dealing effectively with ideas and concepts.

2. F.P. Magoun has noted the epistolatory form of the *Preface* in "Some Notes on King Alfred's Circular Letter on Educational Policy Addressed to His Bishops," *Mediæval Studies* 10 (1948) : 93–107, and in "King Alfred's Letter on Educational Policy according to the Cambridge Manuscripts," *Mediæval Studies* 11 (1949) : 113–22. My own observation that the *Preface* was in the form of an epistle

was made independently. Professor Magoun does not consider the actual structure of the epistle in ordering his
comments.

3. R.L. Poole, *Lectures on the History of the Papal Chancery*
   (Cambridge, 1915), pp. 41–48.

4. Paul E. Szarmach in an article awaiting publication, "The Meaning of Alfred's *Preface* to the *Pastoral Care*," has made an
   important, detailed analysis of Alfred's thoughts as presented in the *Preface*.

5. The noncurrent term "clausule" I adopt from my method of
   rhetorical-structural analysis of Old English Poetry in *The
   Web of Words* (Albany, 1970) pp. xviii–xx. As in the
   analysis of poetry, the analysis of prose appears to require
   some term to describe the basic rhetorical units which
   constitute the elements of a rhetorical period.

6. See F. Klaeber, "Zu König Aelfreds Vorrede zu seiner Ueber-
   setzung de Cura Pastoralis," *Anglia* 48 (1923) : 57–58.

7. Caesarius of Arles, Sermon 16, CCL 103 (ed. Morin), p. 77.

8. F. Klaeber, "Zu König Aelfreds Vorrede," p. 62.

9. Reference is to the line numbers in the Bright 3rd edition.

10. Grammar (singular—plural) to Rhetoric (metaphor) provides
    the unstated transition from the three angels to Abel's blood
    crying.

𝒢.R. LETSON ❧ THE POETIC CONTENT
OF THE REVIVAL HOMILY

It is commonly asserted that there are three distinct periods of
artistic resurgence in Anglo-Saxon England. The first of these is
associated with the late seventh- and early eighth-century North-
umbria of Venerable Bede. During Bede's lifetime relatively com-
prehensive libraries were established in England, so that the
writings of the Church Fathers became systematically available,
thereby providing the basis for the *florilegia* of Bede and simultaneously for the development of the insular pericope homily.
Although Bede was a young man when an inspired cowherd sang
the first Christian poem in the English vernacular, the Age of
Bede was a time for recording serious Latin composition both in
prose and in poetry so that few lines of Anglo-Saxon verse can
confidently be assigned to this period. England's second intellectual
renaissance arrives approximately one hundred and fifty years
later in Wessex under the patronage of King Alfred. Alfred pro-
moted a general artistic awakening involving both Latin and the
vernacular, both prose and poetry, but it is in the tenth and early
eleventh centuries under the initial impetus of Oswald, Dunstan,
and Aethelwold that Anglo-Saxon England enjoys its most per-
manently productive intellectual revival. It is during the Benedictine Revival that almost all of the presently extant Anglo-Saxon
poetry was collected and preserved in the Junius, Vercelli, Exeter,
and *Beowulf* manuscripts; similarly, the bulk of the vernacular
homilies composed in Anglo-Saxon England are Revival homilies
either as collections (the Vercelli and, apparently, the Blickling)
or as compositions (the Aelfrician and Wulfstanian). It is noteworthy that at this time when the monastic scribe is avidly recording his countrymen's doctrinal compositions both in English poetry
and in English prose, the monastic author is showing a keen
interest in adorning prose instruction with vernacular poetic embellishment. The revived interest in regular monastic discipline
apparently included a stress on the teaching of Christian truths in

a pleasing fashion, though what begins as pragmatic adornment evolves into the near convergence of the poetic and prose traditions in late Anglo-Saxon England. This stylistic convergence is the natural outgrowth of established rhetorical tradition and a popular affection for poetry. There is, for example, Augustine's influential directive to the preacher that he make limited use of rhyme and rhythm both for *delectare* and for rhetorical effect (*De doctrina christiana,* IV.xx.41), so that poetic embellishment becomes quite widespread.[1] In fact some of Anglo-Saxon England's most revered homilists (Aldhelm, Bede, Alcuin, Cynewulf, Dunstan, Aelfric, and Wulfstan) shared the esteem with which all strata on Anglo-Saxon society regarded vernacular poetics. Scribal practice also suggests a conscious relationship between the poetic and predicatory traditions, since some of our best Anglo-Saxon poetry appears in homiliaries, notably the Vercelli. Ultimately the Anglo-Saxon homilist begins to borrow directly from Anglo-Saxon and Latin poetry (Napier 29, for example) and even shares general rhetorical and structural devices with the poet: balance, catalogue, cohesion and emphasis through alliteration, all found even in the favored pericope and hagiographic homiletic forms.

But the poetic homily is not peculiarly an Anglo-Saxon phenomenon, nor is its origin simply ninth and tenth century. Early examples appear during the fourth century in the Syrian church, such widely imitated Latin homilists as Augustine and Gregory used rhyme and rhythm to enhance the effectiveness of their preaching, and the poetic homily seems to have been popular in France, at least during the twelfth century, since Alanus de Insulis found it necessary to censure the use of rhythmic melody and poetic harmony (*rhythmorum melodias et consonantias metrorum;* PL 210, 112), thereby implying a tradition of metrical or quasi-metrical homilies.[2] Significantly, French connections that predate Alanus surface in such places as Alcuin's Latin verse discourse on St. Willibrord, the apostle of the Franks (*PL* 101, 713–24), and in Aelfric's use of Haymo. It is an influence which increased after the Battle of Hastings, when rhymed homilies in the vernacular began to proliferate.[3]

Within the Anglo-Saxon homiletic tradition Aelfric's and Wulfstan's poetic prose homilies are far from isolated phenomena. The earlier Vercelli homilists often break into poetry, especially in descriptive passages and particularly in depictions of heaven and hell.[4] In the second of these homilies, for example, there is an extended section of regular verse displaying both rhyme (II. 50, 52, 60) and complex alliteration (II. 64, 68, 70):

se opena heofon 7 enȝla þrym
7 eall-wihtna hryre 7 eorþan for-wyrht,
treowleasra ȝe-winn 7 tunȝla ȝefeall,
þunor-rada cyrm 7 se þystra storm,   50
þæra lyfta leoma 7 þæra liȝa blæstm
7 ȝraniendra ȝesceaft 7 þæra ȝasta ȝefeoht
7 sio ȝrimme ȝe-syhð 7 þa ȝod-cundan miht
7 se hata scur 7 hell-warena dream,
þæra beorȝa ȝeberst 7 þara bymena sanȝ,   55
7 se brada bryne 7 se bitera dæȝ
7 se micla cwyld 7 þara manna man
7 seo sarie sorh 7 þara sawla ȝedal
7 se deað-berenda draca 7 diofla forwyrd
7 se nearwa seaþ 7 se swearta deaþ   60
7 se byrenda ȝrund 7 se blodiȝa stream
7 mycel fionda fyrhto 7 se fyrena ren
7 hæðenra ȝranunȝ 7 hira heriȝa fyll,
heofon-warena menȝo 7 hiora hlafordes miht
7 þæt mycle ȝemot 7 seo eȝesfulle fyrd   65
7 sio reðe rod 7 se rihta dom
ure fyrena edwit 7 þara feonda ȝestal
7 þa blacan ondwlitan 7 bifiendan word,
se forhta cyrm 7 þara folca wop
ond se scamienda here 7 se synniȝa heap,   70
seo graniende neowelnes 7 sio for-ȝlendrede hell
7 þara wyrma ȝryre.[5]

This same affection for rhyme and alliteration is present to some extent in a large number of Old English homilies and is especially to be found in Vercelli IV, XXI, XXII, and Blickling X.[6] In each case alliteration is the predominating poetic device and rhyme an

accompanying adornment, so that the poetic influence is clearly
Germanic and vernacular, and not Latin.

The functional identity which the Anglo-Saxon envisions between homilist and poet also appears in the mixing of quasi-poetic
homilies and pure poetry within the Vercelli manuscript. In this
instance regular prose, poetically enriched prose, segments of
poetry, and whole poems are arranged side by side in a collection
whose principle of organization, as in many Old English MSS, is
far from haphazard.[7] Most of the Vercelli homilies center on the
pivotal Christian feasts of Christmas and Easter or on the eschatological theme usually associated with these two related feasts. The
Dream of the Rood fits well into such a collection, as does *Elene,*
a poem which Cynewulf explains is about the victorious cross (*be
ðære rode,* 1240; *be ðam sigebeacne,* 1265), not about Elena.
Andrew's designation as Apostle of the Cross accounts for the
inclusion of *Andreas,* as does the poetic unravelling of the theme of
redemption, in which Andrew explicitly imitates the salutary passion of Christ. *The Soul and Body I* fits naturally into the
eschatological framework and is even thematically echoed in
several of the homilies (e.g., II, pp. 50f; IV, especially pp. 87ff,
92ff; XXII, folios 117vff). Only the Martin and Guthlac homilies
do not seem to fit easily into the organizational pattern. They are,
however, perfect companion pieces. Both saints were worldly
warriors turned soldiers of God (*godes cempan*), and both overcame satanic forces and were taken gloriously to heaven. As such
they provide concrete examples of the fulfillment of the esachato-
logical theme of the manuscript. Although the Vercelli book is
principally an organized selection of quasi-poetic homilies, the
pieces of pure poetry fit comfortably into the overall design and
are essential constituents of the homiliary.

There is a further hint of a possible kinship between the poetic
and predicatory in the fondness a significant number of homilists
reveal for vernacular and classical poetry. This fondness is evident
from the Age of Bede up to and including the Benedictine Revival.
It is, in other words, ubiquitous both historically and geographically in Anglo-Saxon England. Aldhelm's competence in vernacular
poetry, attested to by King Alfred, results in an ability to attract
an eager congregation through the singing of popular Germanic

lays.[8] His skill in Latin poetry, his reverence for style and the classics are clear evidence of his interest in poetry, and his riddles are exercises in poetic wit. That Bede was learned in native songs (*doctus in nostris carminibus*) is perhaps of greater significance, since Bede was destined to become a major source of homiletic inspiration for Anglo-Saxons, although his "Death Song" stands as a lone witness of a talent in the vernacular. Like Aldhelm, Bede looked upon poetry as a potential aid to religious instruction, so that his admiration for Cædmon's contribution to effective Christian pedagogy is unqualified (*Historia Ecclesiastica* IV.xxiv). Furthermore, just as Aldhelm had reshaped his prose *De laudibus virginitatis* to its poetic form in *De laudibus virginum,* Bede transformed his prose Cuthbert into a second, poetic version, and, in like manner, Alcuin provided both a prose and a poetic life of Willibrord, lives he expressly calls sermons. Alcuin has often been considered an adversary of vernacular poetry because of his famous challenge "Quid Hinieldus cum Christo?", yet his alliterative epistolary style implies Germanic influence, and even the famed letter to Higebald is heavily alliterative.[9] Alcuin admits to being "more moved by the tears of Dido than by the Psalms of David," with the result that both his letters and his poetry reveal an admiration for the classics, particularly Ovid and Virgil.[10] The embellished prose of the Revival writers is therefore a cumulation of a long-standing affection for delectable pedagogy and not the development of a new form. Aelfric's alliterative style and Wulfstan's metrical catalogues reflect this traditional attraction for vernacular poetry and suggest an appreciation for the power of poetry as a means of appealing to English congregations. Wulfstan had even tried his hand at political propaganda in the Edgar and Edward poems, which appear in the *Anglo-Saxon Chronicle*.[11] Throughout the Anglo-Saxon period the homilist nourished a general admiration for poetry and an appreciation of its potential role in the effective presentation of the teachings of Christ. Both Augustine and Gregory had argued that the good preacher should adapt his teaching to suit the tastes of his audience, so that for homilists and congregations traditionally moved by the pleasant rhythm of poetry the dissemination of doctrine through poetic prose is simply good pedagogy.

For an explicit demonstration of the essential relationship between the poet and homilist in Anglo-Saxon England, Napier 29
provides a good example. In this homily it is possible to trace a
compositional progression wherein Bede's *De die iudicii* is ver-
nacularized by an Old English poet (*Anglo-Saxon Poetic Records*
VI, pp. 58–67) and is subsequently incorporated into a pseudo-
Wulfstanian homily. The inspiration moves historically through
the Age of Bede to the Revival homilist, thereby revealing a continuity in image and idea as well as an evolution from private
scholarly devotion to popular poetic homily. The Old English poem
is faithful to Bede's original, though the poet expands his source
with characteristic Old English embellishment.[12] The homilist has
incorporated lines 92–207 of the poem into the body of his homily
(p. 136 l. 29 to p. 140 l. 1), the description of the torments of hell
and the joys of heaven being a time-honored homiletic preoccupation. That the homilist has borrowed from an Old English translation and not the Latin original is unmistakable.[13] Krapp even
emends his poetic text on the basis of the homiletic interpolation.

The homily as a whole is well suited to the poetic insertion,
since alliteration and rhyme are used to greater and lesser degrees
throughout the prose sermon. Conversely *Judgment Day II* employs typically homiletic exhortatives which are incorporated
naturally into the sermon. Bede's *Sis memor illius* (CCL 122,
p. 441, l. 62), for example, becomes *ic bidde, man, þæt þu gemune*
in the poem, and, characteristic of the Old English homily, it appears as *nu, leofan men, uton habban us on mycelum gemynde* in
the sermon. The homiletic exhortation is formulaic, and the singular monastic scholar has become an Anglo-Saxon popular congregation.

Besides literal borrowing, the homilist apparently takes thematic
cues from the translation of Bede. The opening admonition to confess, for example, parallels Bede's introductory monologue, in
which the narrator struggles with the necessity to reveal his
wounds to the Physician.[14] Similarly the exemplum and the soul's
moralizing address to the body (Napier, pp. 140–42), both of which
follow the poetic interpolation, merely amplify identical addresses
within the poem.[15] The homilist now brings his discourse full
cycle, returning to his plea for the sinful to confess. Only the

summary prayer and the final doxology seem not to have been inspired by *Judgment Day II,* though even here there is a likeness, since the poem does conclude with a prayer and a closing doxology. Napier's 29, therefore, does not merely borrow from the poetic tradition; rather, the content of the homily is formally inspired by it, verbally and thematically. There is here a real fusion of the art of the homilist and that of the poet. They share similar aims, similar images, similar turns of phrase, and they do so in no accidental way. Equally important, these same aims, images, and phrases are presented both to learned and popular congregations without essential modification.

This natural affinity between the poetic and predicatory arts in Anglo-Saxon England is, therefore, long standing and merely matures during the Benedictine Revival. It is moreover an affinity that surfaces quite demonstrably on the stylistic level. The catalogue, for example, is one of the many structural devices common to the media and is a rhetorical effect which lends itself naturally to poetic flourish, even in a prose text. The rhetorical and metrical flourishes Wulfstan achieves with this embellishment, especially in those homilies Bethurum categories as "Evil Days," are well known. There are, however, other homilists who make notable use of the poetic catalogue, homilists such as the authors of Blickling X and Vercelli II. Similar catalogues appear in Hrothgar's homily, Cynewulf's homiletic *Christ II,* and they constitute much of the "homiletic segment" of *The Wanderer.* The theme of earthly transience, which is catalogued in *Beowulf* and *The Wanderer,* reappears in poetic form in Blickling Homily X.[16] In this instance the theme, the transience of middle-earth, moves from generalized biblical signs of impending doom to particular, immediate application. The homilist has introduced nothing extraneous and has perfectly interlaced the well-known exemplum by allusion to the body and soul motif as well as the *ubi sunt* catalogue. In fact a series of catalogues follow in close proximity. The *we sceolan* (p. 111), *hwær beoþ* (pp. 111f), and *nu is* (p. 115) series rely heavily on alliteration and rhyme to enchance the effect. This reliance is particularly true in the contrasting *we sceolan* and *hwær beoþ* instances, in which the nature of the eternal is convincingly juxtaposed with that of the temporal.

Likenesses in style are not limited to alliteration, catalogue, or other minor rhetorical effects, but extend also to literary unity (it is thematic) and to specifically homiletic forms (the pericope and the hagiographic). In the case of form, Augustine himself seems to provide the rationale for homiletic disjointedness. Aside from his exposition on the allegorical method, perhaps, the most significant formal advice he has to offer is a forthright encouragement to digress. As one subdivides main questions, says Augustine, further difficulties may come to mind. When this happens he considers it advisable that the preacher answer all questions even if in so doing he lose sight altogether of the main topic. This distraction is preferable, Augustine reasons, to permitting the timid to leave with unresolved doubts (*De doctrine christiana,* IV.xx). Beryl Smalley's comment on Gregory seems to imply that Gregory's attitude towards formal homiletic unity was similar to Augustine's. She points out that

> Everything in St. Gregory's teaching is attached, however loosely, to the thread of the text, which precludes any attempt at coherence or logical arrangement. But if we take a series of two or three homilies, or one of thirty-five books of the *Moralia,* we can see how suitable it was for educational purposes. In two or three addresses, or hours of study, St. Gregory's hearers or readers would get a series of lessons on doctrine, prayer and ethics, in a well-arranged and carefully varied time-table.[17]

Digression, therefore, was inherent in the allegorical method and was recommended by the best of authorities. Yet, as Adrien Bonjour's treatment of the digressions in *Beowulf* convincingly suggests, unity in Anglo-Saxon literature may well be a matter of motif and thematic balance so that the appearance of digression may well be the result of a twentieth-century perspective.[18] More recently with his theory of interlace John Leyerle has taken a fresh direction in the study of literary form in the Middle Ages. His concept is of particular importance because it establishes a frame of reference which is restricted by design neither to *Beowulf* nor to a single method of artistic expression.[19] Though in some ways more complex, Bernard Huppé's analysis of *Vainglory, The*

Wonder of Creation, The Dream of the Rood, and *Judith* seems similar in inspiration to Leyerle's, appealing as Huppé does to illustrations from *The Book of Kells* and suggesting "the rational thread" as a principle of poetic organization.[20] Recent critics have traced the notion of thematic unity to the exegetical and Cædmonian process of intellectual *ruminatio,* and Thomas Hill has applied the theory to the structure of *Christ I.*[21] Although the idea of thematic unity has most often arisen in analyses of *Beowulf,* thematic unity, however we define it, was consciously or unconsciously an intellectual and organizational conviction which was widespread, if not universal, in the Christian Middle Ages.[22] As a result, even the digressive pericope homily often reveals an identical unifying principle. An examination of an Aelfrician episodic pericope will serve to reveal of the homily what has generally been formally associated primarily with Old English poetry.

Aelfric's homily for the Third Sunday after Epiphany begins with a formal evangelical introduction to the Old English pericope, "Matheus se eadiga godspellere awrat on þissere . . . ." (CH I, pp. 120–34). There is no formal exordium. Aelfric follows the Old English semialliterative rendering of Matthew's account of the healing of the leper with an orientation naming Haymo as the source of the exegesis (*PL* 118, 137–47); then he begins the characteristic point-by-point interpretation. The mountain symbolizes the heavens from which the Healer descends, the multitude signifies the faithful who follow their Healer, the leper typifies sinful mankind, and his leprosy represents sin. The healing of the leper demonstrates the humility of the Healer, who could have effected a cure without physical contact as he later does when healing the centurion's servant in the parable which serves as the pericope for the second half of the homily. The conclusion succinctly follows. "Christ . . . ure sawle fram synna fagnyssum gehælan mæge" (p. 122). Finally, the hand of Christ represents his physical nature, the admonition that the leper keep his cure secret teaches man not to boast of good deeds, and the informing of the priest instructs man to confess to *þam gastlican læce.*

From the viewpoint of allegoresis Aelfric has thus far merely abridged Haymo, though he has also made full use of images and concepts with which the Old English audience would have been thoroughly familiar. Wherever possible Aelfric seems to be providing interpretative "translation." Within the pericope, for example, there is an alliterative pattern that suggests a relationship between the *hreoflig mann* and *se hælend*. One only need examine a few lines of the pericope to see this pattern. For example:

> Se *H*ælend astrehte *h*is *h*and, and *h*ine [þone *h*reoflig mann]
> *h*repode, and cwæð, ic wylle; and sy þu geclænsod.
> Þa sona wearþ *h*is *h*reofla eal geclænsod, and *h*e wæs
> ge*h*æled. Ða cwæð se *H*ælend *h*im to . . . (CH I, p. 120)

Note the profusion of "h" sounds and the final use of *Hælend* juxtaposed with *wæs gehæled*. Even in his first series of his *Catholic Homilies,* Aelfric is using alliteration to adumbrate ideas to follow; namely,

> Crist . . . ure sawle from synna fagnyssum
> gehælan mæge . . . (CH I, p. 122)

and the physical/spiritual duality which is fused in the image referring to the spiritual physician (*ðam gastlican læce,* p. 124). Consequently the *eal* of the phrase *eal geclænsod* (p. 120) suggests an ambiguity and a cleansing which is more than physical, even when the phrase appears in the pericope, so that traditional images are reinforced by alliterative patterns and the process of interpretation is anticipated through the linking of letters.

Throughout the development of the first half of the pericope Aelfric is interlacing the tropological unfolding of the meaning with the dual significance of the *Hælend* concept. He emphasizes the salutary nature of the Incarnation and carefully underlines the means by which the Christian may be healed. The multitude signifies the faithful Christians (*ða leaffullan cristenan,* p. 120), and Christ's touch is healing for the faithful (*halwende geleaffullum,* p. 122). By logical extension the leper betokens mankind befouled with various sins, so that the first half of the pericope provides a carefully organized thematic study of the salutary effects of the virtue of faith. The congregation is admonished to believe (*gelyfan*) in Christ that he may heal their souls (*gehælan*) from the ulcers of sin:

We sceolan rihtlice gelyfan on Crist, þæt he
ure sawle fram synna fagnyssum gehælan
mæg . . . (CH I, p. 122)

In the complementary miracle which constitutes the second half
of the pericope (especially as Aelfric simplifies, augments, and
interprets it), this thematic lesson on the virtue of faith is continued and carefully elaborated. The miracle, the curing of the
centurion's servant, originally suggests several virtues: faith
("speak but the word"), humility (*non sum dignus ut intres sub
tectum meum*), wisdom (his recognition of the divinity of Christ),
and charity (he asked for another, not for himself). At this point
Aelfric introduces a biblical exemplum also used by Haymo and
taken from John 4: 46–53. Its lesson, as Aelfric develops it, contrasts the imperfect faith of the official introduced in the exemplum
with the exemplary faith of the centurion. The official asks Christ to
come and cure his son, whereas the centurion merely prays that
Christ may utter a salutary word for the benefit of his servant.
Consequently when Christ tells the official to go home, his son
will live, he believed (*gelyfde,* p. 128), but his faith was not as
great as the centurion's. Aelfric stresses this by concluding his
discussion of the exemplum with Christ's praise of the centurion:
"In truth I say to you, I have not met such great faith (*swa
micelne geleafan,* p. 128) in the land of Israel." Aelfric now introduces a second exemplum, one not to be found in Haymo, who
concludes his homily with his allegorizings on the centurion. In
this second digressive biblical narrative Aelfric says that Mary
and Martha had a strong faith in God (*swiðe on God belyfde,*
p. 130.). Yet they duplicated the official's error by complaining that
had Christ been present their brother would not have died. The two
exempla clearly reinforce the tropological theme of the salutary
effects of faith around which the homily is organized.

Aelfric now returns to his exegetical analysis by explaining the
anagogic significance of *fram east-dæle and west-dæle,* p. 130. As
a metaphor the phrase is meant to demonstrate how the young and
old alike have been gathered from the four corners of the earth.
The wealthy are cast into external darkness and the virtuous are
at rest with the patriarchs. In particular the faithless have been

exiled into the eternal prison where each suffers on an hierarchial scale according to his offence.

Christ's final words to the centurion, "Go home, and may it happen to you according to your faith" (*swa swa ðu gelyfdest*, p. 132), both follow from this scene of retributive justice and lead directly to the summary exhortation: "Let us believe" (*Uton gelyfan*, p. 134). The formulaic doxology follows and the congregation is left with the tropological importance of the homily: have faith and you will receive the salutary cleansing. The message perfectly recapitulates the second half of the homily and blends thematically with the first.

Aelfric's techniques of structural organization and the images with which he reinforces them are significant. He has made Haymo his own by adapting, abridging, and adding. He has done his job so well, in fact, that the general assumption that pericope homilies must be digressive, various ideas running off like rivulets from the main flow, is not true of this homily, even though it employs the pericope form, actually contains a double pericope, and has digressive exempla.[23] The thematic interlace reflects a structural approach often associated with the Anglo-Saxon poet; conversely there are elements of design with which a Christian poet may well be assumed to be familiar, such as the movement from description to interpretation and the total significance of narrative and descriptive detail. There is also an organizational concern for balance and for total rational explication extending even to the hierarchical sufferings endured by the damned. Finally each of the two pericope segments has its own unifying principle, though each coalesces into a unified whole. In spite of the point-by-point development demanded by the pericope form, there is a steady progression in the tropological development leading unmistakably to the concluding *Uton gelyfan*.[24]

Just as principles of structural unity are assimilated and commonly used by the poet and the homilist, so are literary forms. The pericope is the preacher's favored means of homiletic expression, it is a form with which congregations have become thorougly familiarized, and it is a form, therefore, which the poet can use with absolute assurance that Christian audiences will react meaningfully. The structure to which audiences of *Physiologus* respond, for example, is not merely Greek, Latin, or Physiological, but is also homiletic. As a result, when composing *Physiologus* the poet reverses the accustomed stress of the Physiological tradition as it appears in Christian writings, and the emphasis is moved from interpretation to description. The Christian poet expects his audience to dwell on description and narrative and to allegorize from it just as congregations would in the case of the biblical pericope. *Phoenix* and *Exodus* display the same general structure and verbal anticipation.[25]

It seems logical to me, therefore, that when one considers that the homilists of Anglo-Saxon England often served also as her Christian poets, one should naturally anticipate a convergence of the two traditions, especially when the end of each is moral instruction. It is a convergence that apparently begins early in the Christian tradition and that flourishes in Anglo-Saxon England during the Benedictine Revival. It is surely in keeping with the spirit of the Fathers that the best homilists should concern themselves with the *delectare* of doctrinal composition. Hence alliteration, occasional rhyme, rhetorical catalogue, a balance of thought and expression, all are elements of design which the Revival homilist shared with his poetic counterpart. The modern reader can appreciate the work of neither the poet nor the homilist, if he considers either in isolation from the other.

NOTES

1. J.D.A. Ogilvy, *Books Known to the English, 597–1066* (Cambridge, 1967), p. 84, notes that *De doctrina christiana* is quoted by both Bede and Alcuin. For a note on the transmission of Augustinian and classical rhetoric into the Anglo-Saxon period, see Dorothy Bethurum, *The Homilies of Wulfstan* (Oxford, 1957), p. 87, n. 2. See also the Jurovics essay in this volume.
2. See Yngeve Brilioth, *A Brief History of Preaching,* tr. Karl E. Mattson (1945; rpt. Philadelphia, 1965), p. 27, for comment on early forms, and for specifically Syrian influences on Old English, see Rudolph Willard, "Vercelli Homily

VIII and the *Christ," Publications of the Modern Language Association* 42 (1927) : 329; and A.S. Cook, *The Christ of Cynewulf* (1900; rpt. Hamden, Conn., 1964), p. 210. One might mention here that various critics have explicitly categorized specific Old English poems as homilies. See, for example, Richard L. Hoffman, "The Theme of *Judgment Day II*," *English Language Notes* 6 (1969) : 161–64; J.E. Cross, "The Conception of the Old English *Phoenix,"* in *Old English Poetry: Fifteen Essays,* ed. Robert Creed (Providence, 1967), pp. 129–52; and F.A. Blackburn, "Is the 'Christ' of Cynewulf a Single Poem?" *Anglia* 19 (1897) : 94. Th. M. Charland, *Artes Praedicandi* (Ottawa, 1936), pp. 153ff discusses the poetic and stylistically ornate homily of the medieval period with particular stress on the late medieval. See also Dorothy Bethurum, "The Form of Aelfric's *Lives of Saints,"* *Studies in Philology* 29 (1932) : 515–33.

3. The *Speculum Ecclesiæ* (*PL* 172, 815–1108) attributed to Honorius of Autun provides evidence of the poetic homily in the twelfth century in Germany. Perhaps more importantly the *Speculum Ecclesiæ* also demonstrates the influence of the homily on art forms other than poetic: see Emile Mâle, *The Gothic Image,* tr. Dora Nussey (1913; rpt. New York, 1958), pp. 39–46. There is also an implication in *Romance of the Rose* that in thirteenth-century France metrical homilies were not unknown; F.N. Robinson, *The Complete Works of Geoffrey Chaucer* (Boston, 1957), 2nd ed.: 5745–56. For examples of purely metrical homilies, see John Small, *English Metrical Homilies from Manuscripts of the Fourteenth Century* (Edinburgh, 1862) ; and for more nearly Anglo-Saxon examples, see the religious tracts in Richard Morris, ed., *Old English Homilies,* EETS OS 29, 34, #18, and the related version in EETS OS 53, #35. The popularity of such homilies eventually drew John Wycliffe's derision. See G.R. Owst, *Preaching in Medieval England* (Cambridge, 1926), p. 276. For a more detailed discussion of the homilist's use of alliteration and rhyme, see Otto Funke, "Studien zur alliterierenden und

rhythmisierenden Prosa in der älteren altenglischen
Homiletik," *Anglia* 80 (1962) : 9–36.
4. The joys of heaven and the sorrows of hell seem so often to be
emphasized through poetic embellishment that a similar
discussion in *Phoenix* (14b–20a) becomes uncharacteristically ornate for Old English poetry.
5. Max Förster, ed. *Die Vercelli-Homilien* (1932; rpt. Darmstadt,
1964) (emendations not shown). Reference to Vercelli
homilies IX–XXIII is to the facsimile edition prepared by
Celia Sisam, *The Vercelli Book* EEMF 19 (Copenhagen,
1976).
6. E.g.:
7 þu eart blindra manna leoht 7 dumra ȝesprec
7 deafra ȝe-hyrnes 7 hreofra clænsunȝ 7 healtra
ȝang. 7 eallre biternesse þu eart se sweta swæc.
7 ealle ȝe-unrette maȝon on þe ȝe-blissian. 7
ðu eart ealra worca wyrhta 7 ealra wæstma fruma
7 eallra þystra onlihtinȝ. (Vercelli IV, p. 89)
Ic wæs þin eacnunȝ 7 þin cenninȝ ; 7 þa ic wæs
ȝast, fram ȝode to þe cumen. Ic wæs þin wlite
7 þin wunsumnes. Ic wæs þin spræc 7 þin swæcc
7 þin fnæst 7 þin hawunȝ 7 þin ȝe-hyrnes 7 þin
ȝlædnes 7 þin onmædla. Ic wæs þin ȝe-þanc 7 þin
fæȝernesse 7 þin lufu 7 þin ȝestæðþiȝnes 7 þin
ȝe-treownesse . . . (Vercelli IV, pp. 98–99)
on worulde wyrðan wyrmum to æte 7 of eorðan
sceolan eft arisan on domes dæȝe 7 dryhtne sylfum
eall ætywan þæt we ær dydon . . . . we sceolon
symle herian heofones ȝod se us healdeð a wið
feonda ȝehwæne ȝif we hine soðfæstlice mid eaðmettum
eallunȝ lufiað. Witudlice he sylð þam ece blisse
earmum ȝe eadiȝum þe hyt ȝearniað . . . . (Vercelli
XXI, f. 114ᵛ)

The same type of alliterative pattern continues in homily
XXI up to and including 116ʳ with interruptions of non-
alliterative prose of variously long and short passages.
Similar alliterative passages appear in Vercelli XXII

folios 118ᵛ–19ʳ, in addition to briefer segments elsewhere.
& we sceolan gelyfan synna forlætnessa & lichoman
æristes on domos dæg; & we sceolan gelefan on
þæt ece lif & on þæt heofonlice rice . . . . (BH, p. 111)
Nu is æghwonon, hream & wop, nu is heaf æghwonon,
& sibbe tolesnes, nu is æghwonon yfel & slege,
& æghwonon þes middangeard flyhþ from us mid mycelre
biternesse, & we him fleondum fylgeaþ & hine feallendne
lufiaþ. (BH, p. 115)
BH X is a homily which makes extensive use of catalogue
so that alliteration comes naturally to a very large propor-
tion of it.

7. D.G. Scragg, "The compilation of the Vercelli Book," *Anglo-
Saxon England 2* (1973) : 190, argues to the contrary by
suggesting that "it is difficult to discern any principle of
arrangement in the items of the collection," adding that "the
poems are distributed amongst the homilies in a way that
is difficult to understand." Kenneth Sisam implies a thematic organization to the *Beowulf* MS when he states that
it is "a collection of marvellous stories" to which *Judith*
has been added since Judith "resembles Beowulf in her role
of saviour of an oppressed people," *Studies in the History
of Old English Literature* (Oxford, 1953), p. 65 ; and
Angus Cameron has taken some convincing though still unpublished steps towards demonstrating thematic groupings
in the Exeter Book. In a paper read at the Learned
Societies in Toronto, 28 May 1974, Professor Cameron
discussed *"Deor* as a Poem in the Exeter Book," in which
he demonstrated philosophical similarities between *Deor*
and the poem which precedes it in the Exeter Book, *Soul
and Body II*.

8. A.H. Smith, *Three Northumbrian Poems* (1933; rpt. London,
1968), p. 18 points to Alfred's comment that Aldhelm "was
without equal in the composition of English poetry."

9. *Monumenta Germaniae Historica,* Epistola Karolini Aevi,
Tomus II, Epistolarum Tomus IV, epistle 124, pp. 181–84.

10. See G.H. Putnam, *Books and Their Makers During the Middle
Ages,* I (1896–97; rpt. New York, 1962), p. 62.

11. Dorothy Bethurum, *The Homilies of Wulfstan,* pp. 47ff. Miss Bethurum, pp. 87–98, provides an excellent summary of all phases of Wulfstan's rhetoric. James Ure, *The Benedictine Office* (Edinburgh, 1957), pp. 25–46, indirectly presents a similar summary. For a more stylistic examination of Wulfstan's prose, see O. Funke, "Some Remarks on Wulfstan's Prose Rhythm," *English Studies* 40 (1962) : 311–18, wherein he discusses two-stress phrasing and its variations.

12. For an exegetical interpretation of these embellishments, see Bernard F. Huppé, *Doctrine and Poetry* (New York, 1959), pp. 80–94. For a more conservative statement, see L. Whitbread, "The Old English *Judgment Day II* and its Latin Source," *Philological Quarterly* 44 (1966) : 645–46.

13. This is so in spite of the scribal heading:
    Her is halwendlic lar and ðearflic læwedum mannum, þe þæt læden ne cunnon.

14. Bede, CCL 122, pp. 440–41 *Judgment Day* ll. 43–81. See Richard L. Hoffman, "The Theme of *Judgment Day II,*" *English Language Notes* 6(1969) : 161–64 for a discussion of the poem and the patristic development of the medical imagery.

15. Bede, pp. 442–43; *Judgment Day II* ll. 176–84; Napier p. 138 ll. 17–23.

16. *The Wanderer* provides several examples of the poetic catalogue set in a homiletic context: *ne to* . . . ll. 66a–69b; the fortunes of men, ll. 80a–84b; *hwær cwom* . . . ll. 92a–3b; *eala* . . . ll. 94a–5a; *Her bið* . . . ll. 108a–9b. Vercelli Homily II uses similar techniques of balance and repetition of organizing phrases. There are, for example, series beginning *in þam dæge* (ll. 1–23, 46–76), *La, hwæt* (ll. 23–46), *hwæt* (ll. 76–93), *Ac uton we* . . . *Lufigen we* (ll. 93–110), *Hwæt we* (ll. 111–37), *Utan we* (ll. 138–51). This homilist relies on alliteration, rhyme, and a section of regular poetry to reinforce the effect of his quasi-poetic construction.

17. *The Study of the Bible in the Middle Ages* (1952; rpt. Notre Dame, 1964), p. 34.

18. *The Digressions in Beowulf* (1950; rpt. Oxford, 1965).

19. "The Interlace Structure of *Beowulf*," *University of Toronto Quarterly* 37 (1967) : 1–17.

20. *The Web of Words* (New York, 1970), p. xvi.

21. "Notes on the Imagery and Structure of the OE *Christ I*," *Notes and Queries*, 207 n.s. xix (1972) : 88–89.

22. See Edward B. Irving, *A Reading of Beowulf* (New Haven, 1968), Chapter Five, "The Hero Departs," pp. 192–246.

23. The image is Gregory's and is discussed by Smalley *The Study of the Bible in the Middle Ages*, p. 33.

24. For a comment on thematic structure in one of Bede's homilies see Philip J. West, "Liturgical Style and Structure in Bede's Homily for the Easter Vigil," *American Benedictine Review*, 23 (1927) : 3.

25. I make this observation in spite of the convincing argument presented by Cross in "The Conception of the Old English Phoenix." Cross argues that the Lactantian segment of *Phoenix* is equivalent to the historical level of exegetical analysis. What I am suggesting is that the training of the interpretative mind in the Middle Ages made it impossible for almost anything to be accepted simply as historical or literal. In fact the Anglo-Saxon's view of history itself was neither simply linear nor literal. See my "The Old English Physiologus and the Homiletic Tradition," to appear in *Florilegium*.

ANN ELJENHOLM NICHOLS ❦ METHODICAL ABBREVIATION: A STUDY IN AELFRIC'S FRIDAY HOMILIES FOR LENT

It is generally agreed that Aelfric not only abbreviated his sources, but that he articulated a theory for the brief style as well.[1] This paper summarizes the results of an analysis of Aelfric's method of abbreviation in the Friday homilies for Lent. Four of the homilies are available with critical apparatus in Pope's edition; the fifth was edited by Assmann.[2]

1st Week	John 5:1–15	Bethsaida Miracle	SS 2
2nd Week	Matthew 21:33–46	Vineyard Parable	SS 3
3rd Week	John 4:5–42	Samaritan Woman	SS 5
4th Week	John 11:1–45	Resurrection of Lazarus	SS 6
5th Week	John 40:47–54	Plots against Jesus	Assmann 5

These homilies were apparently written as a part of Aelfric's plan to expand his Temporale, and since it is at least possible that they were composed as a unit, we can look for some uniformity of method.[3]

There is, of course, a disadvantage in working with these homilies, since we would expect their alliterative style to entail amplification rather than abbreviation, as is illustrated by two of the translations of John 5:14b, the first, the most literal, from CH I, the second, more amplified, from the homily for the First Friday of Lent:

> Ecce sanus factus es: iam noli peccare, ne deterius
> tibi aliquid contingat. John 5:14b
> Efne nu ðu eart gehæled, ne synga ðu heonon-forð,
> þylæs ðe ðe sum ðing wyrse gelimpe. CH I, p. 350
> Efne nu þu eart gehæled, heald þe nu heonon forð,
> þæt þu ne syngie, þy læs þe sum þing
> wyrse gelimpe . . . . SS 2.55–57

However even an amplified translation like the last can provide an important textual norm to which abbreviations within the homily can be compared.[4] Thus when Aelfric comments on the above text, he reduces a clause to a prepositional phrase: "heald þe nu heonon forð, / ðæt þu ne syngie" > "geheald þe wið synna" (SS 2.278). Furthermore the five Lenten homilies when compared to their sources provide adequate evidence of methodical abbreviation.[5]

Four of the five Lenten homilies explicate Johannine pericopes, and hence we can look for Augustinian features of style that Aelfric consistently cuts or abbreviates. The elaborate word play of Augustine's *In Ioannis Evangelium* is one such feature.[6] In the opening lines of the homily for the Third Friday Aelfric presents the paradox of Christ's fatigue, Christ who "on þam micclan weorce" of creation "gesceop / ealle gesceafta buton geswince" (SS 5.106, 103–4). Augustine begins the corresponding section of his tractate as follows:

> Iam incipiunt mysteria. Non enim frustra fatigatur Jesus;
> non enim frustra fatigatur Virtus Dei; non enim frustra
> fatigatur, per quem fatigati receantur; non enim frustra
> fatigatur, quo deserente fatigamur, quo praesente firmamur.
> Fatigatur tamen Jesus, et fatigatur ab itinere, et sedet, et
> juxta puteum sedet, et hora sexta fatigatus sedet. . . .
> Tibi fatigatus est ab itinere Jesus. (xv.6; CCL 36, p. 152) [7]

Even for Augustine this is a fairly heady brew of anaphora, homoeoteleuton, polyptoton, and a variety of other verbal figures. Aelfric condenses all this to the rare distillation of: "Se Hælend wæs werig, þeah þe hit wundorlic si" (SS 5.102).

In the homily for the Fourth Friday Aelfric radically cuts Augustine's hour-day metaphor in the explication of John 9:9. "Nonne duodecim horae sunt diei?"—"Quo ergo pertinet?" asks Augustine.

> Quia ut diem se esse ostenderet, duodecim discipulos
> elegit. Si ego sum, inquit dies, et vos horae, numquid
> horae diei consilium dant? Horae diem sequuntur, non dies
> horas. Si ergo illi horae, quid ibi Judas? Et ipse
> inter duodecim horas? Si hora erat, lucebat; si luce-
> bat, quomodo diem ad mortem tradebat? . . . [Discussion
> of succession of Matthias follows.] Sequantur ergo

horae diem, praedicent horae diem, horae illustrentur a
die, horae illuminentur a die, et per horarum praedicationem credat mundus in diem. (xlix.8; CCL 36, p. 424) [8]

Aelfric reduces this to:

He is se soða dæg, and þæt soðe leoht . . . .
His twelf apostoli synt þa twelf tida
þe ðam dæge folgiað Drihtne Hælende. . . .
[Discussion of Matthias] and wearð eft gefylled
þæt twelffealde getel on þam twelf apostolum. (SS 6.346,
349–54)

It is difficult to know whether Aelfric rejected this elaborate metaphor because of its word play or because of its inherent complica-
tions.[9]

Elsewhere it seems likely that Aelfric may have rejected imagery
in his source because of its complexity. In the homily for the
Third Friday, for example, Aelfric rejects Augustine's explicit
development of the eating and drinking imagery. Augustine is
explicating Christ's request that the Samaritan woman give him
water to drink. At the close of his paragraph he says: "Ille autem
qui bibere quærebat, fidem ipsius mulieris sitiebat" (xv.11; CCL
36, p. 154). Instead Aelfric has:

Se Hælend bæd drincan, swa swa ge gehyrdon ær,
æt þam Samaritaniscan wife, for ðan ðe he gewilnode
hire geleafan, þæt heo gelyfde on hine . . . . (SS 5.118–20)

Paragraph 17, from which Aelfric quotes elsewhere in his homily,
opens with "Promittebat ergo saginam quamdam et satietatem
Spiritus sancti" (CCL 36, p. 156), with its nuances of nourishment and satiety. Aelfric ignores this line altogether. Augustine,
commenting on 5:34 ("Meus cibus est ut faciam voluntatem eius,
qui misit me") says:

Ergo et potus ipse erat in illa muliere, ut faceret
voluntatem eius, qui miserat eum. Ideo dicebat,
Sitio, da mihi habere [sic]; scilicet ut fidem in ea
operaretur, et fidem eius biberet, et eam in corpus
suum traiiceret: corpus enim eius Ecclesia. (xv.31; CCL
36, p. 163) [10]

Aelfric glosses the same line with "Hys gastlica mete ys mancynnes alysednyss, / and him þyrste on þam wife hyre geleafan . . ." (.242–43). Did Aelfric feel that the "baroque" overtones of this image were too difficult for his audience? Only .243 retains something of the image, and in the preceding line he notes that it is *"gastlica* mete" that Jesus speaks of. Aelfric's abbreviation of Augustine's amplified imagery is in line with his preference for "apertis verbis," for one of the descriptions Alcuin gives for *verba aperta* is "non nimis procul ductis translationibus." [11]

Rhetorical questions are another characteristic feature of Augustine's style. Frequently they are set up in elaborate parallels, as in the passage quoted above on the hour-day metaphor. Although Aelfric uses rhetorical questions elsewhere, there are none in the five Lenten homilies. The following translations consistently transform question to statement.

> Audito, *Ego sum qui loquor tecum,* et recepto in cor Christo
> Domino, quid faceret, nisi iam hydriam dimitteret, et
> evangelizare curreret?
> Mid þam þe heo gehyrde of þæs Hælendes muþe,
> Ic hit eom, se ðe to ðe sprece,
> þa efste heo swiðe ham to ðære byrig,
> and began to bodienne þam burhwarum embe Crist.
>   (SS 5.216–19)
> Quid est ergo quod prophetavit Caiphus? (xlix.27 ; CCL 36,
>   p. 432)
> Caiphus witegode . . . . (Assmann 5.106)
> Ideo *fatigatus ab itinere* quid est aliud, quam fatigatus
> in carne? . . . Illius infirmitas nostra est fortitudo.
> . . . ac Crist wæs werig swaþeah
> on þære menniscnysse, æfter mannes gecynde,
> and his untrumnys is ure trumnys. (SS 5.106–8) [12]

Aelfric's preference for statement over rhetorical question can also be found in his handling of other authors. For example, he translates Gregory the Great's "quis vero patrisfamilias . . . quam conditor noster?" (*PL* 76, 1154) as "Se hiredes ealdor is ure Scyppend." [13] What principles guided Aelfric in his rejection or use of rhetorical questions? One suspects that he rejected them whenever they were *merely* rhetorical, whenever they suggested "artful" flourish as in Augustine's hour-day metaphor. However a much larger corpus of material must be studied before any firm conclusion can be drawn.

Two other minor characteristics of style that Aelfric typically deletes from Augustine's commentaries are first-person transitional phrases, such as "videamus proinde iam quo sacramento iste languidus curetur a Domino" (xvii.7.1531), and hortative exclamations, such as "O si possemus excitare homines, et cum ipsis pariter excitari, ut tales essemus amatores vitae permanentis, quales sunt homines amatores vitae fugientis!" (xlix.2.1747) Aelfric prefers his own brand of first person transitions, and he limits their use. They commonly occur between the pericope translation and the homily. His most common transitional formula is "swa swa we sædon ær/ ge gehyrdon ær," but he does not use it more than three times per homily. His brevity formulas are another common sort of transition. They occur at the beginning of a homily (e.g., 2.59–62), within a homily (e.g., 5.159–61), or at the end as a closing formula (e.g., 6.367–69).

Augustine regularly fills his homilies with exhortations. The exhortative passage that begins with the "O si possemus" formula quoted in the preceding paragraph runs to eleven sentences in length (five are rhetorical questions). Aelfric ignores the entire passage. Augustine's interruptions are not always so long, e.g., following his discussion of the Samaritan woman as a type of the church, he says: "Audiamus ergo in illa nos, et in illa agnoscamus nos, et in illa gratias Deo agamus pro nobis (xv.10.CCL 36, p. 154)." This sort of hortative interruption is rare in Aelfric, and in the five Lenten homilies they are always independent of his sources.

Aelfric restricts the *uton* + infinitive exhortation to the closing prayers. There is one short passage using the modal *sceal* in the homily for the First Friday, but although it can be interpreted as an exhortation, it certainly does not have the emotional force that characterizes Augustine's exhortations: "Ure ælc sceal mid lufe oðrum flystan, / and eac ure yfelnysse us betwynan forberan, / þæt Godes æ on us swa beo gefylled" (SS 2.203–5). The other two passages both occur in the homily for the Fourth Friday. The first runs to six lines and begins "Ondræde swa þu ondræde, se deað þe cymð to" (SS 6.154–59). The second occurs near the end of the interpolation:

> Nu sceolon we biddan mid gebigedum mode
> þone ælmihtigan Fæder, þe us ðurh his Wisdom gesceop,
> and us eft alysde ðurh ðone ylcan Sunu,
> þæt he ure synna fram us adylegie
> þurh ðone Halgan Gast, and us gehealde wið deofol,
> þæt we him gegan þe us aer geworhte. (SS 6.278–83)

This passage comes very close to the tone of a closing prayer.

The homily of the Fourth Friday is unusual in that it deals with only nine of the forty-five verses of the pericope. Perhaps because of the proximity of Holy Week Aelfric felt the long sections on sin and forgiveness were more appropriate than line-by-line exposition. This possibility may also account for the unusual occurrence of two exhortations within one homily. It is also true that five lines of the earlier exhortation (.155–59) verge on exposition, the hortative subjunctive "ondræde swa þu ondræde" (.154) alone having the emotional force one associates with Augustine's exhortations.

One final comparison will show how Aelfric's abbreviation of Augustine, his preference for statement rather than rhetorical question, and for first person plural rather than second singular results in a totally different tone.

> O si invenirem, dicebas, montem aliquem altum et solitarium!
> Credo enim quia in alto est Deus, magis me exaudit ex alto.
> Quia in monte es, propinquum te Deo putas, et cito te ex-
> audiri, quasi de proximo clamantem? *In excelsis habitat,* sed
> *humilia respicit. Prope est Dominus.* Quibus? forte altis?
> *His qui obtriverunt cor* [Psalms 33:19]. Mira res est; et in
> altis habitat, et humilibus propinquat: *humilia respicit,*
> *excelsa autem a longe cognoscit* [Psalms 137:6]; superbos
>   longe
> videt, eo illis minus propinquat, quo sibi videntur altiores.
> Quaerebas ergo montem? descende ut adtingas. Sed ascendere
> vis? ascende: noli montem quaerere. *Ascensiones,* inquit, *in*
> *corde eius* (hoc Psalmus dicit), *in convalle plorationis*
> [Ps. 83:6,7]. Convallis humilitatem habet. (xv.25; CCL 36,
>   p. 161)[14]

Nu ne þurfe we astigan to sticolum muntum
mid earfoðnysse, us to gebiddanne,
swilce God si gehendor on þam hean munte
þonne on þaere dene, for hyre deopnysse.
Se heaga munt getacnað þa heagan modignysse,
and seo dene eadmodnysse, þe ure Drihten lufað,
and we sceolon us gebiddan mid soðre eadmodnysse,
gyf we willað þæt us gehyre se heofonlica God,
se ðe on heannysse wunað, and behylt þa eadmodan,
and byð symble gehende þam ðe mid soðfæstnysse
him to clypiað on heora gedrefednysse. (SS 5.174–84)

Aelfric abstracts the essence of Augustine's passage in a straightforward declarative sentence (.174–77) in contrast to Augustine's
exclamation and rhetorical questions.[15] He also focuses clearly on
the main point of the passage with the more specific *gebiddanne*
(.175 and .180) rather than the more general *clamantem* and the
explicit explanation of the symbolism involved: "se heaga munt
getacnað þa heagan modignysse, and seo dene eadmodnysse"
(.178–79, italics mine). He translates the *humilia respecit* quotation
only once (.182). The entire passage is considerably more direct
and straightforward than Augustine's; one senses the difference
between the teacher and the preacher.

It is easier to discuss general techniques of abbreviation than
specific syntactical techniques. The ideas in a given passage may be
clearly derivative, but unless the vocabulary and syntax are close
enough to suggest rewriting rather than remembering, the text
will not serve. The safest material to deal with is a paraphrase of
the pericope translation, e.g., the one at the close of the homily for
the Third Friday. For brevity I shall refer to the translation as
A and the paraphrase as B.

A. Of þære burhware þa Samarian byrig
manega menn gelyfdon on þone lifigendan Hælend
for ðæs wifes gecyðnysse þe heo cydde be him,
þæt he hyre sæde swa hwæt swa heo gefremode.
Þa þa seo burhwaru him com to, þa bædon hi hine georne
þæt he þær wunode, and he wunode þær twegen dagas,
and micele ma gelyfdon for hys mæran lare,

    and to ðam wife cwædon, þæt we for þinre spræce ne
        gelyfað;
    we sylfe gehyrdon and soðlice witon
    þæt þes is soðlice Hælend middaneardes. (SS 5.88–97)
B. Seo burhwaru gelyfde, swa swa we sædon ær,
    ærest þurh þæt wif; and eft, þa þa hi comon
    to Criste sylfum þær þær he sæt,
    þa bædon he þæt he wunode þær sume hwile,
    and he him getiþode, and twegen dagas þaer wunode,
    lærende þæt folc, oððæt hi gelyfdon fullice,
    and to ðam wife cwædon þe him cydde ær be him,
    We ne gelyfað nu þurh þine gecyðnysse;
    "we sylfe gehyrdon and to soðan witon
    þæt þes ys Hælend soþlice middaneardes." (SS 5.279–88)

At first glance there appears to be little difference in the length
of the two passages; each has ten lines, and the number of words in
each is almost identical, eighty-five in A and eighty-one in B. However some of the phrases in B are purely transitional, such as
"swa swa we sædon ær," and others refer to details in the Gospel
that do not occur in A, such as "þær he sæt." B also adds commentary not in A to focus on the personal response of the Samaritans, e.g., "and he him getiþode" (.283), "lærende þæt folc,
oððæt hi gelyfdon fullice" (.284), and the intensive pronoun "to
Criste *sylfum*" (.281) to parallel that in .96 and .287, "we sylfe
gehyrdon." When this material is subtracted from the total of the
original eighty-five words, we have only sixty-one. The total length
may not be significantly altered, but Aelfric had to use the syntactical techniques of abbreviation in order to add new material
without substantially increasingly the length of B.

    The first sentence is radically abbreviated in the final version. The
modified subject, "Of þære burhware þa Samarian byrig manega
menn," becomes "seo burhwaru," and except for the verb all the
other material in the predicate is either cut or rearranged.
"Gecyðnysse" replaces "spræce" at .95 (.286), and the relative
clause "þe heo cydde be him" (.90) which modified "ðæs wifes
gecyðnysse' 'is rearranged to modify *wife* in .285. The *þæt* clause in
.91 is cut altogether, probably because Aelfric does not deal with

Christ's revelations about the Samaritan woman's husbands. The *manega/micele ma* contrast of A is replaced by the adverbial contrast *ærest/eft* (.280), a change probably suggested by the *primo/postea* succession in Augustine.[16] All these changes shape the final presentation of a key theme of the homily, belief. Aelfric focuses on the fact that belief is a personal response to Jesus himself, not merely to the testimony of those who bear witness to him. This difference accounts for both the rearrangement of material in the paraphrase and also for the deletion and addition of other phrases with the immediate focus on the Samaritans coming "to Criste sylfum" (.281). From this final rewriting Aelfric immediately moves to testify to the believing response of his audience and quickly closes with the final prayer "On þone we eac gelyfað, se ðe alysde us. / Si him wuldor and lof a to worulde, amen" (.289–91).

This passage illustrates three techniques common in Aelfric's methodical abbreviation: deletion of material, rearrangement, and a special sort of embedding I shall call splicing. Embedding is an essential syntactic tool for the prose stylist.[17] The good writer uses it intuitively; the reviser uses it consciously. Splicing occurs when the same word (or a noun and its antecedent) occurs in different sentences. Thus in the Samaritan passage, Aelfric simply rearranges a relative clause from one sentence with *wife* to another sentence in which the same noun occurs. In the following example he reduces two clauses to one: "Super lapidem cadit, id est super Christum, qui peccando illum offendit" > "Se fylþ uppon þone stan, se ðe syngað on Crist" (SS 3.152). (There are other syntactical changes here as well, e.g., the more general "offendit" is dropped in favor of the more specific "syngað," with the common translation of the participle as a finite verb.) In the next example Aelfric deletes the double oxymoron and the parallel sentences are reduced to one: "Laborat ne moriatur homo moriturus, et non laborat ne peccet homo in æternum victurus. . . . si autem peccare nolit, non laborabit, et vivet in æternum" > "and hi nellað swincan þæt hi ne singian, / þæt heora sawla lybban on þam ecan life / buton geswince" (SS 6.149–51).

In the following examples Aelfric embeds independent sentences as relative clauses:

"Et ædificavit turrim." Turrim, id est templum . . . .>
Se stypel þe he getimbrode, þæt wæs þæt stænene tempel . . . .
(SS 3.83),
Spiritualiter vero Rachel . . . Ecclesiam
significat . . . . Plorat ergo Rachel filios suos . . . . >
heo getacnode Godes gelaðunge, þe bewepð hire gastlican
 cild.[18]

The next passage is expanded independently to meet the needs of
alliteration, but it also involves relative embedding of the under-
lined clause:

Due namque sunt mortes, una corporis et altera anime.
Sed mortem corporis nemo evadit. . . . >
an is ðæs lichaman deað, þe eallum mannum becymð, / oðer is
ðære sawle deað, þe þurh synna becymð. . . . (SS 11.130–
 31)

When the verb of a sentence is *be*, relative clauses are also re-
ducible to appositives or to adjective modifiers, e.g., "heora an
cwæð þa, Caiphus gehaten, / se was sacerd" > "Caiphus se sacerd
cwaeð" (Assmann 5.9–10 and .96). or "prurigo . . . intolerabilis
erat" > "unaberendlic gyhða." [19] The deletion of *be* is also involved
in the following translations; in each case Aelfric's translation has
the rhetorical figure *zeugma,* while the Latin is characterized by
hypozeuxis.

Messias autem unctus est; unctus græce Christus est;
hebraice Messias est.
Messias on Ebreisc, Christus on Grecisc, unctus on
Leden, ys on Englisc gesmyrod. (SS 5.208–09)
Non est sapientia, non est prudentia, non est consilium
contra Deum. (Proverbs 21 :30)
Nis nan wisdom ne non ræd naht ongean God. (ASR. xiv
 82–3)

In the following examples Aelfric reduces clauses to prepositional
phrases, a type of abbreviation particularly common with adverbial
clauses:

cum sero autem factum esset > on æfnunge (ASR. xiii.17).
heald þe nu heonon forð, / þæt þu ne syngie >
geheald þe wið synna. (SS 2.55–56 and .278)
Omnia per ipsum facta sunt, . . . et sine labore facta sunt >
His heofonlica Fæder þurh hine gesceop
ealle gesceafta buton geswince. (SS 5.103–04)

This sort of abbreviation is apt to occur where the syntax is repetitive, as in the last example, or in "se witega . . . bæd þone ælmightigan God . . . þæt he renscuras forwyrnde to feorðan healfan geare" for "oravit ut non plueret super terram, et non pluit annos tres et menses sex" (SS 8.79–81).

In the next example a *cum* clause has been reduced to a *for* prepositional phrase:

Sepelire autem mortuorum corpora, nec morientium mul-
titudo, nec virium debilitas permittebat. . . . Cum-
que fetor intolerabilis de mortuorum cadaveribus in
civitate crescere coepisset, extra muros eadem eiicebant.
And man þa deadan ne mihte . . .
nateshwon bebyrgean for heora mægenleaste
ac wurpon fela hundreda forð ofer þone weall
for þam yfelan stence, þe him of eode. (Assmann 5.77–81)

There is also an interesting variation in subjects here, with *debilitas* becoming the object of *for* in *for heora mægenleaste*.[20]

When Aelfric rearranges the order of clauses in his source, it commonly involves significant cutting and rewriting, not just syntactical variation. Yet seldom are the deletions and rearrangements arbitrary. Rather they are made in order to support the thematic structure of individual homilies. There is ample material in all five homilies to substantiate this generalization, but I shall concentrate on two passages from Aelfric's homilies for the First and Third Fridays.

The following passage from the homily for the Third Friday explicates verses 7b and 9. Christ speaks to the Samaritan woman:

and se Hælend hyre cwæð to, Syle me drincan.
Þæt wif him cwæð to andsware, Hwi wilt þu me þæs biddan,

þonne þu eart Iudeisc, and ic Samaritanisc wif?
Nellað þa Iudeiscan mid nanum Samaritaniscum
etan oððe drincan. (SS 5.13–17)

Augustine explicates these lines from John in the context of a running commentary. His preceding paragraph deals with John 4:7a
and the following paragraph with verse 10. He explicates verses
7b and 9 as follows:

> Videtis alienigenas: omnino vasculis eorum Judaei non ute-
> bantur. Et quia ferebat secum mulier vasculum unde aquam
> hauriret, eo mirata est, quia Judaeus petebat ab ea bibere,
> quod non solebant facere Judaei. Ille autem qui bibere
> quaerebat, fidem ipsius mulieris sitiebat. (xv.11; CCL, 36
> p. 154) [21]

The first sentence states the prohibition against common use of
dishes. The second, long and balanced sentence frames the discussion of the woman with references to Jewish customs. The paragraph ends with a typical Augustinian reversal from *res* to
sacramentum. As noted above, Aelfric cuts this final sentence. He
also "fits" the rest of Augustine's material into quite a different
context, namely, that of the true belief of the Jews versus the false
of the Samaritans, this independent context (.120–22 and .127–29)
acting as a frame for the borrowed material. Christ willed

[the woman's] geleafan, þæt heo gelyfde on hine,
and þæt gedwyld forlete þæs deoflican bigengas   ⎫ Frame
þæra hæþenra goda þæt hi oð ðæt wurðedon.   ⎭
Þa wundrode þæt wif þæt he wolde drincan
of hyre fæte, for ðam ðe þa Iudeiscan
noldon næfre brucan nanes þinges mid þam hæþenum,
ne of heora fatum furðon næfre drincan,
and hi rihtlice swa dydon, for þam soðan biggenge   ⎫
þæs ælmihtigan Godes þe hi on gelyfdon,   ⎬ Frame
þæt hi ne wurdon befylede þurh þa fulan hæþenan.   ⎭
                                    (SS 5.120–29)

Aelfric also handles Augustine's second sentence with considerable syntactical freedom. Aelfric begins with *eo mirata est:* "þa

wundrode þæt wif." He cuts the initial *quia* clause, but embeds its object *vasculum* as the prepositional object of *drincan*. To his main clause Aelfric adds a modifying *for ðam ðe* clause with a compound predicate. This clause translates the first sentence in Augustine, although *vasculis eorum* in transfered to the second predicate, while Aelfric's new general phrase ties the entire passage to the heathen framework.[22] The final *quod* clause is cut except for its residual presence in *næfre*. The directness of Aelfric's sentence results from the use of a typical pattern of clauses in English, main clause plus an adverbial of reason. The peculiar balance of the Latin sentence is replaced by one more suitable to English. So natural is Aelfric's syntax that the casual reader of the passage might miss the artful opposition at the line ends: *wolde drincan* vs. *næfre drincan* (.123, 126) and *Iudeiscan* vs. *hæþenum* (.124, 125).

The homily for the First Friday of Lent provides another good example of Aelfric's rearrangement of material. The Gospel (John 5:1–15) deals with the healing of the paralytic at Bethsaida. As might be predicted of a commentary on a healing miracle, the central theme of the homily is spiritual versus physical health. In Aelfric's homily this theme is dealt with in .68–138 and .276–89. The sections are clearly unified by the central metaphor: man lies ill, and the Healer comes to make him physically hale and spiritually whole. Augustine opens his tractate on this passage as follows:

> Mirum non esse debet a Deo factum miraculum, mirum
> enim esset si homo fecisset. Magis gaudere quam
> mirari debemus, quia Dominus noster et salvator
> Jesus Christus homo factus est, quam quod divina
> inter homines Deus fecit. Plus est enim ad salutem
> nostram quod factus est propter homines, quam quod inter
> homines: et plus est quod vitia sanavit animarum, quam
> quod sanavit languores corporum moriturorum.
> (xvii.1; CCL 36, pp. 169–70) [23]

Rather than begin with generalizations as Augustine had, Aelfric puts the details of the Gospel story into immediate focus with the explanation that has no exact parallel in the sources: "Swa wæron þa Iudei wanhale on mode" (.70).[24] He then borrows from Alcuin the catalogue of illnesses, translating "caeci" as "blinde *on mode*" and "claudi" as "healte *on heortan*" to clarify the symbolism. He also expands the catalogue by adding the parallel sentence on the deaf:

> Þa beoþ blinde on mode þe ne magon geseon
> þæs geleafan leoht, þeah hi locion brade;
> and þa beoð healte on heortan þe þæs Hælendes beboda
> unrihtlice farende ne gefyllað mid weorcum;
> and þa beoþ deafe þe Drihtnes hæsum
> nellað gehyrsumian, þeah þe hi þa gehyron. (SS 2. 76–81)

Only after this straightforward verse paragraph does Aelfric turn to Augustine's opening paragraph. He adapts paragraph 1, sentence 5 for .90–94 and then etymologizes on the meaning of *Hælend*. Line 91 focuses on the *res* of the gospel situation, .92–97 on the *sacramentum*. "Se ælmihtiga Hælend" comes to heal man "on sawle and on lichaman."

> Hys nama is Hælend, for þan þe he gehælþ his folc,
> swa swa se engel cwæþ be him, ær þan þe he acenned wære:
> He gehælþ hys folc fram heora synnum. (.95–97)

Only now does Aelfric use Augustine's two opening generalizations about the proper evaluation of God's wondrous works. He makes the point more explicit by adapting the *visibiliter/invisibiliter* contrast from Alcuin (.98–104).[25] Whereas Augustine had only introduced the *res/sacramentum* parallel at the close of his third sentence ("et plus est quod vitia sanavit animarum, quam quod sanavit languores corporum moriturorum"), Aelfric has dealt with it at length before introducing the generalizations. "Micele mare wundor" is thus projected for his audience.

> Micele mare wundor is þæt he wolde beon mann
> on þisum life, and alysan us þurh hine,
> þonne þa wundra wæron þe he worhte betwux mannum;
> and selran us wæron þa ungesewenlican wundra
> þurh þa he adwæscte þa dyrnan leahtras
> urra sawla, þonne þa gesewenlican wundra,
> þurh þa ðe wæron gehælede þa þe eft swulton. (SS 2.98–104)

Aelfric has rearranged the sentences from Augustine's opening paragraph with considerable freedom.[26] In the process of using the paragraph for material in .105–14, he also condenses in ways that we have seen are typical of his methods of abbreviation. Sentences 9 and 10 in Augustine involve a great deal of parallel structure, both rely heavily on anaphora and homoeoteleuton, and both deal at length with the ironies implicit in the health/sickness imagery.

> 9 Corporum enim salus quae vera exspectatur a Domino, erit in fine in resurrectione mortuorum: tunc quod vivet, non morietur; tunc quod sanabitur, non aegrotabit; tunc quod satiabitur, non esuriet aut sitiet; tunc quod renovabitur, non
> 10 veterascet. Nunc vero in illis factis Domini et salvatoris nostri Jesu Christi, et caecorum aperti oculi, morte clausi sunt; et paralyticorum membra constricta, morte dissoluta sunt; et quidquid sanatum est temporaliter in membris mortalibus, in fine defecit: anima vero quae credidit; ad vitam aeternam transitum fecit. (xvii.i; CCL 36, p. 170)[27]

Aelfric generalizes the details of sentence 10 in .507–08 and abbreviates sentence 9, and yet for all these deletions Aelfric conveys the essential sense of Augustine's text.

> Witodlice seo sawul þe fram synnum bið gehæled,
> and on geleafan þurhwunað færð of þisum life to Gode;
> and se brosnigenda lichama, þeah þe he beo gehæled,
> bið mid deaþe fornumen and to duste awend.
> He bið swaþeah gehæled to ansundre hæle eft
> on Domes-dæg, þonne he of deaþe arist,
> and syþðan ne swylt, ne seoc ne gewyrð,
> ne him hingrian ne mæg, ne him þurst ne deraþ,
> ne he ne forealdað, ac bið ece syþþan,
> on sawle and on lichaman, orsorh deaþes. (SS 2.105–14)

In sentence 9 Aelfric reduces the parallel structure by half:

tunc quod vivet, non morietur;	þonne he of deaþe arist and syþðan ne swylt,
tunc quod sanabitur, non aegrotabit;	ne seoc ne gewyrð,
tunc quod satiabitur, non esuriet aut sitiet;	ne him hingrian ne mæg, ne him þurst ne deraþ

tunc quod renovabitur, non   ne he ne forealdað . . . .
veterascet.

From Augustine's first paragraph Aelfric cuts six of the sentences altogether; five of these deal at length with the health/sickness metaphor. Yet with Aelfric's personal kind of rearrangement, his consistent focus on the *res et sacramentum* of the miracle, his judicious addition of material (some of it dependent on Alcuin, but some independent) and his restrained use of word play, Aelfric produces a commentary that is every bit as forceful as Augustine's. The one style is elaborately Augustinian, the other restrainedly Aelfrician, if I may be permitted a bit of homoeoteleuton myself.

Although Aelfric typically cuts or abbreviates extended imagery and word play, he will also expand a figure or trope if necessary, for abbreviation is never an end in itself, and Aelfric's balanced style relies on artful repetition. For example the polyptoton in Augustine's "tot iacebant, et unus curatus est, cum posset uno verbo omnes erigere" is expanded with alliterative focus on the one/all contrast:

Ænne he gehælde þa of eallum þam untrumum
se ðe mid anum worde eaðelice mihte
hi ealle gehælan; ac he wolde swiþor
þurh þæt an wundor awreccan heora mod,
and heora sawla onlihtan þurh þæt syllice tacn. (SS 2.134–38)

Aelfric similarly expands the *an/nan* word play in .125–29 of the same homily.

The next passage is a translation of Augustine's relatively uncomplicated sentence: "Voluerunt enim consilium dare Domino ne moreretur, qui venerat mori, ne ipsi morerentur":

Þa halgan apostoli woldon þam Hælende
þone ræd tæcan þæt he ne þorfte sweltan
se þe sylfwilles com þæt he sweltan wolde,
þæt hi sylfe ne swulton, ne we eac soðlice,
þam yfelan deðe þe he us of alysde. (SS 6.338–42)

Line 241b and 242 are Aelfric's addition, and he repeats the phrase *þam yfelan deaðe* at .366. In this particular homily Aelfric expands considerably on the death/life opposition inherent in the

Gospel account of the resurrection of Lazarus. When he does so, the expansions typically involve the words *deað, Domes-dæge, ondræde* ("Ondræde swa þu ondræde, se deað þe cymð to"[.154]). In the final passage, which is a close translation of Augustine, Aelfric is able to add paronomasia to the verbal figures in Augustine's passage because of the useful *lybbað/gelyfð* sound correspondence in Old English.

> . . . non est Deus mortuorum, sed vivorum. . . . Crede
> ergo; et si mortuus fueris, vives: si autem non credis,
> et cum vivis, mortuus es.
> Nis na God deadra manna, ac is libbendra;
> ealle menn him lybbað. Se þe on hine gelyfð,
> þeah þe he dead si, he sceal libban swaþeah,
> and se ðe ne gelyfð on hyne, þeah þe he lifes si,
> he ys dead swaþeah þam yfelan deaðe. (SS 6.362–66)

Sometimes Aelfric will even expand a verbal figure where there is only a suggestion of word play in his source. In the homily for the First Friday Aelfric picks up the etymological reference in Alcuin to servile work: "omnis, qui facit peccatum, servus est peccati (John 8:34), patet liquido, quia peccata recte opera servilia intelliguntur." Aelfric develops this as follows:

> On þam ealdan resten-dæge, þe we ær embe spræcon,
> ne worhton þa Iudei nan *þeowtlic* weorc,
> and se an getacnode eal ure lif,
> þe is gastlic ræsten-dæg, on þam we Gode sceolon
> symle *þeowian* and synna forbugan,
> þe synd *þeowtlice* weorc, and on *þeowte* gebringað
> heora wvrcendras a to worulde. (SS 2.256–62, italics mine)

Still, compared with Augustine, the polyptoton is so restrained as to seem pallid by comparison. Even if we choose a restrained passage in Augustine, Aelfric's translation stands out for its prosaic quality.

> Et illa nondum intellegebat; et non intelligens, quid
> respondebat? . . . Ad laborem indigentia cogebat, et
> laborem infirmitas recusabat. . . . Hoc enim ei dicebat
> Jesus, ut iam non laboraret; sed illa nondum intellegebat.
> (xv.17; CCL 36, pp. 156) [28]

Heo wolde þa iu beon buton geswince,
ac heo ne gehyrde þa gyt hwæt se Haelend cwæð . . . . (SS
5.154–55)

The final balancing clause Aelfric cuts. Though Augustinian, it does not suit Aelfric.

It seems reasonable to assume that Aelfric was guided in his use of word play by some conscious as well as intuitive sense for decorum. Bede in his treatise on tropes and schemes notes that Gregory was particularly fond of homoeoteleuton and continues, "I believe this is the type of address which Jerome refers to as the elegant declamation of orators." [29] An inventory of Aelfric's use of rhetorical figures in a large corpus might provide evidence for the principles of decorum at work. Anaphora, for example, is a figure that Aelfric seems to use in passages of heightened emotion. Pope notes its "incantatory effect" in the description of the liturgical year in the homily for the Octave of Pentecost. Aelfric uses it independently in his description of the penitent woman in the homily for the Fifth Friday:

and mid hyre tearum hys fet aþwoh,
and mid hyre fexe hi forhtlice wipode,
and mid deorwurðre sealfe hi syððan smyrode. (SS 6.307–09)

A proper understanding of Aelfric's achievements in English prose would involve a close study of verbal word play—the types, their extent, the literary contexts in which they are used. It would also involve a study of the consistent revisions Aelfric made, many in the direction of amplification.[30] Ultimately, however, Aelfric's plain style rises on the foundation of methodical abbreviation.

NOTES

1. It would be tedious to list all the articles dealing with this subject. In *Continuations and Beginnings: Studies in Old English Literature,* ed. E.G. Stanley (London, 1966), see P.A.M. Clemoes, "Aelfric," pp. 176–209 and Rosemary Woolf, "Saints' Lives," pp. 62–64; also my "Aelfric and the

Brief Style," *Journal of English and Germanic Philology* 70
(1971) : 1–12.
2. All references will be to SS I and B. Assmann ed., *Angelsächsische
Homilien und Heiligenleben* (Kassel, 1889), pp. 65–72;
arabic numerals refer to homily and line number (emendations not shown).
3. P.A.M. Clemoes, "The Chronology of Aelfric's Works," in *The
Anglo Saxons: Studies in some Aspects of their History
and Culture* (London, 1959), pp. 221 and 228. Clemoes
thinks that these homilies belonged to an initial phase of
Aelfric's expansion. Pope assigns the composition of the four
Friday homilies he edits to an early phase. "We may reasonably suppose that during the period from 992–998 or so
Aelfric produced . . . a certain number of homilies that he
did not wish to include among the *Lives.* Among the relatively early pieces I should place . . . the four homilies for
Fridays in Lent . . ." (SS I, p. 147).
4. The pericope translations in these five homilies are literal ones,
except for amplifications demanded by the alliteration.
Minor variations, e.g., the deletion of *quae dicitur Sichar* in
the description of the Samaritan town (SS 5.3), are without
interest, since Aelfric typically deletes exotic geographical
facts or adds identifications his audience would have needed.
Such changes have been adequately discussed by many
critics.
5. The sources for these homilies are relatively sure. The quotations
in Pope are in most cases adequate to establish indebtedness
not merely in general ideas but also in vocabulary and syntax. The deletions discussed in this paper are from such
secure passages. The homily for the Fifth Friday (Assmann
5) alone poses some difficulties because I have been unable
to locate all the sources Aelfric used. He relied on Augustine
(*PL* 35 nos. 49 and 50), borrowed a detail from Bede (*PL*
92, 785), and used Haymo's treatment of Luke 11 :42–57
(*PL* 118, 654) and reused some of the same material he had
treated before in CH I, pp. 402–04. This homily is the short-
est of the five, and the pericope is handled briefly in the
sources.

6. Augustinus, *In Ioannis Evangelium Tractatus* CXXIV, CCL 36
   (Turnbolti, 1934). Unless stated otherwise all references to
   Augustine will be to this volume. When numbers are listed,
   the order is tractate number, paragraph number, and p. citation to CCL 36. I will not cite references for quotations included in Pope. Translations for extensive passages are
   taken from James Innes tr., *The Works of Aurelius Augustine* Vols. X–XI, ed. Marcus Dods (Edinburgh, 1873).

7. Augustine, tr. Innes, Vol. X, p. 212: "Now begin the mysteries.
   For it is not without purpose that Jesus is weary; not indeed without a purpose that the strength of God is weary;
   not without purpose that He is weary, by whom the wearied
   are refreshed; not without a purpose is He weary, by whose
   absence we are wearier, by whose presence we are strength-
   ened. Nevertheless Jesus is weary, and weary with His
   journey; and He sits down, and that, too, near a well; and
   it is at the sixth hour that, being wearied, He sits down.
   . . . It was for thee that Jesus was wearied with His
   journey."

8. Augustine, tr. Innes, Vol. XI, p. 129: "Just that to point Himself
   out as the day, He made choice of twelve disciples. If I am
   the day, He says, and you the hours, is it for the hours to
   give counsel to the day? The day is followed by the hours,
   not the hours by the day. If these, then, were the hours,
   what in such a reckoning was Judas? Was he also among the
   twelve hours? If he was an hour, he had light; and if he had
   light, how was the Day betrayed by him to death? Let the
   hours then attend upon the Day, let them preach the Day, be
   made known and illuminated by the Day, and by the preaching of the hours may the world believe in the Day."

9. Cecily Clark notes similar cutting of elaborate figures of speech
   in Aelfric's handling of Abbo of Fleury's *Passio Sancti
   Eadmundi,* e.g., "velut lupis vespertinis mos est clanculo
   ad plana descendere, repetitis quantocius noctis silvarum
   latibulis" > "swa swa wulf." "Aelfric and Abbo," *English
   Studies* 49 (1968): 32–33.

10. Augustine, tr. Innes, Vol. X, p. 227: "therefore, in the case of
    that woman, it was even His drink to do the will of Him that

sent Him. That was the reason why He said, "I thirst, give me to drink:" namely, to work faith in her, and to drink of her faith, and to transplant her into His own body, for His body is the Church."

11. *The Rhetoric of Alcuin and Charlemagne,* ed. Wilbur Samuel Howell (Princeton, 1941), p. 132.

12. Many other examples from the Friday homilies could be cited, but they commonly involve quoting very long passages, such as that on the hour-day metaphor. Aelfric's prosaic reduction of Augustine's passage is a good example of his rejection of three characteristic traits of Augustine's style, word play, rhetorical questions and expanded metaphor. After all Aelfric did not wish "laudari artificiosi sermonis compositione" (CH II, p. 1).

13. Sweet's *Anglo-Saxon Reader,* ed. Dorothy Whitelock (Oxford, 1970), xiii.39–40, henceforth cited as ASR with selection and line number.

14. Augustine, tr. Innes, Vol. X, p. 224: "Would I could find, thou didst say, some high and lonely mountain: For I think that, because God is on high, He hears me the rather from a high place. Because thou art on a mountain, dost thou imagine thyself near to God, and that He will quickly hear thee, as if calling to him from the nearest place? He dwells on high, but regards the lowly. 'The Lord is near.' To whom? To the high, perhaps? 'To them who are contrite of heart.' Tis a wonderful thing: He dwelleth on high, and yet is near to the lowly; 'He hath regard to lowly things, but lofty things He knoweth from afar:' He seeth the proud afar off, and He is the less near to them the higher they appear to themselves to be. Didst thou seek a mountain, then? Come down that thou mayest come near Him. But wouldest thou ascend? Ascend, but do not seek a mountain. 'The ascents,' it saith, 'are in his heart, in the valley of weeping.' The valley is humility."

15. I have so far avoided the question of *how* Aelfric used his sources. Did he work from memory or from a text at hand? Whatever the historically accurate but unascertainable situation, it is clear in passages like these that Aelfric is indebted

to Augustine. Whether Aelfric did his abbreviating at the time of conscious or unconscious memorization, or at the time of composition, the method is essentially the same.

16. Pope does not provide a source for .279–88, labeling this passage "a mere summary of the gospel with conventional ending" (p. 300). In his final paragraph of his commentary on this passage Augustine comments following the quotation of v. 42: "primo per famam, postea per praesentiam" (xv.33; CCL 36, p. 164).

17. Some of the terms used in this paper correspond roughly to the terminology of transformational grammar. The syntactical discussion in this paper could be handled in strict trans-formational terms, but since not all Anglo-Saxonists are transformationalists as well, it seemed preferable to write this paper "non ignotis sermonibus, sed puris et apertis verbis" of traditional philology.

18. ASR.xiv.130–31 and *PL* 118, 80.

19. ASR.xiv. 147 and *PL* 118, 80.

20. *PL* 118, 655.

21. Augustine, tr. Innes, Vol. X, p. 215: "You see that they were aliens: indeed the Jews would not use their vessels. And as the woman brought with her a vessel with which to draw the water, it made her wonder that a Jew sought drink of her,—a thing which Jews were not accustomed to do. But He who was asking drink was thirsting for the faith of the woman herself."

22. Source studies can provide interesting evidence for Aelfric's handling of Latin verb forms. In this passage the imperfect seems to correspond to the use of modals: *noldon* . . . *brucan* for *non utebantur,* and perhaps *wolde drincan* for *petebat* . . . *bibere.* Another interesting possibility is *ongunnon hi to ceorigenne* for *murmurabant* (ASR.xiii. 23–4).

23. Augustine, tr. Innes, Vol. X, p. 236: "It ought not to be a matter of wonder that a miracle was wrought by God; the wonder would be if man had wrought it. Rather ought we to rejoice than wonder that our Lord and Savior Jesus Christ was made man, than that He performed divine works

among men. It is of greater importance to our salvation
what He has made for men, than what He did among men:
it is more important that He healed the faults of souls, than
that He healed the weaknesses of mortal bodies."

24. The homily proper begins at .63, where Aelfric devotes five
lines to the symbolism of Bethsaida. This material has been
rearranged from Augustine's second paragraph.

25. Pope cites the Alcuin passage as the source for .115–16
(p. 235), but the *visibiliter / invisibiliter* contrast is not
used in those lines. It seems likely that Aelfric has shifted
the contrastive adverbs to this preceding section.

26. Sentences 1–3 are handled in .98–104, sentence 5 in .91–94,
sentence 7 in .134–38, sentence 9 in .105–14. Sentences 4, 6,
and 10–13 are cut.

27. Augustine, tr. Innes, Vol. X, pp. 236–37: "For that which is
the real health of bodies, and which is looked for from the
Lord, will be at the end, in the resurrection of the dead.
What shall live then shall no more die; what shall be
satisfied shall no more hunger and thirst; what shall be
made new shall not grow old. But at this time, however,
the eyes of the blind, that were opened by these acts of our
Lord and Saviour Jesus Christ, were again closed in death;
and limbs of the paralytics that received strength were
loosened again in death; and whatever was for a time made
whole in mortal limbs came to nought in the end: but the
soul that believed passed to eternal life."

28. Augustine, tr. Innes, Vol. X, p. 218: ". . . but the woman did
not yet understand and not understanding, how did she
answer? . . . Want forced her to labour, and her weakness
was pleading against the toil. . . . This is, in fact, what
Jesus was saying to her, that she might no longer labour;
but she did not yet understand."

29. Gussie Hecht Tanenhaus, "Bede's De Schematibus et Tropis—
A Translation," *Quarterly Journal of Speech* 48 (1962):
243.

30. Clemoes, e.g., has shown that in the punctuation of Royal there
is evidence of consistent revision to add parallel grammatical forms. He cites four examples in which an original

prepositional phrase with a compound object is revised with
the repetition of the preposition before the second object,
e.g., "mid godum 7 claenum geþohtum" 7 "mid godum 7 mid
clænum geþohtum" (53v/22), and "mid fæder 7 halgum
gaste" > "mid fæder 7 mid halgum gaste" (173/24). see
Aelfric's First Series of Catholic Homilies, British Library
Royal 7 C XII, ff. 4–128, EEMF 13 (Copenhagen, 1966),
p. 33.

KEITH A. TANDY ❦ VERBAL ASPECT AS A NARRATIVE STRUCTURE IN AELFRIC'S LIVES OF SAINTS

In a number of recent studies critics have begun using modern linguistic approaches to language in analyses of poetry. Roger Fowler, for example, has presented detailed discussions of the proper uses and limitations of linguistics as a critical tool, including a study of Wulfstan's *Sermo Lupi*.[1] Stanley Greenfield has extended the discussion further, evaluated much of the early criticism, and applied some of the thinking to Old English poetry.[2] So far as I am aware, this approach has not been used on Aelfric's work, nor has anyone yet concentrated fully on the aspectual features of verbs in literary works.[3] After illustrating the major categories of aspect and the devices by which it is expressed, I shall demonstrate that Aelfric was well informed on the subject of aspect, as his *Grammar* shows, and that he uses aspects as a theological metaphor in the homily on "The Nativity of Our Lord Jesus Christ" which follows the preface to his *Lives of Saints*. Finally, I shall show how, in his "Life of St. Eugenia," he distributes verbs carrying different aspectual features in patterns that characterize Christians as opposed to pagans, in effect using such patterns of verbal aspect —as Greenfield says of syntax and verse form—to "provide a kind of 'formal meaning' that may be helpful, even necessary, for interpretation. . . ."[4]

Aspect studies have never enjoyed the kind of academic industry that has been created around tense studies.[5] Indeed, so long as the major scholars in linguistics focussed their efforts exclusively on surface grammar, on morphological systems of language, and rigorously excluded semantic analysis, a strong prejudice against aspect studies in English existed—and still exists.[6] For in English aspect is not expressed overtly, in a morphological system, but covertly, in modifiers, periphrastic verb structures, and lexical meaning, and consequently aspect is accessible largely through the semantic analysis that was forbidden by formal grammarians.

Still, most grammarians will admit that English forms progressive, inceptive, and iterative aspects by special verbal phrasings, as in sentences like "I am writing," "He began to work," and "He keeps on going to work on the bus every day." The other systems for expressing aspectual categories are less overt. Lexical embedding is one: "to rule" is necessarily durative aspect, while "to jump" is necessarily punctual; "ruling," by its meaning, has to occupy a span of time, while "jumping" has to occupy a point in time, Punctual and durative aspects are paired categories in languages of both types—the *Aspekt* languages with morphological systems, such as Semitic, as well as the *Aktionsart* languages like English, with covert aspect systems.

Adverbial modification is an additional system for marking aspectual features. In "I often play tennis," the adverb marks the verb strongly for iterative (sometimes called frequentative) aspect. The lexically embedded aspectual features can be illustrated by the refusal of some verbs to accept inappropriate adverbs from the modification system, as in * "He ruled suddenly." Ruling has such a powerful durative force that it resists even the aspectual forces of tense markers. For example, in past form—"He ruled England"— the tense carries with it a logical termination point, called terminative or perfective aspect. But the primary aspectual force is probably still durative; if we wish to stress perfective aspect, we choose a modifier like "until" plus a date and still do not succeed in obliterating the durative sense.

Several observations on the operations of aspect can now be made. First, two or more aspectual features may be present in the same verb form, and often we must decide which is the most strongly felt. Second, a rough logic operates in verbal aspect, according to which, for example, we can apply punctual modifiers to punctual, but not durative verbs, and conversely, durative modifiers to durative, but not punctual verbs. "Suddenly he tripped" is English, * "He tripped slowly" is not. In "He punched him for a a long time," we immediately understand the impossibility of taking a long time to execute a single, punctual punch and translate the apparently durative modifier into an iterative aspect, roughly equivalent to "over and over again." Third, aspect logic overlaps with the logic of the other verbal features such as tense, especially in the areas of present tense/characterizing and gnomic aspect (compare "He smokes" for present tense as characterizing aspect to "Cork floats" as gnomic aspect),[7] of past tense/terminative (or egressive) aspects,[8] and of perfect tense/perfective and imperfective aspect, and also with agency, which shares with aspect the systems of verbal phrasing (voice) and lexical embedding. Contrast, for example, "to jump" and "to trip," both punctual aspect, the first necessarily agentive, the second necessarily not agentive. These overlapping areas have been inadequately explored, but need not complicate the present study.[9] They are analogous to what John Robert Ross calls a "squish," "a quasi-continuum" where traditionally we have thought of "a fixed, discrete inventory of syntactic categories . . ."[10] Finally, in contrast to the complexity of the "squishes" with tense and agency, aspect as lexically embedded in individual verbs is an *ad hoc,* but pervasive, feature of verbs. That is, it changes from verb to verb and from sentence to sentence, but is always present in some form.

The terminology of aspect studies is complicated, and the list of major categories above—duration, punctuality, iteration, gnomic, characterizing, termination, inception, and progression—is by no means exhaustive.[11] To the three major systems of expressing aspect—verbal phrasing, adverbial modification, and lexicalization —we should add the phonesthemic clusters in English, of the kind in "wr-" words like "wrap, wrestle, wrench, write," where the initial sound itself carries a consistent marker of twisting motion; we should also note the marking of aspect by syntactical units larger than single adverbs, as in sentences such as "He walked across the ice," which is perfective, contrasted with "He walked out on the ice," which is imperfective.

Fortunately Aelfric, in the process of translating Priscian's grammar into Old English, demonstrates that he is fully aware of much of what has just been discussed. In the "Praefatio de Partibus Orationis" of his work, Aelfric discriminates between three kinds of verbs:

> VERBVM is word, and word getacnaðweorc oððe
> ðrowunge oððe geþafunge.
> weorc byð, þonne ðu cwest: *aro* ic erige; *uerbero* ic swinge.

þrowung byð, þonne ðu cwyst: *uerberor* ic eom beswungen;
ligor ic eom gebunden. geðafung byþ, ðonne ðu cwyst: *amor*
ic eom gelufod; *doceor* ic eom gelaered.[12]

While the distinction between *ðrowunge* and *geþafunge* is less
clear in the terms than in the examples, Aelfric clearly understands
the need to discriminate between passives involving received action
and surface or quasi-passives involving states.

After discussing the "QVINQUE DECLINATIONES NOMI-
NUM," Aelfric returns to verbs and establishes another kind of
distinction:

VERBUM EST PARS ORATIONIS CVM TEMPORE
ET PERSONA SINE CASV AVT AGERE ALIQVID
AVT PATI AVT NEVTRVM SIGNIFICANS,
VERBVM ys word, an dæl ledenspræce mid tide and hade
butan case getacniende oððe sum ðing to donne oððe sum ðing
to þrowigenne oððe naðor.
VERBVM HABET SEPTEM ACCIDENTIA word
hæfð seofon gelimplice ðing. him gelimpð SIGNIFICATIO,
þæt ys, getacnung, hwæt þæt word getacnige, dæde oððe
þrowunge oððe naðor; TEMPUS tid, MODVS gemet,
SPECIES hiw, FIGVRA gefegednyss, CONIVGATIO
geþeodnyss, PERSONA had, NVMERVS getel. we wyllað
nu secgan endebyrdlice and gewislice be eallum þissum.
SIGNIFICATIO ys getacnung, hwæt þæt word getacnige.
ælc fulfremed word geendað on *o* oððe on *or*.
on *o* geendiað ACTIVA VERBA, þæt synd dædlice word,
þa ðe geswutliað, hwæt men doð. *amo* ic lufige geswutelað min
weorc; ealswa *doceo* ic tæce, *lego* ic ræde. *audio* ic gehyre: on
eallum þisum wordum ys min weorc geswutelod. þas and
ðyllice synd ACTIVA gehatene, þæt synd dædlice, forðan ðe
hi geswuteliað dæda; do ænne *r* to ðisum wordum, þonne beoð
hi PASSIVA, þæt synd ðrowiendlice; na swylce hi æfre
pinunge getacnion, ac þonne oðres mannes dæd befylð on me
oððe on ðe, þonne byþ þæt on lendenspræce PASSIVVM
VERBVM . . . þa word, þe geendiað on *o* and ne magon
æfter andgyte beon PASSIVA, þa synd NEUTRA gehatene,
þæt is nadres cynnes: *uiuo* ic lybbe, *spiro* ic orðige, *sto* ic

stande, *ambulo* ic gange, *sedeo* ic sitte. ne mæg her beon nan
PASSIVVM on ðisum wordum, forðan ðe heora getacnung
ne befylð on nanum oðrum menn, buton on ðam, ðe hit
cwyð.[13]

Here we may note Aelfric's comprehension of a fundamental principle of language: the limitations imposed on morphological and
syntactical variation by lexical meaning. The "neutra" verbs do
not form passives "æfter andgyte," and "forðan ðe heora getacnung
ne befylð on nanum oðrum menn, buton on ðam, ðe hit cwyð."
As he completed his discussion of Latin passives Aelfric expressed
this lexical limitation in yet another way: "þas word and ðyllice
ne beoð na ledenword, gif se *r* byð aweg gedon." [14] Though he
does not say so explicitly, Aelfric seems aware that despite syntactical dissimilarities between Latin and English, many of the
lexical determinants of syntax are operative equally in both languages, "æfter andgyte," so that one would not form a passive of
an English verb used to translate a Latin "Neutra" verb, any
more than he would form a Latin passive in this class.

Aelfric takes up the Latin conjugations after treating mood,
person, and number, and then turns to "Specie," or "hiw":

SPECIES is hiw, PRIMITIVA frumcenned and
DIRIVATIVA ofgangende. ealle ða eahta PARTES fornean
habbað þas twa hiw. *lego* ic ræde is frumcenned. þonne cymð of
ðam *lecturio* me lyst rædan. þis hiw is gehaten MEDITATIVA
SPECIES, þæt is smeagendlic hiw, and ealle ða word gað æfter
ðære feorðan geðeodnysse, ðeah ðe þa word, ðe hi of cumað,
beon mislicra geðeodnyssa. *amo* ic lufige, *amaturio* me lyste
lufian; *dictaturio* me lyste dihtan; *docturio* me lyste tæcan;
esurio me hingrað. . . .[15]

Here Aelfric begins to describe the morphological structures by
which "primitive" Latin verbs are varied to form "derivative"
verbs signalling specific aspectual features. It is not his purpose to
comment in the *Grammar* on the form of OE, but to explain and
illustrate the Latin structures in OE, and this is no easy task. In
finding names and illustrations to match the Latin categories he
seems forced into special, narrow usage of OE words. In this

process especially, in this translating of Priscian's grammar, as in his constant occupation with translation of many texts, it would be odd to think that Aelfric would have missed the universal experience of language students—of learning as much about their own language as the new one. Here, as Aelfric builds a vocabulary in his English for talking about Latin aspectual categories, we may fairly assume that he is forced, in choosing terms and illustrations, to form some perceptions of English aspect, or "hiw," as well as of Latin "Species."

Aelfric illustrates the overriding morphological structure in Latin (the formation of derivative, aspectually marked verbs by adding syllables to primitive verbs) with an example of such a formation, the "meditative species" or "smeagendlic hiw." In illustrating this aspect, which appears to range between desiderative and characterizing frequentative aspect, Aelfric is almost consistent in framing a periphrastic of "lyst" plus infinitive, yielding a special sense, "It pleases me to . . ." which sometimes can probably be rewritten as "I am accustomed to/in the habit of . . ." The exception is "me hingrað," a verb already marked (lexically) for desiderative aspect, making the periphrastic marker redundant.

In the section which follows Aelfric again uses this periphrastic resource of English (compare modern "I kept . . . ; I used to . . ." expressing past iterative aspect) as an aspectual marker in the absence of English morphological structures:

> Oðer hiw is gehaten INCHOATIVA, þæt is onginnendlic,
> forðan ðe hit getacnað weorces anginn, and cymð of oðrum
> wordum. *caleo* ic wearmige and of ðam *calesco* ic onginne to
> wearmigenne; *horreo* ic andðracige, *horresco* ic onginne to
> andðricignenne . . . ealle ðas word and ða oðre
> MEDITATIVA nabbað næenne PRAETERITUM
> PERFECTVM ne PLVSQVAMPERFECTVM ne towerde
> tide on SVBIVNCTIVO. . . .[16]

The usual modern term for this aspectual feature is, of course, inceptive aspect. Again Aelfric notes tense formation limitations, though he does not specify the lexical reasons for them.

In the section which follows Aelfric uses yet another structure by which English expresses aspect in the absence of morphological variations—the use of a modifier (here, "gelome," often,) for frequentative aspect:

> Sume word synd gecwedene FREQVENTATIVA, þæt synd gelomlæcende, forðan ðe hi getacniað gelomlæcunge, þonne man sum ðinge gelome deð. *rogo* ic bidde and of ðam *rogito* ic bidde gelome. *uolo* ic fleo, *uolas; uolito* ic flicerige. . . .[17]

Aelfric has more to say about aspect, but the preceding discussion may suffice to establish his general competence in several important areas. He is aware of asymmetrical features in language systems (in the logical, lexical limits of certain passives and the similar tense limitations of "incohoativa" and "meditativa" verbs). This is the same principle which underlies Aristotle's division of verbs into *energeiai,* activities, and *kineseis,* movements.[18] Aelfric further is certainly aware, through the process of explaining his text in English, of the fact that English, lacking morphological variations to mark aspect, must often resort to modification or periphrastic structures to express aspectual features where they are not in fact already embedded, lexically, in the signification of the verb.

These principles have not changed since Aelfric's time, though many specific features of individual words and structures of course have. For in the frequent absence of either modification or periphrastic structures, we must often resort to what Aelfric calls "andgyte"—our understanding of the word, whether in Old or modern English, to describe its aspectual features.

Beyond the few periphrastic structures like "I am . . ." plus present participle for progressive aspect, or the inceptive "I begin . . ." plus infinitive which Aelfric and modern speakers of English share, or "I used to . . ." plus infinitive for past frequentative (compare "I keep . . ." plus present participle as a quasi-present frequentative or iterative), English speakers in Aelfric's time and our own recognize many verbs as inherently marked for specific aspect because of the way we perceive the actions to take place. The major problem here, then, is to show what use Aelfric made of his knowledge of aspect.

That the various features of verbs were very much in Aelfric's mind when he wrote the *Lives of Saints* is demonstrable. He discriminates, on a basis that is essentially aspectual, between beasts, men and angels, and God, in the section on "The Nativity of Our Lord Jesus Christ," which follows his preface:

Ðreo þing synd on middanearde. an is hwilendlic. þe hæfð
ægðer ge ordfrumman ge ende, þæt synd nytenu.
and ealle sawullease þing þe ongunnan þa þa hi god gesceop.
and æft geændiað and to nahte gewurðaþ. Oðer þing is ece.
swa þæt hit hæfð ordfruman and næfð nenne ende. þæt synd
ænglas and manna saula. þe ongunnen ða þa hi god gesceop. ac
hi ne geendiað næfre. Ðridde þing is ece swa þæt hit næfð naðor
ne ordfruman ne ende. þæt is se ana ælmihtiga god . . .
(LS 1.25–32)

In explicit aspectual terms, soul-less things have punctual inception and termination and durative lives; men and angels have punctual inception at their creations, but eternal duration of their souls; God is eternally durative, with no inception and no termination. In the same passage Aelfric notes God's transcendence of time and tenses:

Þæs an scyppend wat ealle þing. and gesihð ge þæt gedon is.
ge þæt þe nu is ge þæt ðe toweard is. . . . ne he nan þing
ne forgit . . . (LS 1.41–43)

Aelfric returns to these distinctions twice in the homily, at the latter place distinguishing man's temporally located, sequential knowledge from God's tenseless omniscience:

Witodlice god ælmihtig wat ealle þing togædere. and ealle þing
hæfð on his andwerdnysse. and hi æfre beoþ on his gesihþe.
and næfre him uncuþe. and þis is þæt gecwæden is þæt god is
æghwær eall. forðan ðe ealle þing þe æfre wæron oððe nu
synd. oþþe ða towearde synd. ealle hi synd on godes gesihðe.
andwearde. na æne. ac æfre. (LS 1.136–41)

The remainder of this section deals with an analysis of the soul, its proper domination over the body, the functions of the mind, and—with special stress—the obligation of the soul to exercise will properly, in seeking God.

If in this first section varieties of verbal features have formed part of Aelfric's statements on theological issues, in the "Life of St. Eugenia" which follows after the homily we should not be surprised to find patterns of verbal aspect functioning as an important narrative structure.

In Aelfric's life of St. Eugenia pagans and Christians are distinguished, but the characterization of Christians is more richly developed than in Cynewulf's *Elene,* for example. While pagans are limited to punctual, inceptive, perfective acts, the distinction between their world of space and time and the permanent and morally defined world of Christians is more sharply drawn, and Christians are not limited to minimal agency, static postures, and abstract moral action : they appear in the world capable of action in it, and they change and grow ; of course their actions and their growth are both given moral contexts, while pagan actions have temporal and spatial contexts. In these respects Aelfric moves closer to the Latinate hagiographic tradition—a move probably made possible by the great monastic reform in England—yet he retains much of the earlier dichotomous view of acts and states, as we shall see.

Four verbal units occur in the four lines which introduce the life of St. Eugenia :

> Mæg gehyran seþe wyle be þam halgan mædene
> eugenian philyppus dæhter
> hu heo ðurh mægðhad mærlice þeah
> and þurh martyrdom þisne middaneard oferswað.
> (LS 2.1–4)

> He who wishes it, may hear concerning the holy maiden
> Eugenia, the daughter of Philip ;
> how she by her virginity gloriously flourished,
> and by martyrdom overcame this world. (tr. Skeat, p. 25)

In the first verbal unit of these lines (1.1a : "Mæg gehyran . . .") Aelfric has an echo of the introductory practice, in Cynewulf and *Beowulf,* of calling attention to the present situation, the relationship between poet, audience, and poem. But he introduces a significant new element, pursued in the second verbal unit

(1.1b–2: "seþe wyle. . ."), by using modal verbs: "He who wishes it, may hear" about Eugenia. (Aelfric's interest in "will" as a theological problem in the materials with which he introduces this collection makes "He who *wills* it" the appropriate translation here.)

These modals draw distinctions between the moral decisions of mankind and his occupancy in the world of time and space and yet signal at the same time that moral decisions are made within that space and time framework. (That position is held consistently in the distribution of verbal attributes between pagans and Christians for the first forty lines of the poem.) That is to say, by way of adding aspectual features to the verbs, Eugenia's accomplishments, now perfective, are available at any time or at any point in time, partly by virtue of their spiritual excellence, for hearing by any human who at any point in time makes the moral choice of willing to hear.

In lines 3 and 4 Aelfric eliminates any possibility of suspense in the plot of Eugenia's life, telling us that we may hear (if we will it), "how she by her virginity gloriously flourished,/and by martyrdom overcame this world." The two phrases giving means ("ðurh maegðhad" and "þurh martyrdom") by which verbal action is accomplished may be characteristic of Christians; I find no "means" phrases applied to pagans in the early sections here, perhaps yielding a sense of the relative simplicity of acting in the pagan realm of time and space, as compared to the complexity of achieving in the moral realm of Christianity.

A verb like "þeah"—"flourished"—raises troublesome questions of agency and time. The past form has a minimal logical terminative aspect, scarcely felt before the dominant aspectual feature, indefinite duration: flourishing must occupy a span of time. Normally agency would be an open question, but here the means phrase imposes a sense that virginity is a state subject to agency, presumably by the choice of preserving it, whether in the presence or absence of a threat to it. It may be significant that when Scyld Scefing in *Beowulf* (line 8) "flourishes," we are not informed directly as to the means; my sense is that in flourishing he advances as a paradigm of the secular ethic, while Eugenia, having made a moral choice, advances as a spiritual paradigm.

The aspectual features of line 4 reflect back on this flourishing, partly because of the parallelism of the means phrases: by martyrdom she overcame this world. In this structure perhaps more than any other considered so far, the need for contextual and lexical subtlety in the analysis of aspect is manifest. "Oferswað" is clearly terminative or perfective; in connection with martyrdom as a means, it is clearly punctual. Without that context it appears to be agentive and nonpunctual; but the "means" phrase recasts it and forces a kind of double perspective.

At one level, namely, the space-time context of the pagans, the line is a euphemistic and circuitous way of saying that Eugenia was killed. Her death is punctual, within that physical context, but that is only an implicit element in the structure. The perspective is moral rather than physical, focusing on a victorious conquest of worldly things and thus allowing the quality of agency most at odds with the temporal and physical reading.

Further, while this "overcoming" occurs in an instant of time, and is in that sense both temporally located and punctual, as a moral victory it is immediately displaced out of the temporal context altogether and becomes an eternal, morally defined state. Thus the paradox: to be martyred is to suffer a punctual act at the hands of others and at the same instant to choose an eternal and nontemporal victorious state.

Aelfric turns from these complexities surrounding Eugenia to relatively simple aspectual features delineating pagans in line 5–11:

> Sum æþelboren þægn wæs philippus gehaten
> ðone asende se casere commodus
> þe on ðam dagum rixode fram rome byrig
> to ðære byrig ðe is gehaten alexandria
> and he hine gesette to heahgerefan
> ofer alexandrian and ægyfto lande
> and het þæt he heolde þa romaniscan gesætnysse. (LS 2.5–11)

> A certain nobly-born thane was named Philip,
> whom the emperor Commodus sent—
> he who in those days ruled—from the city of Rome
> to the city which is named Alexandria;
> and he appointed him as chief ruler

over Alexandria and the land of Egypt,
and commanded him to observe the Roman law. (tr. Skeat,
   pp. 25, 27)

In this section there are six verbal units, and they are of two
kinds. The first is located in line 5, which contains the generic,
durative, agentless "wæs gehaten"; this has a parallel in line 8,
but with a contrast in tense. The certain nobly born thane *was*
named Philip, but the city *is* named Alexandria. Line 5 is perfective, line 8 is not; rather it conveys a generic fact enduring into
Aelfric's time. Thus while association with geography is one of
the elements of worldly pagan character, even geographical features are more durable than mere non-Christian men.

The other verbs in this section are perfective, punctual, inceptive,
and agentive; they involve pagans in acts of commanding. Commodus sent Philip, appointed ("gesette") him as ruler, commanded ("het") that he maintain or preserve Roman law. Absent
from all these verbs is any explicit duration (being an "heahgere-
fan" will occupy time, of course, but being appointed one does not;
the duration of Philip's journey to Alexandria and of his observing
Roman law are also implicit: the focus of the verbs is elsewhere).
Present in each is a strong sense of agency, and of control over
worldly affairs.

One verb in the lines does show duration: at 7a Commodus is
described as "he who in those days ruled. . . ." But the modifier—
"in those days"—functions to place heavy stress on the perfective
and terminative features of "rixode"—ruled—so that even those
actions of pagans which have duration come to an end, and one
ruler is followed by another. The contrast between the aspectual
features of line 4—"how she by martyrdom overcame this world"
—and line 7a—"he who in those days ruled"—is some measure of
how different two apparently perfective verbs can be.

One other characteristic of pagans exhibited here is their movement, typically, from one specified geographic location to another
specified location. Just as "in ðam dagum" places Philip and
Commodus in a temporal context, and just as their punctual acts
define the quality of their lives in that temporal context, so Philip's
being sent "from the city of Rome to the city which is named

Alexandria" fixes him in worldly space. Christians, by contrast, do not move from place to place, but from moral climate to moral climate, as we shall see below.

In three additional lines Aelfric extends the characterization of pagans by placing them in a negative relationship to Christianity:

> Ðæs ðægn philippus næs na gefullod on gode
> forþan þe cristendom næs þagyt geond eall cuð
> and seo reþe æhtnyss þagyt næs gestylled. (LS 2. 12–14)

> This thane Philip was not baptized unto God,
> because Christianity was not yet known everywhere,
> and the cruel persecution was not yet stilled. (tr. Skeat, p. 27)

In these three verbal units we see the negation of three moral states, one personal to Philip, but linked to the other two broader, historical states both by the parallel negation and by the "forþan" —because—structure, even though the latter link is not fully logical, especially in application to the second subordinate clause.

Baptism for Aelfric is a turning point in the progress of a human being through distinct stages. Before it one merely occupies time and space; after it one is engaged in moral concerns, and time and space are irrelevant. Baptism seems to me potentially more strongly agentive than martyrdom, though either may be regarded as a happening, and both have the special aspectual feature of being punctual, with contrasting states on either side of the instant of accomplishment. In this they are like "being found" in *Beowulf* (lines 6–7), but unlike that verb, being martyred and being baptized involve the inception of moral stages that have no temporal delineation or limitation. Neither of the moral states, once achieved, can be negated.

The two subordinate clauses employ the anticipatory "þagyt"— "yet," or "still"—which Aelfric uses also to describe Eugenia's condition at line 27b: "heo þagyt hæðen wære"—"she was still a heathen." By virtue of the anticipation imposed by this modifier, the states described—Christianity not yet known, persecution not yet stilled—those states carry an implicit termination and an implicit inception of an opposite state, in each case a morally positive one. That implicit punctual inception of positive states exactly parallels the condition of Philip, who is not baptized—yet. Illogically associated with his negative state is the condition that the cruel persecution continues; more logically associated with it is the condition that Christianity is not everywhere known.

Aelfric next provides biographical material:

His wif wæs gecyged claudia
be þære he gestrynde twægen suna
auitum and særgium and ane dohtor
eugenian þe we embe spræcaþ (LS 2. 15-18)

His wife was named Claudia,
on whom he begat two sons,
Avitus and Sergius, and one daughter,
Eugenia, of whom we now speak. (tr. Skeat, p. 27)

In these lines I sense no particular intensity, nor any of the special characterizing purpose (and patterns) which has gone before; yet the generic, perfective, and durative qualities of "wæs gecyged" at line 15, and in line 16 the inceptive, perfective, agentive qualities of "gestrynde" are consistent with the worldly contexts of paganism of the earlier passages.

At line 18b—"þe we embe spræcaþ"—Aelfric interjects himself as author for the first time, imposing the special time of the poem-author-audience relationship; the indefinite duration and agency of the verb are thus outside the patterns established, but the half-line signals the end of the introductory materials and recalls Eugenia to the foreground in a graceful transitional move.

As the next set of lines opens, Aelfric uses the typical structural signal "þa":

Þa befæste se fæder philippus to lare
þæt heo on woruldwysdome wære getogen
æfter greciscre uðwytegunge and lædenre getingnysse.
Eugenia þa þæt æðele mæden
wel þeah on wisdome and on uðwytegunge.
Þa becom hyre on hand þæs halgan apostles lar
paules þæs mæran ealles manncynnes lareowes.
Þa wearð hyre mod mycclum onbryrd

þuruh þa halgen lare þeah ðe heo þa gyt hæðen wære.
(LS 2. 19–27)

Then her father Philip put her to school
that she might be educated in worldly wisdom
according to the Greek philosophy and Latin eloquence.
Eugenia then, that noble maiden,
well increased in wisdom and in philosophy.
Then came into her hands the holy apostle's doctrine,
[the words of] St. Paul, the famous teacher of all mankind.
Then was her mind greatly aroused
by the sacred doctrine, though she was still a heathen (tr.
    Skeat, p. 27)

In line 19, the first in this section, Philip assumes the commanding role which characterized Commodus earlier—he "put her to school, that she might be educated in worldly wisdom. . . ." Aelfric's respect for classical learning and education shows in the next few lines. Philip acts, as agent of a punctual verb inceptive of a process, and Eugenia submits to that action and process. She does well at her studies, "flourishing" at line 23—"þeah" again having indefinite duration and a minimal sense of agency.

At line 24 Aelfric moves Eugenia into a new stage of development: her studies shift from worldly wisdom to "þæs halgan apostles lar." The verb at line 24a—"becom"—is punctual, inceptive of a state, and nonagentive; indeed it signals a pure happening, since neither Eugenia nor anyone else appears to have any control over the event. Of course a Christian audience does not require explicit reference to the divine agency behind morally significant happenings.

Line 25 seems to modify the punctuality of "becom" in a temporal and eternal mixture parallel to the first line of the work. "Paul, the famous teacher of all mankind" contains a suppressed verb of indefinite duration: his teaching, like the story of Eugenia's life, became available in the past and will continue to be available in the future, just as it became available to Eugenia. Paul as "the famous teacher" has the same quasi-agency as martyr; the real agents are Paul's "lar" and Eugenia's story. Just as Paul's teaching came into Eugenia's hand, so Eugenia's story has come into the hands of Aelfric's readers, since "He who wishes it, may hear concerning the holy maiden Eugenia" at any point in time. In both these features—in the temporally perfective and even punctual moral achievement which becomes perpetually available and in the shifting of agency from the actor to the act, Paul and Eugenia are in perfect contrast to the transient, terminative, punctual, and perfective agency of the pagans, all of whose deeds are dead.

Lines 26 and 27 describe the consequences of Paul's "lar": with the "halgen lare" as agent, Eugenia's mind became "mycclum onbryrd"—greatly aroused. This phrase is almost always a positive sign in Aelfric; it is followed by further study of Christian doctrine, leading to baptism, in a regularly detailed series of stages. In line 27b—"þeah ðe heo þa gyt hæðen wære"—Aelfric defines the "stirred up" stage precisely and recalls the lines on Philip (12–14) where "þagyt" signalled anticipated improvements in moral states. If "wearð . . . onbryd" is punctual, it is also inceptive of a state and agentless. So the section ends with Eugenia in two states: stirred up, but still a heathen.

Eugenia acts in the next section:

> Heo bæd þa hyre fæder þæt heo færen moste
> geond his hames on alexandiscre scyre
> wolde swa cepan þære cristenra lare
> forðan þe heo næfde on ðære byrig nænne
> geleaffulne mann þe hi læran cuþe
> forðan philippus aflygde þa cristenan
> of alexandrian ealle on ær. (LS 2. 28–34)

> Then prayed she her father that she might go
> away from his house in the city of Alexandria;
> she thus desired to seek after the Christians' doctrine,
> because she had no one in that city,
> no believing man who could instruct her,
> seeing that Philip drave away the Christians
> from Alexandria beforehand, all of them. (tr. Skeat, p. 27)

Perhaps it is by way of stressing her still heathen state that Eugenia, in agentive and punctual aspect, prays to her father— and in a modal phrase, prays "that she might go/away from his house in the city of Alexandria. . . ." Certainly the passage stresses her geographic location and the moral condition of that location, as well as her submissive relationship to her father.

Despite these limitations, Eugenia's going is from a place (which is heathen) but to a morally defined goal: "She thus desired to seek after the Christians' doctrine"—which is not located by physical marker at all. The journey thus very neatly defines her condition: being "greatly aroused," she is directed toward a moral goal; while being still a heathen, she is leaving a heathen city.

Explanatory clauses and negatives as a sign of heathen conditions mark lines 31 and 32, as Aelfric elaborates on the defects of spiritual life in Alexandria. Literally read, she is leaving Alexandria to seek Christian doctrine "because she had not in that city not any/believing man who could teach her." Of course the multiplication of negatives has the function of stressing the negation, and modern grammatical logic by which they cancel does not apply. Alexandria is emphatically devoid of Christianity and of the teaching that could fulfill Eugenia's need. Yet another "forðan" clause at line 33 recalls Philip to the scene as the reason: exercising typical agency in punctual manner, inceptive of a negative moral state, he "drave away the Christians"—again, *from* the place, the city, the geographical point in space, in a physical world which, Aelfric is showing us, has of itself no moral interest. Since Eugenia is in this place, and since it is negatively defined, she must move; but since the movement is inspired by a moral state (being "greatly aroused"), it is only quasi-physical in nature, or perhaps physical (and concrete) if seen as movement *from,* and moral and abstract if seen as movement *towards.*

These distinctions apply as Eugenia makes her journey in the lines which follow, and the goal of her journey is described:

Hwæt þa Eugenia ardlice færde
oð þæt heo becom þær ða cristenan sungen
mid mycelre blisse þus mærsigende god.
Omnes dii gentium demonia dominus autem caelos fecit.
Ealle þære hæðenra godas syndon deofla
and dryhten soðlice heofonas geworhte. (LS 2. 35–40)

So then Eugenia quickly journeyed
until she arrived where the Christians were singing
with great joy, thus glorifying God:

Omnes dii gentium demonia ; dominus autem celos fecit :
'All the gods of the heathen are devils,
and verily the Lord created the heavens.' (tr. Skeat, p. 27)

"Hwæt" at the opening of the section may be regarded as a signal
of the real beginning of Eugenia's spiritual story, though that may
place too much weight on it. That she eagerly journeyed would
seem to involve her in agency, in temporal action, and in the same
sort of motion that Philip makes when he is sent from Rome to
Alexandria. But—as stated above—while she moved from Alexandria, she journeyed "until she arrived where the Christians were
singing," a moral *locus* rather than a physical place. Where in the
world these Christians are, we are never told, and by now we
know why: they are "located" spiritually, and their geographic
address is of no interest.

Eugenia's journey ends when she "becom"—the same verb used
at line 24 of the happening by which Paul's lore came into her
hands. If punctual, again it is inceptive of a state which is morally
defined. She arrives at a *locus,* then, which is characterized by two
progressive aspect processes: the Christians were singing and
praising God. Again, the contrast between the punctual commands
and acts of the pagans and the abstract processes of Christians
should be noted. These processes derive from and define the
moral state of the Christians, and that state is further characterized
in the specific song quoted.

Aelfric states the words of the song, first in Latin and then in
Old English. Each of the lines affirms a moral judgment about
states, each announces a generic truth: if "all the gods of the
heathens are devils" contrasts with "the Lord created the heavens"
in that the latter is agentive, perfective, and punctual, this is
essentially a surface distinction, though perhaps it points implicitly
at the distinction between agency at the human level and the
agency of God. Creation, even if punctual, is inceptive of a permanent state. The lines balance in subject and in moral valence, the first
affirming the evil of heathen gods, the second affirming the glory of
the true God. This too serves as a characterizing feature, since,
having arrived for the first time in a Christian *locus,* we are being
shown Christians about their characteristic activities—singing and

praising God, making morally significant discriminations and affirming those choices. Thus to sing and praise the Lord are Christian acts and the song which is sung, viewed as an affirmation and choice, is a moral act appropriate to a moral state.

These first forty lines may suffice as a preliminary sketch of Aelfric's scheme. In that scheme pagans and Christians are distinguished, the former characterized as active, punctual, imperative, nondurative; the latter are virtually nontemporal, all their actions having moral goals and contexts. The distinctions drawn arise from a dichotomous view of acts and states, from a complex range of aspectual features, and from careful variations of agentive features of verbs. The patterns thus arranged serve as a strong but subtle narrative structure, delineating the characters of Christians and pagans and marking out the spiritual values of the narrative.

These patterns emerge under careful linguistic analysis, once we are equipped with a clear understanding of aspectual features. That they should appear in hagiography, especially that written by Aelfric, with his combination of theological and grammatical interests, should not surprise us. Any thoughtful grammarian translating the *acta sanctorum* with homiletic purpose is likely to find himself seriously involved in the meaningful nuances of verbs.

NOTES

1. Roger Fowler, *The Language of Literature* (London, 1971), and ed., *Essays on Style and Language* (London, 1966).
2. Stanley B. Greenfield, "Grammar and Meaning in Poetry," *Publications of the Modern Language Association* 82 (1967): 377–87; *The Interpretation of Old English Poems* (London, 1972), pp. 109–32.
3. There are two exceptions to this statement: George T. Wright, "The Lyric Present: Simple Present Verbs in English Poems," *Publications of the Modern Language Association* 89 (1974): 563–79, discusses an aspectual problem in poetry, but calls it tense; Julian and Zelda Boyd, in an un-

published article, deal with aspect, action, and motion in
Tennyson's poetry.

4. Greenfield, *The Interpretation of Old English Poems,* p. 110.

5. See, for example, William Diver, "The Chronological System
   of the English Verb," *Word* 19 (1963) : 141–81 (which
   attempts to resolve aspect and tense into one system) ;
   Hans Reichenbach, *Elements of Symbolic Logic* (New
   York, 1947), pp. 287ff. ; Richard M. Gale, *The Language
   of Time* (London, 1968) ; Arthur Prior, *Past, Present and
   Future* (Oxford, 1967).

6. R.W. Zandvoort, "Is 'Aspect' an English Verbal Category?" in
   Contributions to English Syntax and Philology, ed. Frank
   Behre, Gothenberg Studies in English 14 (1962), for ex-
   ample ; Zandvoort concludes that "the plain statement
   'Aspect is a conception which does not exist in English
   grammar' may be hard to digest for some linguists who, like
   Mossé, refuse to take the character of aspect in Slavonic
   as an absolute standard." Zandvoort's reasons for taking
   Slavonic aspect, which is morphologically expressed, as an
   "absolute standard" are that he believes early studies of
   English aspect borrowed terminology from Slavonic gram-
   mars and that morphology is the only kind of grammar that
   can be discussed by linguists. The latter position led
   Leonard Bloomfield to assert that

> In English, iteration plays no part in the verb-form: *he
> played tennis every day* (punctual) and *he was playing
> tennis every day* (durative) are like *he played a set of
> tennis* (punctual) and *he was playing a set of tennis*
> (durative).

This appears in Bloomfield's *Language* (New York, 1933),
p. 272. The position, as Bloomfield states it, is technically
correct: "iteration plays no part in the verb-form"—that is,
it plays no *morphological* part. But this qualification is not
always made clear. L.S. Limar, in *Ucenye Zapiski,* 28,
C. 2-ja (Moscow, 1963), pp. 159–74, admits context and
adverbial modification as aspectual systems, then denies any
system of aspect in English:

> In languages where the aspectual differences are not part
> of the very *form* of the verb the decisive influence of

context and, in particular, of adverbs on the aspectual meaning of the given verb is frequently encountered. This is precisely the condition which we find in Old English.
. . . In Old English essentially there was no form for the imperfective aspect, and since there was no imperfective aspect, that is, one of a correlative pair was absent, there obviously could be no system of aspects, since the system is built on correlatives.

The quotation is given in J.W. Richard Lindemann, *Old English Preverbal Ge-: Its meaning* (Charlottesville, Va., 1970). The argument is untenable: iteration is an unpaired aspectual category in all sorts of languages and is not seen thereby as a threat to the existence of aspect systems.

7. For a fuller discussion of literary uses of these aspectual features, see George T. Wright's article cited in note 2.

8. Terminative aspect can be expressed periphrastically, as in "he finished working." But note the mixture of terminative and characterizing aspects in the present tensed verbs in "he begins things but he never finishes them."

9. For philosophical investigations of tense/aspect relations, see Terry Penner, "Verbs and the Identity of Actions—A Philosophical Exercise in the Interpretation of Aristotle," in *Ryle: A Collection of Critical Essays,* ed. Oscar P. Wood and George Pitcher, and Anthony Kenny, *Action, Emotion and Will* (London, 1963), pp. 172ff. For discussions of aspect and voice, see H.V. Velten, "On the Origin of the Categories *Voice* and *Aspect*," *Language* 7 (1939): 229–41, and Emile Benveniste, *Problems in General Linguistics,* trans. Mary Elizabeth Meek, Miami Linguistics Series 8 (Coral Gables, Fla., 1971), pp. 145–215.

10. John Robert Ross, "The Category Squish: Endstation Hauptwort," *Papers from the Eighth Regional Meeting, Chicago Linguistic Society* (Chicago, 1972), p. 316.

11. For a wide range of aspectual categories in both Indo-European and other languages, see Louis H. Gray, *Foundations of Language* (New York, 1939), pp. 203–08, 359, and 400.

12. Julius Zupitza, ed., *Aelfric's Grammatik und Glossar* (Berlin, 1880), p. 9.

13. Ibid., pp. 119–21.

14. Ibid., p. 122.
15. Ibid., p. 211.
16. Ibid., pp. 211–13.
17. Ibid., pp. 213–14.
18. Aristotle, *Metaphysics* 6. Cf. Penner and Kenny, cited in note 9. For stimulating set of theoretical statements on aspects, see Jerzy Kurylowicz, *The Inflectional Categories of Indo-European* (Heidelberg, 1964), pp. 90–135.

RAACHEL JUROVICS ❦ SERMO LUPI &
THE MORAL PURPOSE OF RHETORIC

Because of its style and subject Dorothy Bethurum argues that
the *Sermo ad Anglos,* though the best known of Wulfstan's works,
is in some respects the "least characteristic" of him.[1] But when
the *Sermo* is considered in the light of Wulfstan's lifework as
churchman and lawmaker, the *Sermo* stands, I believe, as his most
characteristic work.[2] Wulfstan was, above all, a man of practical
morality. All of his activities reflected the dominant purpose of
his career, which was the moral regeneration of the English nation.
He believed that such regeneration would heal the political and
social maladies of his people. All his legal codes, those for clergy
and those for laity, as well as many sermons, testify to his intense
concern for "an orderly arrangement of society." [3] To this end he
brought to his episcopal duties enthusiasm and energy both for
conveying the basic teachings of Christian faith and for establishing practical "rules of conduct for canons, for monks, for priests
living in the semi-converted part of the Dane-law, and for all conditions of men." [4]

As catalogued by Bethurum, for example, the list of Wulfstan's
occupations reinforces one's impression of his intensity and devotion in encouraging and enforcing moral regeneration; not only a
reforming homilist and lawmaker, Wulfstan was also a prominent
statesman, canonist, orator, translator, and collector of books,
especially of regulatory works, penitentials, and writings of the
Church Fathers.[5] In seeking to correct the abuses of his days in
accord with his vision of an ordered society, he worked to raise
the levels of learning and morality among the clergy and to provide
clerk and layman alike with livable injunctions formulated in a
closely related body of Anglo-Saxon and Christian law.[6]

In eleventh-century England a near union of church and secular
power permitted able prelates, such as Dunstan and Wulfstan, to
exert considerable influence in affairs of state. Wulfstan's *Institutes of Polity,* a definition of all classes' social duties, is the only

Old English work to deal with the limits of political power and
the interrelationship of church and secular authority.[7] Character-
istically Wulfstan conceived of the civil good as dependent on the
welfare of the church, for he believed that political facts reflected
God's judgment on the nation's moral behavior. Among Wulfstan's
legal formulations are the later codes of Ethelred (*V–X Ethelred*),
which sought to enforce moral regeneration by instituting legal punishments for breaches of Christian ethics, the *Canons of Edgar,*
which provided rules for the secular clergy, and the *Laws of
Edward and Guthrum,* which attempted to establish English
ecclesiastical practice in the Danelaw. Wulfstan's legislative influence continued during the reign of Cnut; he prepared *I–II Cnut,*
which set penalties for various minor infractions previously un-
punished (although known to be disapproved), and the *Northumbrian Priests' Law* (c. 1021–23) was probably drawn up at his
instigation.[8]

This last code, both a priests' law and religious regulations for
the laity, reveals that in Wulfstan's day heathen practices still
competed with Christian practices in the north:

> 48. If, then any man is discovered who henceforth
> carries on any heathen practice, either by sacrifice or divina-
> tion, or practices witchcraft by any means, or worship of
> idols, he is to pay, if he is a king's thane, 10 half-marks,
> half to Christ, half to the king. . . .
>
> 54. If there is on anyone's land a sanctuary round a
> stone or a tree or a well or any such nonsense, he who
> made it is then to pay *lahslit,* half to Christ and half to the
> lord of the estate.

Twice the code stipulates that "we must all love and honour one
God and zealously hold one Christian faith and entirely cast out
every heathen practice" (47, 67).[9] There is no doubt that much
of Wulfstan's characteristic concern for social organization and
for the proper interrelationship of the various ranks derived from
his keen awareness of the social upheavals caused by the Danish
invasion. This disruption was especially pronounced in the north,
where heathen cults initiated in the tenth century by Norse invaders from Ireland had not been subdued to Christian control.

Even earlier than in the *Northumbrian Priests' Law,* which gradu-
ates the fines for heathen practices according to the various social
ranks, Wulfstan refers several times to forbidden activities such as
idola wurðinge. The Latin text of *VI Ethelred* refers to *idolorum
cultores* and *idolatrie,* Napier X (Bethurum X C) includes *ne
ænig man idola weorðie æfre,* and a Latin addition to this text in
mss. C and E mentions *idolatria.*[10] Wulfstan's attacks against the
laxity of marriage practices in his province, both from the pulpit
and in legal writings, were probably provoked by the Danish
reintroduction of such easy divorce settlements as had formerly
been common in parts of England.[11]

The Danish presence posed a clear threat to English Christianity. Wulfstan hoped not only to prevent apostasy among his own
people, but also to Romanize and modernize the English church
and to reform ecclesiastical practices according to the best models.
He expected bishops to undertake an active role in the reformation
of English morals. In his attempts to define ecclesiastical power and
obligations Wulfstan "takes . . . [bishops'] rights for granted
and emphasizes their duties . . . . the section of Polity headed
'Be Ðeod-witan' is devoted to directing bishops to study and teach
diligently, rather than to defending the episcopal position." [12] The
evidence remaining of Wulfstan's own studies reflect his faith in
the ability of moral regeneration to cure social and political ills,
his faith that peace and order will reign when there is no longer
a discrepancy between Christian teaching and individual behavior.
Wulfstan seeks to define the meaning of Christian life and to teach
it to his flock, *7 utan God lufian 7 Godes lagum fylgean,* thereby
repairing wrongs, ending the present sufferings under God's ire,
avoiding eternal damnation, and attaining to heavenly glory.[13]
Wulfstan would have the knowledge of God translated into direct
action.

For all the range of his activities, however, Wulfstan is remem-
bered primarily as a homilist and orator. Wulfstan frequently
insisted on the episcopal responsibility to preach against the sins
of the people. The *Sermo Lupi* is an especially apt example of his
contribution to medieval pulpit oratory, as it shows so clearly the
interrelationship of his sociolegal and religious concerns. Those
catalogues of sins and crimes which make up such a large part of

the *Sermo* (included by Wulfstan as evidence that the English deserved the providential punishment then afflicting them) illustrate those very breaches of faith and loyalty between members of a society that Wulfstan's laws attempted to regulate and reduce. Even more than his law codes, the *Sermo* exhibits Wulfstan's intense reforming impulse: as law sets forth practical rules of conduct, the sermon sets forth the Christian imperative for moral action, the underlying reason for an individual's accepting and following a law enjoined both by state and church.

In framing his imperatives for moral action Wulfstan drew his rhetorical inspiration and tactics from the tradition represented by Cicero, Augustine (especially), Boethius, and the later manuals based on their theories, such as those of Alcuin, Isidore, and Rabanus.[14] This Christian rhetorical tradition applied the devices of eloquence to moral purposes, to the teaching of virtue. In considering the major tenets of the Augustinian rhetorical tradition and Wulfstan's application of them, my evaluation of the *Sermo Lupi* and of its relation to the other homilies of Wulfstan's canon will differ somewhat from Bethurum's. The topicality of the *Sermo* does not provide sufficient grounds to separate it significantly from the rest of the canon, nor do its rhetorical methods violate the decencies of public address, at least as these decorums might be construed by a Christian preacher. The style departs only in degree, not in kind, from Wulfstan's usual practice, while the actual subject does not depart at all from "the central concern of life"—moral regeneration. The details of style, large and small, are those characteristic of his work in general, and the specific topic is a near epitome of his political and religious concerns.

St. Augustine's *De doctrina christiana* defines for the medieval Christian teacher the rules and attitudes of the new, anti-Sophistic rhetoric.[15] Based on Ciceronian principles, this manual emphasizes above all the responsibility of the Christian orator to persuade his listeners to act virtuously. So much more important is content than style that a teacher incapable of eloquence "dicat sapienter, quod non dicit eloquenter, potius quam dicat eloquenter, quod dicit insipienter" (IV.28.61; CCL 32, p. 165).[16] Three styles—subdued, moderate, and grand—serve the three ends of Christian oratory: teaching, pleasing in such a way as to encourage willingness, and

obedience, or action. Augustine does not insist, however, that one
of the three styles be attributed exclusively to one of the three ends,

> ut ad submissum intellegenter, ad temperatum libenter,
> ad grande pertineat oboedienter audiri . . . ut haec
> tria semper intendat et quantum potest agat, etiam cum
> in illorum singulo quoque versatur. (IV.26.56; CCL 32,
> p. 161) [17]

Above all the orator must succeed in persuading his audience to
act on his words:

> Cum vero id docetur, quod agendum est, et ideo docetur
> ut agatur, frustra persuadetur verum esse, quod dicitur,
> frustra placet modus ipse, quo dicitur, si non ita
> dicitur, ut agatur. Oportet igitur eloquentem eccle-
> siasticum, quando suadet aliquid, quod agendum est,
> non solum docere, ut instruat, et delectare, ut teneat,
> verum etiam flectere, ut vincat. (IV.13.29; CCL 32,
> pp. 136–37) [18]

Effective ecclesiastical oratory adjusts itself to the needs and
accomplishments of each specific audience. In preaching, as in
study of Scripture,

> . . . sciamus alia omnibus communiter praecipi, alia
> singulis quibusque generibus personarum, ut non solum
> ad universum statum valetudinis, sed etiam ad suam
> cuiusque membri propriam infirmitatem medicina
> perveniat. (III.17.25; CCL 32, p. 93) [19]

A preacher should never speak so as to force his audience to attempt an interpretation of his words, but rather he should willingly
sacrifice eloquence to clarity in any situation where felicity of
style may obstruct meaning for an unsubtle audience (IV.22.8).
In order to maintain the interest and attention of his audience a
speaker generally needs to vary his style, choosing now one, now
another of the three manners of address (IV.22.51). If, however,
the audience appears reluctant to accept and act upon his words,
the preacher may justifiably heighten his tone throughout, in an
effort to provoke spiritual reform:

. . . cum vero aliquid agendum est et ad eos loquimur,
qui hoc agere debent nec tamen volunt, tunc ea quae
magna sunt, dicenda sunt granditer et ad flectendos animos
congruenter. (IV.19.38; CCL 32, p. 144) [20]

In evaluating the *Sermo Lupi* one must keep in mind St. Augustine's definition of this grand persuasive style, for it emphasizes that the subject-matter of a sermon determines its style and implicitly reiterates the primary importance of content in Christian rhetoric:

Grande autem dicendi genus hoc maxime distat ab isto
genere temperato, quod non tam verborum ornatibus
comptum est, quam violentum animi affectibus. Nam
capit etiam illa ornamenta paene omnia, sed ea si
non habuerit, non requirit. Fertur quippe impetu
suo et elocutionis pulchritudinem, si occurrerit,
vi rerum rapit, non cura decoris adsumit. Satis
enim est ei propter quod agitur, ut verba congruentia,
non oris eligantur industria, sed pectoris sequantur
ardorem. (IV.20.42; CCL 32, pp. 148–49) [21]

In all cases Augustine would have content establish style, and in all cases he would have eloquence, in any of the three styles, serve the moral end of persuasion. In actual practice he makes little distinction between the three, for they do not function separately, but rather work in concert, and at a given moment any one of them may simultaneously instruct, delight, and persuade, as in the case of the grand style:

Iam vero ubi movere et flectere grandi genere opus est
auditorem (quod tunc est opus, quando et veraciter dici
et suaviter confitetur et tamen non vult facere, quod
dicitur), dicendum est procul dubio granditer. Sed quis
movetur, si nescit, quod dicitur? aut quis tenetur, ut
audiat, si non delectatur? Unde et in isto genere, ubi
ad oboedientiam cor durum dictionis granditate flectendum
est, nisi et intellegenter et libenter qui dici, audiatur,
non potest oboedienter audiri. (IV.26.58; CCL 32
p. 163) [22]

In sum, Christian rhetoric aims at inducing virtuous action and at provoking moral regeneration. It adjusts its style and tone to the immediate needs and abilities of its audience and allows the subject to determine form rather than delighting in displays of stylistic accomplishment for their own sake. Since the details of style derive from the specific subject, this subject is itself the arbiter of the decorum of public address. A preacher must use whatever rhetorical means he can in order to persuade his listeners to live in accord with Christian moral teaching.

Wulfstan's application of Augustinian-inspired rhetoric appears in both the larger structural characteristics and smaller verbal details of his sermons and homilies. All aspects of his style contribute to the end of convincing his audience to act rightly, as the following consideration of the *Sermo Lupi* will illustrate. So little does the *Sermo* differ from the rhetorical patterns characteristic of Wulfstan's work that it serves admirably as representative of his canon. His sermons, prepared for public delivery, abound in features of style that contribute to clarity and show a conscious and deliberate adjustment of style to particular purposes and occasions in their use of all three manners of address suggested by Augustine.[23] As Augustine notes, some occasions demand a consistently heightened manner (p. 145). At least three of Wulfstan's works other than the *Sermo* are composed almost entirely in an impassioned style, Homilies III, V, XXI. Conspicuously absent from Wulfstan's works are most *figurae sententiarum,* such as metaphor and simile, as well as analogical interpretations of Scripture. This absence is a clear indication of his careful adjustment of style to his audience:

> This rejection of poetic imagery, of the subtle play of thought over an idea, enriching but often confusing it, is only what is to be expected from a practical moralist, whose gifts, by no means slight, were turned to forceful and clear preaching to a not very subtle audience whose capacities for abstruse thought he did not overestimate.[24]

As noted above, conditions in York during Wulfstan's episcopate demanded fundamental Christian moral teaching rather than generalized philosophical or religious speculation. Christianity in the north held in those days a most precarious supremacy.

Among the small, verbal details of style that reinforce the com-
prehensibility and persuasiveness of those works Wulfstan composed for oral presentation are: rephrasing, as with an explanatory
þæt is . . . , repetition, alliteration, assonance, rhyme, the use of
reiterated intensives and tags, and the joining of nouns into pairs,
often linked by alliteration. Larger verbal or structural units which
serve the same rhetorical aims of clarity and persuasion include
sentence and word parallelism, rhetorical questions, a reflective
pause in the latter part of a sermon to consider an ethical or
religious truth. Significantly for the *Sermo Lupi,* which would
otherwise seem inexplicably imbalanced because of the preponderance of criticism over positive moral injunction,

> the conclusion of Wulfstan's sermons varies in length from
> a sentence to several paragraphs, but it nearly always takes
> the same form, *Uton don swa us micel þearf is,* followed by a
> short recapitulation of the theme of the sermon, with the
> promise of eternal bliss to the faithful.[25]

Wulfstan's *sermones communes* share a particular structure: all
begin with introductory general admonitions, establish their specific
subject, and then develop it through divisions dictated by the
chosen material.[26]

Throughout the *Sermo Lupi* these large and small stylistic details promote a consistent and coherent rhetorical strategy. Nearly
all of Wulfstan's characteristic devices appear in order to reinforce his message and to urge his audience (however dull or
reluctant) to renounce its sins and regain God's blessings for
England. A thematic emphasis on the knowledge both of guilt and
of its consequences runs through the sermon, which falls into a pattern of alternating cause and effect to explain the nation's trials.
In its overall arrangements it conforms to the standard outline of
the *sermones communes.* It opens with a general admonition to understand that worldly conditions deteriorate as the Apocalypse approaches:

> Leofan men, gecnawað þæt soð is: ðeos worold is on
> ofste, 7 hit nealaecð þam ende, 7 þy hit is on worolde
> aa swa leng swa wyrse, 7 swa hit sceal nyde for folces

synnan ær Antecristes tocyme yfelian swyþe, 7 huru
hit wyrð þænne egeslic 7 grimlic wide on worolde.
(4–8)

The specific topic (8–21), so closely related to this eschatological
consideration, arises out of Wulfstan's belief that the English sufferings represent deliberate punishment for their sins, especially for
sins of social and religious faithlessness:

> Understandað eac georne þæt deofol þas þeode nu fela
> geara dwelode to swyþe, 7 þæt lytle getreowþa wæran
> mid mannum, þeah hy wel spæcan, 7 unrihta to fela
> ricsode on lande. . . . (8–11)
> 7 we eac forþam habbað fela byrsta 7 bysmara gebiden,
> 7, gif we ænige bote gebidan scylan, þonne mote we
> þæs to Gode ernian bet þonne we ær þysan dydan.
> Forþam mid miclan earnungan we geearnedan þa yrmða
> þe us on sittað, 7 mid swyþe micelan earnungan we
> þa bote motan æt Gode geræcan, gif hit sceal heonan
> forð godiende weorðan. (15–21)

There is a certain tension between the introductory admonition and
the specific lesson. Wulfstan develops this tension: although a
general decline inevitably accompanies the approach of Antichrist
and the end of days, his listeners can improve their worsening
physical and political situation (as well as gain eternal spiritual salvation) by earning worldly rewards from God. Wulfstan does not
preach apocalypse, although he does place contemporary events
into an ultimately apocalyptic context; indeed, he uses this foremost
example of the operation of God's judgment in the world as frame
and as evidence that God's providence at that very moment justly
afflicts the English.[27]

As transition to the main body of the sermon (21–36), Wulfstan
reiterates that great wrong requires great remedy, in this case the
eager and correct fulfillment of God's laws and appropriate payment
of God's dues for the support of the church. He reinforces the
general exhortation with a specific comparison of the English failure to support their church and to protect its servants with the
Danes' scrupulous attendance to their heathen religious sites and

priests. In so doing Wulfstan blames the English for lacking even so
much religious devotion as the misguided pagan invaders, much as
the Apostle Paul blames Israel in his Epistle to the Romans:

> What shall we say then? That the Gentiles, which followed
> not after righteousness, have attained to righteousness, even
> the righteousness which is of faith.
>
> But Israel, which followed after the law of righteousness,
> hath not attained to the law of righteousness.
>
> Wherefore? Because they sought it not by faith, but as it
> were by the works of the law. For they stumbled at that
> stumbling stone (Romans 9:30–32).[28]

By no means, however, does this comparison imply sympathy for
the Danes; the *Sermo Lupi* amply documents the role these invaders played in scourging and afflicting the English. If anything
they represent an actual, historical embodiment of God's ire.

By extensive example the body of the sermon elaborates on the
main topic of providential retribution for sin with frequent emphasis on the audience's knowledge of sin and on Wulfstan's conviction that the only remedy rests in appeasing God's anger by
"doing what is needful." This portion of the sermon, as in all the
other *sermons communes,* divides into sections dictated by its subject, in this case into alternating enumerations of the causes for
God's anger and the visible manifestations of His judgment. Perhaps because Wulfstan wished to impress his listeners with the extent of their provocation of the Lord, he speaks more fully of the
sins than of the sufferings which they have earned for the nation. In
spite of this imbalance, through its larger structural pattern the sermon gives even now a vivid impression of the chaotic social conditions in the north during the years of Viking raids and devastation. Lines 37–52 reiterate the need for a remedy and describe the
decline of public law, the desecration of churches, and various sorts
of injustice involving the deprivation of individual rights. For
these things, all indications that God's law is despised, the people
in common suffer frequent disgraces from which only God can save
them. The next section (53–60) asserts that clearly the English
have done more evil than good, and therefore nothing has prospered
for them for a long time. Providence has visited on them multiple

disasters, among them war, pestilence, famine, oppressive taxes, storms, and crop failure. Lines 60–101 enumerate at length varieties of injustice and personal disloyalty. Wulfstan seems to me most dismayed by this sort of crime, by the failures of faith between men that have allowed them to betray their kinsmen, their kings, their fellow Christians. Broken vows and perjured oaths have only increased God's ire. The following passage (102–32) opens and closes with rhetorical questions, the first emphasizing the weight of punishment for sin and the second underscoring the fact that such punishment represents undeniable proof of God's dissatisfaction:

> 7 la, hu mæg mare scamu þurh Godes yrre mannum gelimpan
> þonne us deð gelome for agenum gewyrhtum? . . .
> 7 la, hwæt is ænig oðer on eallum þam gelimpum butan
> Godes yrre ofer þas þeode swutol 7 gesæne?

Many of the intervening illustrations of shames endured by the English people appear to be references to notorious incidents with which Wulfstan expected his audience to be familiar, for example, the routing of Christian bands by only two or three Vikings, "to the public shame of us all," or the enslaving of a thane by his former thrall, "through God's anger."

Lines 133–83 turn again to enumerating the causes for punishment, the ways in which the English have earned their sufferings. Evil days are no wonder, because "we witan ful georne þæt nu fela geara mænn na ne rohtan foroft hwæt hy worhtan wordes oððe dæde" (133–35). A staggering list of specific crimes follows, among them murder, betrayal, the selling of men into slavery, heathen vices, sexual crimes, perjuries, nonobservance of church responsibilities, apostasy, scoffing at God's laws. Men now despise good deeds and are shamed by them, while evildoers receive praise:

> hy scamað þæt hy betan heora misdæda swa swa bec tæcan,
> gelice þam dwæsan þe for heora prytan lewe nellað beorgan
> ær hy na ne magan, þeh hy eal willan". (163–65)

Lines 166–83 reiterate the variety and countless number of evil deeds and crimes, the ease with which any man could call them to mind, the reluctance to undertake a remedy, and finally Wulfstan calls on the individual listener to consider his own deeds and ultimate fate, urges each one to do what is necessary, "þe læs we ætgædere ealle forweorðan" (182–83). A short historical parallel (184–94) introduces the concluding exhortation, as Wulfstan repeats the citation from Gildas that Alcuin had used to point out the similarly providential nature of the Anglo-Saxon conquest of the native Britons and the contemporary Viking raids on England.[29] In consequence of the Britons' sins, an enraged God allowed the English to win the country and destroy the inhabitants. The conclusion proper (195–211) draws the obvious moral:

> Ac wutan don swa us þearf is, warnian us be swilcan; 7
> soð is þæt ic secge, wyrsan dæda we witan mid Englum
> þonne we mid Bryttan ahwar gehyrdan; 7 þy us is þearf
> micel þæt we us beþencan 7 wið God sylfne þingian
> georne. (195–99)

Wulfstan speaks in the first person plural throughout this final section, joining all of the audience to himself in his plea that all do as is needful, turn to the right, at least somewhat abandon evil, keep faith with one another, and anticipate the great judgment, so that *we* may save ourselves from hellfire and enjoy the glory "þe God hæfð gegearwod þam þe his willan on worolde gewyrcað" (210–11).

Several of the larger verbal and structural devices characteristic of Wulfstan's prose enhance the clarity and persuasiveness of the *Sermo Lupi*. Wulfstan reinforces his concluding plea for all listeners to turn to the right and to forsake sin by repeating over and over the exhortation "utan don" (or a parallel phrase) in the last forty lines: "utan don swa us neod is" (181), "Ac wutan don swa us þearf is" (195), "7 utan don swa us þearf is" (199), "7 utan God lufian" (201), "7 utan word 7 weorc rihtlice fadian" (204–05), "7 utan gelome understandan" (207). Examples of word parallelism (the repetition of the same or a similar word or short phrase) occur frequently. In the passage comparing Christian Englishmen to heathen Danes, for instance, the reiteration of "inne . . . ute" serves to underscore the seriousness of the English failing:

> 7 ne dear man gewanian on hæþenum þeodum inne ne ute
> ænig þæra þinga þe gedwolgodan broht bið 7 to lacum

betæht bi∂; 7 we habba∂ Godes hus inne 7 ute clæne berypte.
(28–31)

Wulfstan achieves a similar effect in the first part of this same comparison by twice employing the verb "forhealdan" (26, 28). To promote the theme of his listeners' certain knowledge of guilt and its consequences Wulfstan emphasizes throughout the sermon the truth and obviousness of his statements with words and phrases such as "gecnawa∂ þæt so∂ is" (4), "understanda∂" (8), "we witan ful georne" (21), "gecnawe se þe cunne" (50–51), "þeh man swa ne wene" (51–52), "understande se þe wille" (97), "swa hit þincan mæg" (166).[30] Should anyone fail to believe that God in his anger has chosen to punish England, the failure lies in his own will (e.g., 97), for "so∂ is þæt ic secge" (195–96). At least twice in this sermon Wulfstan employs a particular pair of synonyms to support the thematic emphasis on the truth of his matter, "swutal 7 gesæne" (53, 132).

Wulfstan insists on the fact of God's anger (101–03, 109, 114, 121, 123, 130–32). Two rhetorical questions frame illustrations of the disgraces suffered by the English in order to enforce this very point (102–03, 130–32). Sentences based on structural parallels also serve to increase the emotional impact of Wulfstan's words, so that he may move as well as teach (e.g., 71–74 "her syn . . . her syn," 188–94 "þurh . . . þurh . . . þurh . . ." etc.).

The *Sermo Lupi* contains those smaller details of style typical of Wulfstan's work, and these devices, as well as the large structural ones, contribute to the total effectiveness of the sermon. Long accumulations of nouns in lists of crimes or punishments create a clear sense of both the weight of sin and the weight of suffering (167–73, 137–52, 53–60). Nearly all the intensives and tags favored by Wulfstan appear: "mid ealle" (188), "ealles to swy∂e" (39, 155), "georne" (9, 12, 21, 25, 94, 134, 199, 201, 202, 205, 209), "ealles to wide" (14), "ealles to gelome" (28, 66, 156), "mid rihte" (25), "oft 7 gelome" (112–12, 146). Alliteration, assonance, and rhyme are prominent in the *Sermo Lupi* as elsewhere in Wulfstan's canon, as in lists or noun-pairs linked by these devices of sound, for example, 55–58, 137–46, 167–73.

In its style and expression the *Sermo* stands well within the bounds of Wulfstan's characteristic mannerisms, while it also ex-emplifies the archbishop's commitment to the moral purposes of rhetoric. As St. Augustine prescribes, his subject determines his method; in the case of the *Sermo,* the gravity of the subject has determined his choice of the various stylistic details, large and small. All of these details, structural and verbal, contribute to the end of convincing Wulfstan's listeners both of the fact of providential judgment and of the necessity to act virtuously. For a preacher, subject matter is all: eloquence cannot redeem the emptiness of speech that does not embody Christian truth.

The specific content of the *Sermo* epitomizes Wulfstan's major concern, moral regeneration, and expresses his understanding of the way in which Christian eschatology impinges upon daily existence. As Bethurum observes, Wulfstan's sermon, in its treatment of sin and reform, expresses an "ideal of conduct against which he indicts the English of his day." The *Sermo* dwells on the sorts of abuses against which Wulfstan labored as legislator and inveighed as preacher—lapses of faith between men, apostasy, desecration of churches, indifference or hostility toward Christianity and its priests. These crimes, violations of interdependent secular and ecclesiastical prohibitions, provoke direct punishment by God. Belief in the manifest operation of divine providence in the world of men was of course typical of Wulfstan's age. Although many of Wulf-stan's writings reflect this conviction that national calamities repre-sent divine retribution, the *Sermo* is his best, fullest exposition of the close relationship between Christian eschatology and human action.[31] Indeed, sensitivity to this relationship underlies Wulfstan's efforts as lawmaker and preacher, for it is this very fact of present and future judgment according to divine standards that requires men to live well and virtuously.

Placing too much emphasis on the *Sermo*'s unique use of realistic topical detail clouds the more important similarities between this sermon and the others in Wulfstan's canon. In its large structural patterns, its various stylistic details, its eschatological theme and ending, above all its subject matter, the *Sermo* exhibits most of those elements characteristic of Wulfstan's rhetorical manner. Most of the sources of this sermon, moreover, may be found within the Wulfstan canon:

To a fair amount of material from Ethelred's codes Wulfstan added an introductory passage made up of phrases from his eschatological sermons, especially XIII, and this homily supplied also his passage of the decay of kinship and some isolated phrases elsewhere. There is also a general similarity between the list of calamities in the *Sermo ad Anglos* and that in XXVIII, a free translation and expansion of Leviticus XXVI.[32]

Thus only the topical references are untypical of his style, and even these do not detract from the consistent purposes of Wufstan's work, namely, to teach virute and to motivate its pursuit. These topical allusions, especially the ones which seem to refer to some specific notorious events, contribute to the Christian rhetorical ends of this sermon. They support the thematic emphasis on the undeniable truth of Wulfstan's accusations by destroying the excuse of ignorance: no one could deny the notoriety and authority of such examples as the betrayal of Edward (78–79) or the exile of Ethelred (79–80), and several other examples seem, even today, to carry the same weight (e.g., 93–96, 116–21, 123–26). However impassioned, the *Sermo Lupi ad Anglos* exemplifies the controlled application of rhetorical skill to the moral ends of Christian faith, the translation of emotional ardor into Christian persuasion.

NOTES

1. Dorothy Bethurum [Loomis], ed., *The Homilies of Wulfstan* (Oxford 1957), pp. 355, 356.
2. Dorothy Whitelock, "Archbishop Wulfstan, Homilist and Statesman," *Transactions of the Royal Historical Society* s. 4, 24 (1942) : 43n.
3. Dorothy Whitelock, ed., *Sermo Lupi ad Anglos,* 4th ed. (London, 1942), p. 24 (citing Bethurum).
4. Bethurum, *Homilies of Wulfstan,* p. 70.
5. Ibid., pp. 61, 69; Whitelock, *Sermo,* p. 31.
6. R.R. Darlington, "Ecclesiastical Reform in the later Old English

Period," *English Historical Review* 51 (1936): 392; Whitelock, "Archbishop Wulfstan," p. 42.

7. Bethurum, *Homilies of Wulfstan,* p. 76.

8. Ibid., p. 78; Whitelock, "Archbishop Wulfstan," 40–41; D.
Whitelock, ed., *English Historical Documents,* v. I (London, 1953), pp. 434–435.

9. Whitelock, *English Historical Documents,* pp. 434–39.

10. Dorothy Whitelock, "Wulfstan at York," in *Franciplegius:
Medieval and Linguistic Studies in Honor of Francis Pea-
body Magoun, Jr.,* ed. Jess B. Bessinger, Jr., and Robert P.
Creed (New York, 1965), p. 225.

11. Dorothy Whitelock, *The Beginnings of English Society* (Baltimore, 1952), p. 150.

12. Bethurum, *Homilies of Wulfstan,* p. 81.

13. Ibid., p. 162; Whitelock, *Sermo,* lines 201–202. All following
citations from the Sermo will indicate line numbers in
parentheses.

14. Bethurum, *Homilies of Wulfstan,* pp. 87–89.

15. Augustine, *De doctrina christiana* CCL 32 (Turnholti, 1962),
ed. J. Martin. The translation I cite is St. Augustine, *On
Christian Doctrine,* tr. D.W. Robertson, Jr. (New York,
1958).

16. Tr. Robertson, p. 166: "should say wisely what he cannot say
eloquently rather than say eloquently what he says
foolishly."

17. Tr. Robertson, p. 162: "so that the subdued style pertains to
understanding, the moderate style to willingness, and the
grand style to obedience; rather, . . . that the orator always
attends to all three and fulfills them all as much as he can,
even when he is using a single style."

18. Tr. Robertson, p. 138: "But when that which is taught must be
put into practice and is taught for that reason, the truth of
what is said is acknowledged in vain and the eloquence of
the discourse pleases in vain unless that which is learned is
implemented in action. It is necessary therefore for the
ecclesiastical orator, when he urges that something be done,
not only to teach that he may instruct and to please that he

may hold attention, but also to persuade that he may be victorious."

19. Tr. Robertson, p. 94: "some things are taught for everyone in general; others are directed toward particular classes of people, in order that the medicine of instruction may be applicable not only to the general state of health but also to the special infirmities of each member. For what cannot be elevated to a higher class must be cared for in its own class."

20. Tr. Robertson, p. 145: "But when something is to be done and he is speaking to those who ought to do it but do not wish to do it, then those great things should be spoken in the grand manner in a way appropriate to the persuasion of their minds."

21. Tr. Robertson, p. 150; "The grand style differs from the moderate style not so much in that it is adorned with verbal ornaments but in that it is forceful with emotions of the spirit. Although it uses almost all of the ornaments, it does not seek them if it does not need them. It is carried along by its own impetus, and if the beauties of eloquence occur they are caught up by the force of the things discussed and not deliberately assumed for decoration. It is enough for the matter being discussed that the appropriateness of the words be determined by the arbor of the heart rather than by careful choice."

22. Tr. Robertson, p. 164: "Now when it is necessary to move and bend the listener by means of the grand style (which is necessary when he will confess that the speech is true and agreeable, but will not do what it says should be done), one must undoubtedly speak grandly. But who is moved if he does not know what is being said? Or who is held attentive that he may hear if he is not delighted? Whence also in this style, where the hard heart is to be bent to obedience through the grandness of the diction, if what is heard is not heard intelligently and willingly, it cannot be heard obediently."

23. My analysis is indebted to the works of Bethurum (*Homilies,* especially pp. 28–29, 87–98) and Whitelock ("Archbishop Wulfstan," *Sermo*), and to a lesser degree to those of Green-

field (*Critical History*) and Funke ("Some Remarks on Wulfstan's Prose Rhythm," *English Studies* 43 (1962) : 311–318). See also A. McIntosh, "Wulfstan's Prose," *Proceedings of the British Academy* 35 (1949) : 109–142, concerning Wulfstan's characteristic rhythmic patterns.

24. Bethurum, *Homilies of Wulfstan,* pp. 91–92.
25. Ibid., p. 96.
26. Ibid., p. 97.
27. Dorothy Bethurum comments in her edition on the reluctance of Wulfstan's ecclesiastical contemporaries to presume to predict the exact date of the expected apocalypse. For Wulfstan, deciding on a precise prediction of this sort would be less important than convincing his listeners of their immediate and ultimate accountability to God. See pp. 278–82.
28. Similarly, Romans 10:20–21, which refers back to Isaiah 65:1.
29. Whitelock, "Archbiship Wulfstan," p. 43.
30. See also 37, 53, 86, 101, 110, 126–27, 136.
31. Dorothy Whitelock points out that divine retribution is the theme of an ordiance written by Wulfstan as well as a number of his homilies. See Whitelock, "Archbiship Wulfstan," p. 41.
32. Whitelock, *Sermo,* p. 17.

MARCIA A. DALBEY ❦ THEMES & TECHNIQUES IN THE BLICKLING LENTEN HOMILIES

Although it is probably impossible at this point to ascertain fully the nature and purpose of the Blickling homiliary, a careful reading of the extant homilies suggests that the unknown compiler chose his sermons with some care and a reasonably consistent philosophy.[1] An analysis of the Lenten homilies, the most extensive group for a single season in the manuscript, can reveal a great deal about the nature of the homiliarist's beliefs, his overall plan, his parenetic and didactic intent, even his "literary" judgment. For reasons unknown, the homilies for the second and fourth Sundays in Lent do not occur in the collection, but it is possible, as Gatch points out, that the homiliary was designed only for major occasions of the Church year.[2] The homilist has included homilies for the most important Sundays in Lent, namely, the first and third Sundays, Passion Sunday, and Palm Sunday, and he is likely to have found these adequate for his purposes.

In these four homilies, as in the collection as a whole, the emphasis is almost entirely tropological. The preachers are concerned with the immediate practical problem of convincing their hearers to live moral lives in this world. The considerable eschatological emphasis in the homilies is a means of exhortation and of making vivid and immediate to the audience the rewards for virtue and the punishments for inquity. The homilists seem uninterested or unable to explain points of dogma, to speculate on various Christian mysteries, and to develop intricate exegetical arguments. As one might expect, therefore, the hortatory sermons are considerably more effective than the exegetical ones. The anonymous homilists often exhibit a good deal of skill in their hortatory passages, whereas their attempts at exegesis, even when they are following such authorities as Gregory, are often disjointed and unclear.

The homily for the first Sunday in Lent is, in form at least, an exegetical explanation of the Gospel for the Sunday, Matthew 4:11, the story of Christ's temptations in the wilderness. In both subject and form it is an appropriate introduction to the season, for it stresses the need for repentance and the constant need to struggle against the devil's temptations, while offering Christ's actions in the Gospel account as a source of inspiration to mankind. The next two homilies, those for the third and fifth Sundays in Lent, are mainly parenetic, in that they exhort the congregation to continue that struggle against the devil and, by means of fasting, prayer, almsdeeds and other virtuous acts, to renew constantly their commitment to Christian virtue. The third Sunday in Lent is a time for renewing one's awareness of the devil's power and for strengthening the spiritual struggle against an implacable enemy.[3] Hence it is appropriate that the homily for this Sunday urges all Christians to perform the almsdeeds, which are, along with fasting and prayer, the chief means of combating the devil, and that it especially warns the bishops and priests, the leaders of the church, of the dire consequences of corruption.

The homily for Passion Sunday is even more urgently hortatory, for it dwells primarily on those subtle, insidious sins which are not easily discerned. Virtually all the sins discussed in this homily are sins of deception in one form or another, sins which are especially dangerous because the deceiver often fools himself as well as his victims. Some are common sins of omission, namely, the almost universal failure to live up to good intentions. Other are sins of commission, as in the case of a man who wilfully deceives his neighbor or a judge who greedily betrays his calling. It seems as if the homilist is urgently and consistently preparing his audience for the coming of Easter, first by offering them Christ's example as a means of resisting temptation, next by reminding them of their obligations to fight sin by good works, and then by making them urgently aware of those invidious sins which can destroy them.

Although the two hortatory homilies make no direct reference to the gospels for the Sundays to which they are assigned, they work incrementally to prepare the congregation for the climax of the Lenten season. Indeed all of the sermons may derive some of their monitory intensity at least indirectly from the belief that the

Last Judgment would be accomplished at the time of Easter. The Quadragesima I homily begins its textual explanation with these words: "Men þa leofestan . . . halige fæderas & godes folces lareowas . . . sweotollice cyþdon þæt se egeslica domes dæg cymeþ on þa tide þe Godes sunu on rode galgan þrowode." [4] The idea returns with greater emphasis in the Easter homily, where it is discussed extensively in the opening passage and developed dramatically in the homily itself, which combines a vivid account of the harrowing of hell with a lively description of the signs preceding the Last Judgment.[5]

The Palm Sunday homily does not, however, continue this hortatory emphasis, but instead returns to the exegetical mode as the homilist attempts to recount for his audience the major events of Holy Week, as if trying to prepare them intellectually as well as emotionally for Easter. Combining the Gospels for Palm Sunday and Monday of Holy Week, the homilist creates a continuous narrative of the events leading up to Christ's entry into Jerusalem and His eviction of the money changers from the temple. But while its form and its treatment of the story are more strictly exegetical than those of the other homilies, its tropological emphasis and its tone are entirely consistent with the others.

In general the Blickling exegetical homilies utilize the technique of "continuous gloss" developed by the Fathers. The Quinquagesima homily, a rather literal translation of a homily of Gregory, is most successful; the Quadragesima I homily, which departs considerably in style and form from its partial source, Gregory's *Homilia XVI in Evangelia* (PL 76, 1134–38), is somewhat less so.

The Blickling homilist's major concern early in the homily is to accentuate the greatness of Christ's power and glory and the importance of the deeds He performed for mankind. At the beginning he stresses the great mercy and love shown by Christ's action. By taking on our weak nature, Christ the Almighty, Who was in the likeness of God, and coeternal with God, especially favored man over all the other animals:

Us is þonne mid mycelre gemynde to geþencenne þæt se
Ælmihtiga, se þe wæs on Godes hiwe, God Fæder efnece,

onfeng þæt hiw ure tyddran gecynde. Geþencean we eac, gif
oþer nyten wære to haligienne, and geteod to þon ecan life, þonne
onfenge he heora hiwe, ac he wolde urum hiwe onfon, swa he
us ælces godes bysene onstealde. Forþon eal swa hwæt swa
we to gode doþ on mildheortnesse, oþþe eadmodnesse, oþþe
on elne gastlices mægenes, oþþe on gefylnesse Godes beboda,
oþþe on þæm welme þære soþan lufan Godes and manna—ealle
þas god cumaþ of þæm aesprenge Godes mildheortnesse,
and beoð atogen of þæm mægen þære Halgan þrynesse.
(BH, p. 29)

By dwelling on Christ's great majesty, by stressing the magnitude
of His favor to man, and by presenting the long list of human motives whose goodness springs from God, a list made to seem even
more extensive by its carefully parallel phrases and by the final summation "eall þæs god. . . ," the homilist prepares his audience for the
actions they must perform in order to follow Christ's example. The
simplicity of the idea that Christ could have assumed another form,
had He favored a different species, is an effective way of proving
man's privileged status. The hearer is made aware both of his great
good fortune and of the vast distance between his humanity and
Christ's divinity.

In the next section, which is his central exposition, the homilist
tells us why Christ came into the desert and also attempts to explain the threefold nature of his temptation.[6] The passage closes
with a discussion of the devil's lies and his audacity in tempting
Christ, the son of God *se Ælmihtiga from þon Ælmihtigan, and se
Eca from þon Ecan.* Again, the homilist's main purpose throughout
this passage is to accentuate the greatness of Christ and the importance of the deeds He performed for mankind. Finally, to close
this section, the homilist makes explicit the ultimate purpose of his
preceding discussion:

forþon ealra þara gifa þe he middangearde forgeaf þurh his
tocyme, nis nænig mare mægen, ne þisse menniscan tydernesse
nyttre, þonne he þone awyrgdan gast oferswiþe, and þone
wælhreowan feond þisse menniscan gecynd; forðon
hine mæg nu ælc man oferswiþan, and he nænig mehte wið us

nafaþ buton hwylc man þurh ða unanrædnesse his modes him
wiþstandan nelle. Þurh Cristes sige ealle halige wæron gefreol-
sode, þa þe him þeowiaþ on rihtwisnesse and on halignesse;
swa þonne beoþ þa synfullan genyþerade mid heora ordfruman,
swa he genyþerad wearþ. (BH, pp. 31–33)

By overcoming temptations, then, Christ gives us the strength to do
likewise. He is the leader of the Christian army of which we are a
part. By meeting and defeating the devil, He leads us to follow His
example. Structurally the homily offers a pattern of straightforward
exegetical analysis, with a presentation of the scriptural passage and
the explication of each section of that passage. This follows closely
the method of Gregory's homily. Unlike Gregory, however, the
Blickling homilist is not concerned with exegesis or with developing, for example, the typological relationship between Adam's fall
and Christ's victory. His intention is more simply tropological, his
application straightforward. Christ fasted; therefore we must fast.
Christ was patient; we must be also.

When he does try to deal explicitly with exegetical material,
this homilist is not entirely successful. Shortly before his final section, the homilist attempts to explain the meaning of the forty days
of Lent. Gregory's analysis, upon which the Blickling version apparently is based, is typically detailed, coherent, and clear.[7] He
brings together the major patterns of Christian history. His analysis
of the number forty, for example, shows the completion of the Old
Testament in the New and explains how all men have their place in
the divine plan. The Blickling homilist does not, however, make
any connections between the Old and New Testaments. He omits
necessary logical connections and fails to suggest appropriate patterns.[8] Such omissions are perhaps understandable if one keeps in
mind the difference between Gregory's intent and that of the
Blickling homilist. The numerological analysis is an important,
even climactic, point of Gregory's exegetical explanation, while the
Blickling homilist is far more concerned to sway his audience to
good behavior through concrete example and emotional appeal.

The rest of his homily deals with an explanation of right conduct
as it is manifested especially in the Lenten season. In the tone of

rather gentle persuasion frequently encountered in the Blickling
homilies, the preacher exhorts his hearers to purge themselves of
their sins:

> þonne sceolon we nu for þon dæghwamlicum synnum on
> þas tid georne clænsian, mid fæstenne, and mid halgum
> wæccum, & mid ælmessum; swa we sceolon eac ure heortan
> gefyllan mid þære swetnesse godcundra beboda, þæt on
> us ne sy gemeted nænigu stow æmetig gastlicra mægena,
> þæt þær mæge yfelu uncyst on eardian. Ne magon we
> buton þæm medmyclum synnum beon, ah we sceolan on
> þas tid þas feawan dagas on forhæfdnesse lifgean, urne
> lichoman and ure heortan clænsian from yflum geþohtum
> þæs þe we magon; forðon seo blis and seo ofer-
> fyll þæs lichoman getyhþ þone mon to synnum, and seo
> forhæfdnes hine geclænsaþ and gelædeþ to forgifnesse.
> Ne gelyfe þæs nænig mon þæt him ne genihtsumige þæt
> fæsten to ecere hælo, buton he mid oþrum godum hit
> geece; and se þe wille Drihtne bringan gecweme lac
> fæsten, þonne sceal he þæt mid ælmessan and mid mild-
> heortum weorcum fullian. . . . (BH, p. 37)

The opening sentence of this quotation provides the key to the
following exhortation and summarizes the parenetic point of the
entire homily. Through these three acts men can purify both their
bodies and their minds and prepare themselves throughout the
Lenten season for the miracle of salvation prefigured by the death
and resurrection of Christ. The preacher realistically acknowledges
that men cannot achieve perfection; nevertheless each man must do
his best to perform both the private and the public acts of expia-
tion. The rest of this final peroration, while presented in the usual
hortatory imperative, is nevertheless at least as didactic as it is
hortatory. The preacher has until now stressed primarily the
private acts of resisting temptation; he now adds and explains the
importance of almsgiving and other works of mercy. With the
love of God must come love of neighbor, and the acts of love
must come freely and joyfully. His final peroration continues this
emphasis, for the preacher constantly reiterates the importance of
willing and joyous giving with such words and phrases as *bliþe,*

lustfullice, arfæstre heortan and mildre, bliþe mode. Christ is no longer *se Ælmihtiga,* but rather *se mildheorta Drihten.* The preacher's emphasis has appropriately shifted from the powerful Christ who overthrew the devil to the merciful Creator who sees our good deeds and receives us joyfully into heaven. This dual tone, found much less markedly in Gregory, is an almost universal characteristic of these four Blickling homilies. Most of this homily glorifies Christ as the mighty conqueror Who, by His power and glory, defeats the devil to whom we, in our weakness, have succumbed. He is, in effect, the general whose leadership and example we follow as we combat the temptations of the devil. But after we, with His help, conquer the devil and atone for our sins, cleansing ourselves with fasting, prayers, and deeds of mercy, He becomes the loving Lord who will bring us to eternal life.

In structural terms at least, the Palm Sunday homily is more successful than the Quadragesima I homily, primarily because it is in many ways less pretentious and the author seems to have a clearer sense of purpose and of method. The pattern of this homily is more straightforwardly didactic than that of the other, while the exegetical analysis are more logical and precise. Yet its methodical development is somewhat plodding. The homily, moreover, lacks some of the hortatory spirit and the sense of conviction present in the other Lenten homilies.

Contrary to the usual practice in this collection, the author opens his homily with a long preface to the Gospel account, where he relates, as one might expect, the significance of the Sunday, but also attempts beyond this to glorify Christ and to show the greatness of His victory over the devil. In order to create emotional conviction as well as intellectual understanding of Christ's great triumph, the homilist uses imagery of power and victory, describing Christ as *unforhte mode* and *gesigfæsted* and showing how the believing Jews honored Him as heavenly king and conqueror of the devil. To illustrate even more fully Christ's total victory over evil, the homilist alludes to the Harrowing of Hell. This event does not appear in the liturgy until Holy Saturday, but the mention here anticipates the fuller treatment in the Easter homily.

The eclectic nature of the scriptural passage also provides a clue to the author's method and intent. The events related in

John 12, the Gospel for Monday of Holy Week, actually took place on the eve of Palm Sunday, but to narrate them here allows the homilist to introduce a number of figures especially important for tropological emphasis. Most important is Mary, who serves throughout the homily as the major example of positive action. She is both an anagogical figure:

> seo biÞ gefreolsod fram eallum gewinnum, . . . and heo
> resteþ on onsyne ures Drihtnes, and hine hereþ
> unablinnendlice. (BH, p. 73)

and a tropological model:

> Nu we sceolan onherian Marian þære þe smerede
> Hælendes fet, and mid hire loccum drygde; þæt is
> þonne, þæt we sceolan god weorc wyricean, and
> rihtlice libban, þonne fylge we Drihtnes swæþe,
> þæt is gif we oþre men teala læreþ, and hie
> be urum larum rihtlice for Gode libbaþ, þonne
> bringe we Drihten swetne stenc on urum dædum
> and larum. (BH, p. 75)

In her unswerving dedication to Christ, Mary is furthermore the example of the good Christian joined with the Saviour against his enemies.

The latter sentence quoted above closes a long metaphor based on the sweet smell of the oil with which Mary anointed Jesus' feet. The beginning of the passage connects still other deeds with the sweet odor of the oil:

> Cwæþ se writere þæt Maria gename an pund deorwyrþre
> symrenesse, and smyrede mid þæs Hælendes fet, and mid
> hire loccum dregde; þa wæs eal þæt hus gefylled mid
> þon swetan stence. Þeos smerenes wæs geworht of
> ehtatene cynna wyrtum, þær wæron þreo þa betstan ele,
> and nardus, and spica, seo is brunes heowes and godes
> stences, and þæt næfre ne afulaþ þæt mid hire gesmered biþ.
> Þis wæs us gedon to lifes bysene, and gif we nu
> willaþ ure saula smerian mid mildheortnesse ele, þonne
> magon we bringan Drihtne unforwealwodne wæstm

godra weorca. Gemunon we symle þæt we þa god don þe
us Godes bec læraþ, þæt is þonne, fæsten and halige
wæccan, and ælmessylena æfter urum gemete; and mid
manegum oþrum gastlicum mægenum we mægon geearnian
þæt we urum Drihtne bringaþ godra weorca swetne
stenc. (BH, p. 73)

Here the deeds by which we anoint our souls are essentially private
ones, namely the fasts and holy vigils required especially during
the Lenten season. Even almsgiving, the third deed, is a private
act that involves no direct and personal contact with the recipients.
But at the end of this passage the spiritual properties of the oil
are expanded to include those public works, such as teaching
others, which complement acts of private devotion.

The general structural similarities of these two passages with
their nearly identical opening statements, their emphasis on the
swete stenc of good works, and the rhetorical similarity of their
internal sections, emphasize the necessity for both private devotion
and public service. The homilist underscores this a short while
later when, discussing the two disciples who were sent for the ass
on which Jesus was to ride to Jerusalem, he says:

We gehyrdan ær þætte Hælend sende his twegen
þegnas; þa tacniaþ halige lareowas, þæt hie
sceolan þurhwunian on rihtum geleafan
on fulfremdlicum weorcum, and hie sceolan
læran Godes lufan and manna, buton
þæm twam ne mæg nan man becuman to þæm
ecean life. (BH, p. 77)

Without love of both God and man no one can attain salvation.
The message is similar to that of Quadragesima I; only the
exemplars are different.

To say that the presentation of these two loves is the central
theme of this homily would be forcing upon it a kind of structure
which it simply does not have. It would not be difficult to do, for
the interpretation of various parts of the biblical narrative provides
natural examples, either positive or negative, of either kind of love.
Judas, for example, is symbolic of those men who would destroy

God's church; Lazarus signifies this corrupt world; and so on. Such analyses are not particularly unusual. But they are given some cohesiveness by the extended metaphor of the *swete stenc* of good works and by the example of Mary, which dominate the first half of the homily.

From here on the homily is concerned mainly with two subjects; first, the destruction of Jerusalem as punishment for the sins of its inhabitants, and second, the action of the believers who followed Christ and did as He bade them.[9] These contrasting pictures follow the typical pattern of Anglo-Saxon exhortation in which a description of hell precedes a final view of the joys of heaven. The homily thus closes with a positive stress on the rewards of goodness and true belief. The form of the homily remains essentially exegetical and didactic; nevertheless the homilist is obviously trying to impress his audience emotionally as well as intellectually, and so he arranges his homily in the pattern most commonly used in the Blickling manuscript to accomplish parenetic goals.

The account of Jerusalem's destruction opens with a long description contrasting the glory of the city and the evil which, hidden under its external beauty, brings about its total devastation. With many doublets and parallel structures, the homilist develops his description in an almost epic style that heightens the sense of awe inspired by the physical appearance of the city and that underlines by contrast the terrible destruction to come. Noting that God waited forty years after the crucifixion for the people to mend their ways, he recounts the carnage:

Wæs þara manna eallra þe þær ofslegene wæron and
hungre swultan, mid wifmannum and wæpnedmannum,
endleofan siþum hund [teontig] þusenda; and þa hi gyt
genaman þæs folces þe þær to lafe wæs, and him selost
licodan, hund teontig þusenda, and mid him læddon
on haeftned; and ehtatyne syþum hund teontig þusenda hi
tosendon, and wið feo sealdon wide into leodscipas
Ealles þæs folces wæs, þe se casere Titus innon
Ierusalem beferde, þrittigun syþum hund teontig

þusenda, and þæt eal for Godes wræce fordyde and þæt
land gesetton swa hi sylfe woldon. Wæs þæt wite swa
strang, swa Godes geþeld ær mycel wæs. (BH, p. 79)

This passage is much more successful than the "numerical" passage in Quadragesima I. Here the emphasis on the great numbers
of people killed or captured is designed to create a sense of the
disaster which befell Jerusalem, a realization of the enormity of
God's vengeance. The appeal is to the emotion rather than to the
intellect, and the homilist develops this appeal with a fair degree
of rhetorical skill. His emphasis here is on the destruction of
people, who were, after all, the source of the evil, rather than of
the city. Whereas most of the parenetic appeal of the passage lies
in the great numbers of people destroyed, the homilist simplifies
his rhetoric by such phrases as *mid wifmannum and wæpnedmannum,* which are almost poetic formulas in their rhythm and
alliteration and which underscore the comprehensiveness of the
destruction. The final sentence of this passage is very effective.
After the enumeration of punishments suffered by unbelievable
multitudes of people, *Wæs þæt wite swa strang, swa Godes geþeld
ær mycel was* is almost a litotes. It is brief, straightforward, and,
in its very matter-of-factness, especially emphatic. It points up not
only the severity of the punishment, but, more especially, the greatness of God's forbearance. In opening and closing the sentence
with the same word, *wæs,* the homilist stresses grammatically that
central contrast between patience and punishment. Coming as it
does at the end of the passage on Jerusalem, the syntactically
balanced sentence, with its identical opening and closing, produces
an appropriate, climactic summation of the preceding description.

If we view this extended section not simply as a long digression
on a minor, misunderstood portion of the biblical narrative, but as
the negative contrast to a following positive vision, the preacher's
hortatory purpose becomes clear. In the last section of his homily he
includes most of the figures of the Gospel narrative that were not
discussed before. The ass on which Jesus rode symbolizes

þæt geleafulle folc Iudea, and eac oþor manig þa þe beoð
Gode underþeodde on godum willan. . . . (BH, p. 79)

The disciples who did as He asked present a good example for teachers who must obey God's commandments. The crowd which preceded Jesus into Jerusalem signifies the Jewish prophets who foretold Christ's coming. The crowd which followed Him denotes all those who, after His coming, were converted to God. We too are those who follow Him, and we must believe in Him and love Him.

Thus with his final exegesis and exhortation the homilist completes the connection between the biblical figures and his contemporary audience:

> We þonne synt þe þær æfter fylgeaþ; and we witon eall þis
> þus geworden, forðon we sceolan on hine gelyfan, and
> hine lufian, and we eac witon þæt he is toweard to demenne,
> and þas world to geendenne. Nu we habbaþ myccle nedþearfe
> þæt he us gearwe finde. We witon ful geare þæt we sceolan
> on þisse sceortan tide geearnian ece ræste, þonne motan we in
> þære engellican blisse gefeon mid urum Drihtne, þær he leo-
> fað and rixað abuton ende, on ecnesse. (BH, pp. 81, 83)

The homilist has thus progressed through individual acts of Christian love from the deeds of Mary and others in the biblical account to a union with the whole community of believers, past, present, and future, who will be united with God in heaven. More than any other of the Lenten homilies, this piece relies on exegetical analysis rather than exhortation. The homilist has carefully led his audience to an understanding of biblical text and a recognition of how it applies to each of them.

Of the two Lenten homilies which are primarily hortatory, the one for Quadragesima III is the more impressive. Because I have discussed it extensively elsewhere, I shall say only a few words about it here.[10] Based partly on a sermon of Caesarius of Arles, *De reddendis decimis,* it is primarily an exhortation to tithe.[11] In the Blickling homily tithing seems to be mainly a symbolic focus for the obligation of all men, laymen or clergymen, to love God and one another; this general theme animates as well the two homilies previously discussed.

The Passion Sunday homily opens with an extended metaphor based on a quotation from an *æþela lareow:*

Men þa leofestan, ærest us gedafenaþ þæt we gehyron þa
word haligra gewreota, and syþan æfter þon ful medomne
wæstm agifan and agildan. (BH, p. 55)

Adapting Psalms 14: 2–4, the homilist then defines the man who
bears this spiritual fruit:

> "Se mon se þa soþfæstnesse mid his muþe sprecþ, and hie on his
> heortan georne geþencþ, and he hi fullice gelæsteþ, and he
> afylleþ þa inwitfullan word of his tungan, þæt beoþ þa men
> þa þe Godes rices geleafan habbað and healdaþ; forþon hi
> noldan heora nehstan beswican þurh þa facenfullan word."
> (BH, p. 55)

The homilist then illustrates his definition with a series of negative
examples. This first describes the treacherous man who betrays
his neighbor through sweet words, just as the devil betrays the
unwary through the sweetness of sins. The next example concerns
those who hear holy teaching and quickly forget what they have
heard. Here the homilist further develops the metaphor of spiritual
fruit:

> Forþon hie gastlicne wæstm ne beraþ. . .
> forþon þe þæt halige sæd on him gedwan and gewat,
> þæt him ær of þæs lareowes muþe wæs bodad and sægd. . .
> (BH, p. 55)

Those men who begin to do good and abandon it are then compared to those who eat good food and then vomit it up. Just as the
body receives no nourishment and will soon die, so the soul will
perish if it does not retain God's teachings. The fourth and last
example concerns those men who refuse to heed divine instruction.
Unlike the preceding sinners, these men despise God's teaching even
as they hear it. For them no hope exists; unrepentant, they will
suffer eternal punishment. All of these examples reflect the ideas,
though not the wording or structure, of Gregory's *Homilia XVIII
in Evangelia* (PL 76, 1149–51). Gregory's discussion, based on
John 8:47, a verse of the Gospel for Passion Sunday ("Qui ex
Deo est, verba Dei audit. Propterea vos non auditis, quia ex Deo
non estis") is much more abstract than that of the Old English

homilist, with none of his vivid metaphors or analogies. This abstraction is to be expected. Gregory's homily is essentially an exegetical explanation of the Gospel; this Blickling homily is entirely a parenetic sermon based on some of the material contained in the Gospel for the Sunday. Hence the rhetorical structures of the Blickling homilist especially aim to elicit an emotional response.

Concluding that such sins, stemming from a love of this world, cut us off from spiritual life, the homilist then develops a long passage lamenting the transitoriness of the world and the pain and brevity of life. This development reflects several common eschatological themes. The body is first compared to the fruits of the field, which bloom for a while and then fade. Implicit here is the contrast to ever-blooming spiritual fruit, which guarantees everlasting life. Then a description of the body at death and an *ubi sunt* passage follow. The homilist climaxes this section with a vivid comment on the futility of earthly existence:

> On synne[man] bið geeacnod, and on his modor sare he bið
> acenned, on hungre, and on þurste, and on cyle he biþ
> afeded, on gewinne and on swate he leofaþ, on wope
> and on unrotnesse and on sare his lichoma sceal her wunian;
> and þonne se synnfulla on þæm helle fyre cwicsusle his lif
> geendaþ. . . . (BH, pp. 59, 61)

The wicked who end their lives in hell are the subject of much of the rest of the sermon. Beginning with a general warning to those who ignore God, the homilist includes in this admonition a long list of evildoers, namely murderers, perjures, adulterers, thieves, covetous men who cheat others of their property, proud men, and magicians. Those who anger him most, however, are evil judges who accept bribes, give wrong judgments, and otherwise pervert the laws. He grants them a lively and extended, if conventional, vision of hell, a damning comparison with Judas, and a dehumanizing comparison with *slitende wulfas*.

In his choice of subject this homilist resembles the author of the Quadragesima III homily, who condemns to hell the evil priests and bishops who fail to fulfill their obligations. Both homilists are especially critical of those in positions of power who use their offices wrongly or neglect their duties. Both seem especially concerned that the leaders of the people recognize their special responsibility to care for those under their jurisdiction. As does the author of the Quadragesima III homily, this homilist follows his excoriation of evil judges with praise for those who perform their office well. Praising both their motives—they give judgment for fear of God rather than *for feos lufan*—and their actions in guarding themselves from sin and setting right other sinners, he promises them heavenly reward on Judgment Day.

Not only will the judges, both good and evil, be themselves judged, but every man must also at Doomsday account for his deeds before the throne of Christ:

> forþon us syndon nu to bebeorgenne þa myccllan synna, þæt
> we þe eþelicor þa medmyclan gebetan magon. (BH, p. 63)

Murder is the greatest sin, but there are murders of three kinds: homicide, fratricide, and the murder of envy and slander.[12] This last is the worst kind of murder, for those who commit it often do not believe they are guilty of any sin. Hence they never ask God's forgiveness. The homily thus comes full circle, for from the beginning the homilist has emphasized not sins of physical violence, but the more insidious ones of deceit, neglect, hypocrisy, sins which men may not admit, or even know they commit. Failure to recognize and confess such sins leads, of course, to damnation, for it is necessary to repent in this life if one wishes to be saved in the next. The homily thus has more thematic unity than appears at first. The four examples at the beginning explain the types of deception about which the preacher wants to warn his congregation; the middle passages point up in strongly hortatory terms the results of those deceptive practices. Describing the inmates of hell, the homilist excoriates some of the worst deceivers of all, the judges who willfully cheat and accept bribes and otherwise abuse their powers. Finally, as he closes with a reminder that all men, not just judges, must account for their deeds and accept their rewards, he warns his audience again about forms of deception (such as slander) which, because the sinner will not recognize and admit his sin, condemn him to hell's abyss.

To this section the homilist appends, suddenly and without

warning, a traditional closing vision of heaven. Though not unusual in either form or subject, it nevertheless mitigates the
strongly monitory tone of the homily as a whole. Because the
homilist has wished to make his audience recognize that they may
be unknowingly jeopardizing their souls, his admonitions have
generally been harsher than those of most homilies in this collection.
His conclusion offers a vision of hope to counteract his warnings,
or rather to supplement them, an affirmation of the joys which
will result from virtuous behavior.

All of these homilies share common thematic concerns and
rhetorical patterns. Even in a season which stresses the sinfulness
of man's state, the admonition is relatively gentle. All of the
homilists seem more concerned with encouraging than with fright-
ening their audience. Even as they constantly employ reminders of
the Judgment to come, they set forth the means by which men can
gain a favorable verdict. They seem to have faith that men can and
will lead virtuous lives. All of the homilies, especially those for
the third and fifth Sundays in Lent, seem eager to point out that
good men *do* exist. There are good priests and good judges; mankind is not hopelessly sinful. Even when they are most strongly
monitory, the Blickling homilists seem to understand, if not
entirely to forgive, the frailties of mankind. The author of the
first Lenten homily, for example, says in his admonition to perform
fasts, vigils, and almsdeeds:

> Ne magon we buton þæm medmyclum synnum beon, ah we
> sceolan on þas tid þas feawan dagas on forhæfdnesse lifgean,
> urne lichoman and ure heortan clænsian from yflum geþohtum
> þæs þe we magon. . . . (BH, p. 37)

The author of the Passion Sunday homily also acknowledges that
we cannot be free from small sins, though we should try to live our
lives as virtuously as possible.

Nor do these homilies urge a particularly ascetic or unworldly
mode of life. Men can accumulate wealth, so long as they use it
properly. They should give joyfully of their wealth to poor believers and to the church, not because God demands it, but because
all things come from Him and belong to Him. The homilists ask
only a proper recognition of our obligations to God; they do not as-

sume that all men are lustful, avaricious sinners. As the homily for
Passion Sunday tells us, men

> on fruman to Godes hiwunga gesceapen wæron,
> and eac to þon ecan life, næs na to þon ecan deaðe. . . .
> (BH, p. 61)

The homily for Quadragesima I moreover tells us that mankind
was especially favored of God, for Christ took on our form rather
than that of another animal.

All of the homilies emphasize to a considerable degree the social
obligations of men to one another. The rich must give alms to
help the poor; teachers and priests must diligently teach other
men; judges must shield the innocent and punish the guilty. Relatively little is known about the political, religious, or educational
milieu of these homilies, but there is a consistent concern that
those in positions of leadership, whatever their capacity, perform
their duties honestly and faithfully.

Despite his assumption of our humanity, Christ remains throughout the homilies a divine, somewhat remote figure. He is the
glorious leader whose strength, power, and victory over the devil
enable us better to fight the devil in our own lives. Even in the
Palm Sunday homily, which tells of Christ dealing with Lazarus,
with Mary and Martha, and with His disciples, Christ never becomes humanized. Gentle, yet stern and remote, He never seems to
suffer or even to struggle, despite the malevolence of both the
devil and evil men. The vision of Christ returning as Judge to
send men to hell or heaven is constantly in the background.

None of the homilies is particularly unusual in either subject or
form. All treat of common Lenten themes, use their biblical
materials conservatively, and draw upon ideas from established
sources. The parenetic homilies are generally more successful than
the exegetical ones. In general the homilists can with only limited
success meet the demands for order, logic, and coherence which an
exegetical analysis places upon them. But the end of all exegesis
here is less an intellectual understanding of scriptural themes
than an emotional readiness to live virtuously and to merit heaven.

The unknown compiler of this homiliary seems to have great
concern for the daily lives of his congregation. Perhaps even more

than with the relationship between each man and God, he concerns himself with the relationship between man and man, for if that human relationship rests on love and generosity and justice, each man's life will be pleasing to God. If the homilies are unusual in any respect, it is in this consistent, overriding emphasis.

NOTES

1. It is probably a once-complete homiliary from which items for Advent, Christmas, and Epiphany have been lost. Since it has no real analogues either in English or in Latin, we can only speculate its nature and purpose. Milton McC. Gatch, in "Eschatology in the Anonymous Old English Homilies," *Traditio* 21 (1963) : 117–166, discusses these problems more fully.
2. Gatch, "Eschatology," p. 119, n. 8.
3. The Gospel for the Sunday is Luke 11 : 14–28, the account of Jesus casting out devils. It provides ample opportunity to discourse on Christ's power and to oppose the kingdom of God to the kingdom of Hell.
4. BH, p. 27.
5. BH, pp. 83–97.
6. His explanation begins clearly enough, but quickly becomes muddled. There is considerable evidence, as I suggest elsewhere, that a leaf is missing from this portion of the manuscript. See my article, "A Textual Crux in the Third Blickling Homily," *English Language Notes* 5 (1968) : 241–43.
7. PL 76, 1137.
8. Professor Julie Carson (University of Minnesota) and I have discussed these problems in a paper, "An Approach to Semantic and Surface Coherence in the Blickling Homilies," presented in December 1973 to the Old English prose seminar of the MLA.
9. The homilist begins his discussion of Jerusalem's fall with a misunderstanding or deliberate misinterpretation of Jesus'

words to His disciples, "Gaþ on þa wic þe beforan inc standeð." *Wic,* he says, refers to Jerusalem, whereas the biblical passage, even as he has presented it earlier, refers to Bethphage.

10. "Hortatory Tone in the Blickling Homilies: Two Adaptations of Caesarius," *Neuphilologische Mitteilungen* 70 (1969): 641–58. See especially pp. 649–57.

11. Caesarius, *Sermo* 33 *CCL* 103, 142–47. Rudolph Willard identifies this as the source in his essay, "The Blickling-Junius Tithing Homily and Caesarius of Arles," in *Philologica: The Malone Anniversary Studies,* ed. T.A. Kirby and H.B. Woolf (Baltimore, 1949), pp. 65–78.

12. This tripartite division of murder is not original. One of the forged letters in the pseudo-Isidorean False Decretals, attributed in the middle ages to Clement of Rome, discusses it (PL 130, 35), and approximately seventy-five years after the Blickling MS, Geoffrey of Vendome echoes the same idea (*Epistolae XXII,* PL 157, 166). Neither of these asserts, as the Blickling homilist does, that slander is the greatest sin, nor do they dwell as extensively on the consequences of this kind of murder. Their purposes are different; their contexts are different. But the Blicking author is obviously using a relatively long-standing tradition here.

PAUL E. SZARMACH ❦ THE VERCELLI HOMILIES: STYLE & STRUCTURE

The twenty-three Vercelli homilies stand out as important witnesses to the interests of the Benedictine Renaissance and to the vernacular prose tradition that almost a generation later produced the achievements of Aelfric and Wulfstan.[1] The absence of a critical edition of the Vercelli homilies has obscured the fact that the collection offers examples of *vita, homilia* proper, and especially *sermo* whose apparent origins suggest a comparatively developed Mercian school of prose writing, if not a number of different literary centers active before the classical period.[2] This historically important collection has likewise received very little attention for its strictly literary characteristics.[3] In this essay I would like to describe and analyze the style and structure of several prose pieces in the Vercelli Book by discussing almost exclusively examples from the group IX–XXIII, which I have recently edited and which displays a suitable variety of styles and structures. My generally "formalist" method will, I hope, lead to the acceptable conclusion that the prose works of the Vercelli Book are worthy of more appreciation and further profitable study. I will begin with a summary and reading of Homily IX.

Homily IX is not strictly speaking a homily, i.e., a religious discourse that expounds and applies a passage from the Bible, but rather a type of *sermo* known as a *Kompilationspredigt*, i.e., a collection of religious themes for a hortatory purpose.[4] Homily IX thus exhibits a series of linked themes. After an opening paragraph that urges the audience to remember the separation of soul and body and the day of reckoning, the homilist underlines the irrevocable punishments of hell with an allusion to Psalms 6:6. He enumerates the "three deaths" and balances this enumeration with the "three lives," but then dwells on the various qualities of death including its relentlessness and its indiscriminate pursuit of all degrees of men. Pointing out that death is the divider of the soul from the body, the homilist lists four separations at death. The

three separations that survive textual corruption here are the
separations from friends, from all earthdwellers, and from all earthly
bliss. The homilist then lists *fif onlicnessa be hellegryre:* pain, old
age, death, burial, and torments. The reliance on enumeration,
however, yields to narrative at this point. The homilist tells a
Theban legend about an anchorite who, having captured a devil,
was able to make him relate the terrors of hell and the joys of
heaven. Although the manuscript loses a leaf at this point, a
reconstruction from variant versions in Bodley 340 and Cotton
Tiberius A. iii suggests that the lost leaf contained a comparison
of the punishments of hell with those of the earth, a description of
the anguish in hell, a discussion of the size of the earth and hell,
and probably another elaboration on the miseries of hell.[5] The
homilist proceeds to develop his own treatment of the joys of
heaven and then returns to the legend for the extended comparison
that describes the same joys. He interrupts the final exhortation
with a brief, grisly picture of the hound of hell and concludes, as if
in understatement, that *laðlic hit forðy on helle to bionne.*

The homilist's heavy reliance on the list as a rhetorical device to
structure much of the first half of this work looks at first glance
like mere mechanical schematizing. When he balances off the death
that is the sinful life, the death that is the separation of soul and
body, and the death that is in hell against the life in the flesh, the life
in God's glory, and the life in the future world with the saints, he
seems to offer little in the way of complexity.[6] Enumeration is, of
course, a timeworn mnemonic device. Dom LeClercq points out that
the list, be it of Advents, obedience, or spurs, can be seen as a
peculiarly monastic mode of instruction.[7] Such specialized rhetorical
artifice certainly reinforces Margaret Deanesley's comment that the
contents of the Vercelli Book suggest monastic origins.[8] But this
particular double list of three is more than an aid to memory or an
indication of monastic provenance. With this dichotomous list that
opposes the undesirable to the desirable the homilist has begun to
prepare his audience for the contrasting visions of the Theban
legend. The audience will be ready to see things in terms of only
two alternatives, the unspeakably horrible one and the inexpressibly
joyful one, because the homilist arranges his materials, whenever
he can, so that rhetorical order reflects moral choice. To give his

audience the habit of thinking in extremes the homilist orders his paragraph on dreading death by using antithetical adjectives. Death is up and down, multiple and single, noble and base, wise and stupid, for it kills the man in the highest holt and the man in the deepest den, the man in the city or the man in the desert, the king or the slave, the scholar or the dolt. The play on subjective and objective senses of adjectives creates an antithetical point of view in the audience. Earning heaven and *gesæliglice* fleeing hell, the exhortation in the opening, are becoming a way of thinking as well as a subject of thought.

Despite the textual difficulties it is clear that the two subsequent lists that the homilist offers continue the preparation of the audience for the Theban legend. Both the four partings and the five likenesses are incremental lists that heighten the emotional tension that is part of the moral choice the homilist wishes his hearers to make. The separation from earthly joys is pictured as the end of seeing, hearing, speaking, walking, working, and, in the emphatic position, smelling. This emphasis on the life of the body makes for a smooth transition to the five imitations of hell punishments. The third of these imitations, a description of the effects of old age, is indeed so effective that the anonymous author-compiler of Napier 30 elaborates on it almost a century later.[9] A species of the inexpressibility *topos* brings a terrifying conclusion: though seven men live forever, each with seven iron tongues speaking with seventy-two languages, they cannot relate all the hell punishments.

With this introduction to the pains of hell the audience is now ready for the detailed treatment of the Theban legend. This legend, reminiscent of the kind of vision-story that is the stuff of such monastic literature as the *Vitas Patrum* or Rufinus's *Historia Monachorum,* offers alternative full descriptions of hell and heaven. The emphasis on hell effectively inspires a ready identification with and acceptance of the vision of heaven. To determine how verbally close the Tiberius vision is to IX is not as important as to point out that the Vercelli homilist has a similar strategy of moral persuasion. The Theban legend as we have it in the Tiberius manuscript is a self-contained and rounded episode. Aside from omitting several parts of the legend that would encumber his sermon, perhaps the most important rhetorical choice the Vercelli homilist has made in following the legend is to retain the description of the joys of heaven as a statement in dramatic direct discourse. The other parts are related indirectly by the homilist, if the Bodley text is a reasonable guide to the original legend, but he lets the devil relate the joys directly. The implicit elegiac note persuasively strengthens the eye-witness account. Inexplicably the Bodley version of IX omits the devil's comparison. The result is an unbalanced account; the Bodley audience may be terrified by hell, but they have no beckoning vision of heaven to console them and to convert them to righteousness. Homily IX, therefore, has an uncommon structural excellence that implies a thoughtful moral and literary heritage. Direct exhortation, the subtle inculcation of dichotomous thinking, and the incremental list lead the audience to the heart of the homily, the choice between heaven and hell. All is preparation for the presentation of the legend that embodies that choice.

Such a structure, however, is not unique to IX. The formula of introduction, an appropriate number of preparatory motifs, a central narrative episode or exposition, and a closing appears in homilies X, XIX, XX, XXI as well. In XIX the central episode is the story of Jonah; in XX it is the exposition of the eight capital sins; in XXI it is the semipoetic presentation of the Day of Judgment; in X it is an extended presentation of the *ubi sunt motif*. To call this structure a "formula" is not to suggest a mode of technical, mechanical writing, for each of these *sermones* varies from the others in manner and treatment as the difference in content suggests. An analysis of these four sermons demonstrates their formal variety.

Vercelli X is better known as Pseudo-Wulfstan 49 in Napier's groundbreaking collection *Wulfstan: Sammlung*.[10] As a Wulfstanian piece it has received a great deal of attention for the poetic style that is reminiscent of the achievement of Lupus.[11] If it is in fact the best of the anonymous tradition, it is not only because of rhyme, rhythm, and compounding. Unlike IX, where lists and antitheses aggressively assert a coherence and an order, X is a seamless *tour de force* in its structure. As in IX there is a skillful preparation for a rhetorical and a moral center. The homilist begins with an exposition of the Incarnation and its salvific effects on mankind. His doctrinal biography of Christ stresses that men were stepchildren until the only-begotten Son appointed them for the joy of paradise. There is now a covenant between God and man, he says, which must be kept by the avoidance of sin. The idea of covenant or agreement implies in turn the question of compensation and judgment, should the agreement be broken. Just judgment becomes a major ordering principle for the entire homily when the homilist declares of God: *He demð rihtne dom.* The transition to the Last Judgment motif at this point is easy and predictable, but the homilist, using a passage from Paulinus of Aquileia, creates a scene where the devil, not the Lord, is the *accusator* of the sinning soul and the suer for the just judgment. This ironic reversal comes with added effect because the devil's plea carries with it both vigorous supplication (if not demand), *Dem, la dema, rihtne dom 7 emne dom,* and true justice:

> Dem, la Dryhten, rihte domas 7 forlæt me mines rihtes
> wyrðe þæs ðe ic me sylf begiten hæbbe: þæt wæron mine
> þa ðe to þe noldon.[12]

If the devil's direct address is too blatant, then the key image in his speech is not:

> Ac ðonne ic mine hearþan genam 7 mine strengas styrian
> ongan, hie ðæt lustlice gehyrdon 7 fram þe cyrdon 7 to
> me urnon.[13]

The devil is a siren whose music leads men away from the Lord. But there is another music that leads men to the Lord, namely, the kind of rhythmical prose the homilist has used to relate the Incarnation earlier in the homily. Music is thus a link between the matter of the homily and its style.

So cogent an argument by the *daemon accusator* prompts the righteous judge to sentence the accursed into hell and leads the homilist to ask his audience to practice works of mercy because the Lord sees all things. The reference to divine omniscience is the slight but smooth transition that introduces the next major structural unit in the exposition of the theme of just judgment. This unit is another dramatic scene that continues the homilist's moral design for terror by relating how the Lord spoke to a certain proud, rich man who refused to share his wealth with the poor and the wretched. The judgment in this lengthy scene is not the final one of salvation or damnation, but rather a demonstration of man's creatureliness and dependence upon the Lord for everything he is and for everything he may have. Rhetorically the scene consists of the Lord's direct questions to the *wlanca*, which he answers himself, e.g.,

> Wenst du ðæt hit þin sie þæt sio earðe forð bringeð? . . .
> Eall ic nu afyrre minne fultum fram ðe; hafa æt þinum
> gewinne þæt ðu mæge 7 on þinum geswince.[14]

There can be no reply from the proud man to such a question and response, and to what one might call a divine dare: *Ðu liofa butan me, gif ðu mæge*. In a general way this scene recalls the Lord's speech to Job as a vindication of divine authority and a proof of man's dependent nature. Job eventually prospers, of course, but this proud man suffers the curse of death and the loss of his wealth:

> Sona þa on þone welegan mann on þære ilcan nihte deaþ on
> becwom 7 on his bearn ealle. Fengon þa to gestreonum
> fremde syþþan.[15]

The image of the Creator willfully and vindictively extinguishing a man and his possessions, terrible as it is, is an effective complement to the image of the devil seeking souls by appealing to justice.

While the dramatic presentation of a just demon and a vengeful Lord clearly inspire *timor Domini,* this morally valid emotional state is not the homilist's ultimate concern. Rather he intends to move his audience to a renunciation of the transitory world and to convert to the heavenly kingdom. The fate of the rich man shows that *æghwylc heah ham her in woruld bið mid frecnysse ymbseald.* This same mutability, moreover, extends to the natural world. The tallest tree gets buffeted by strong wind, the highest cliffs fall the harder, the greatest mountains suffer the hottest fire: *swa ða hean mihta her in worulde hreosaþ 7 feallað 7 to lore wiorðað.* These images from physical nature prove that mutability and danger are in the natural course of events. The homilist now returns to the pomps of man. All the ornaments of the rich—gold, gems, precious clothing, etc.—*se bitera deaþ þæt todæleð eall.* The imagery and the exposition prepare for the impassioned presentation of the *ubi sunt* motif:

Hwær syndon þa rican caseras 7 cyningas þa þe gio wæron
oððe þa cyningas þe we io cuðon? . . . Hwær coman
middangeardes gestreon? Hwær com worulde wela? Hwær
cwom foldan fægernes? [16]

and the quiet resolution of the tension in these questions in a natural
image and an unadorned, direct, balanced sentence:

> Swa læne is sio oferlufu eorðangestreona: emne hit bið
> gelice rena scurum; þonne he of heofenum swiðost dreoseð
> 7 eft hraðe eall toglideð, bið fæger weder 7 beorht sunne.
> Swa tealte syndon eorðan dreamas, 7 swa todæleð lic 7
> sawle.[17]

The image of the shower and the sun is fundamental to an understanding of the homilist's moral strategy. This image is critical to
the moral persuasiveness of the whole homily. The homilist has
created fear and trembling in a number of ways, but now he presents a pleasant and even hopeful image that comes by surprise. Up
to now physical nature and artifice have been images of natural
decay; here the passing shower is an image of natural process the
end of which is most desirable. That fair weather and bright sun
follow the passing shower at once describe the passing nature of
earthly treasures and suggest a better alternative to them. The
dual function of the image in summarizing the exposition of mutability and yet looking ahead to the conclusion shows this homilist's
characteristic way of linking his major structural units. The
homilist continually presents a major theme from which he develops
the next with a degree of surprise or unexpectedness.

The homily ends on a note of contrast, however. The "fair
weather," so to speak, comes in the form of another speech by the
Lord. Whereas the Lord's first speech was violent and vengefully
just, the second is a divine invitation comparatively full of mercy
and conciliation. The rendering of Matthew 16:26 carries no threat:

> Hwæt hylpeð þam men aht, þeah þe he ealne middangeard on
> his anes æht eal gestryne, gif eft þæt dioful nimeð þa sawle.[18]

The homilist closes with the exhortation *Utan we þænne wendan to
þam beteran 7 gecyrran to þam selran* and the traditional picture
of the bliss and harmony of the *fæderrice*. As a contrast to the pre-

ceeding emphasis on mutability, the recitation of the heavenly joys takes on more than formulaic significance. The audience has heard the devil demand his due, the Lord convict the proud of creature-liness, and the homilist ask *ubi sunt*. Joy and stability come only with the Lord.

The subtle linking of themes in X contrasts with the schematic devices found in IX. As a result, the center of X, the development of the theme of man's mutability, does not stand out so obtrusively as the vision of heaven and hell does in IX. The author of X has a better sense of how to dovetail the parts of his whole, thus, in effect, writing himself out of and beyond the genre of the *Kompila-tionspredigt*.

Homilies XIX, XX, and XXI, however, show a return, so to speak, to the mode of IX. The evidence for dating and composition suggests that these three pieces are most likely a generation later than IX and X.[19] The probability that XIX, XX, and XXI were written by one man is high, but the inferences of scholars are not articles of faith. These inferences do allow the hypothesis that there was a tradition of vernacular composition that continued through-out the tenth century and that XIX, XX, and XXI show the state of that tradition just before the achievement of Aelfric. I will con-sider each of these three homilies separately.

Though clearly writing a Rogationtide homily aimed at fostering penance and penitential observances, the homilist of XIX begins with a general overview of moral history. His opening statement is a confession of faith in the Trinity. From this basic creedal statement he proceeds to relate the Creation, the fall of Lucifer, and the fall of man. This explanation of the origin of sin and of man's sinful nature leads to a general plea for moral conversion, *utan us wendan men þa leofestan to beterum þingum,* and then to a consideration of the specific moral demands of the occasion, *us ys georne to witenne 7 to gehlystenne for hwylcum þingum we ðas gangdagas healdað . . . 7 mid hwylcum þingum we hie healdan sceolon.* This movement from the general or universal perspective to the specific moral mo-ment is the structural principle that now receives vivid application. Borrowing a passage from Caesarius of Arles, the homilist describes Rogationtide's spiritual combat against the devil in dramatic dual-istic terms, the devil contending with the aid of vices and the faithful shielding themselves with virtues.[20] Those who faithfully and religiously observe these holy days despite the devil's attacks will protect themselves before God, and those who turn their hearts to God will gain divine forgiveness. At this point the homilist tells the story of Jonah and the Ninevites to demonstrate divine mercy. His lengthy account of *Jonas* is more moral than narrative because he continually interrupts the action to point out God's power and the binding force of God's command to the fleeing Jonah.[21] Even when the homilist adds a detail to the biblical story, viz., Jonah's ship was checked on all sides by the divinely commanded elements, the point is not for narrative interest but for thematic purpose: a ship motionless in a raging storm is a perfect emblem of human futility in opposition to divine power. After this biblical example of God's powerful mercy the homilist tells how Mamertus of Vienne saved his people from plague by instituting such a three-day fast as the Ninevites practiced. The biblical and historical narratives form the center of this homily. They are the particular precedents of Rogationtide observances, but even more importantly they are actual events that exemplify the core of Christian belief and the efficacy of Christian worship. In beginning with belief, moral history, and Christian observance, and then proceeding to his two exemplary stories, the homilist shows rhetorical control as well as an understanding of moral narrative.

In Homilies IX, X, and XIX the structural center consists of a narrative or dramatic element that embodies the moral themes that appear in the beginning of the homily. Because of its narrative or dramatic nature, this kind of center has an appeal to the literary as well as the moral imagination. XX, however, is an excellent example of how flexible this particular ordering may be.[22] This homily not only has a smaller number of preparatory motifs and themes than the three *Kompilationspredigten* considered so far, but it also has a center that is neither dramatic nor narrative by customary definitions. The center in XX is an adaptation of Alcuin's presentation of the eight capital sins and the four cardinal virtues in the *Liber de Virtutibus et Vitiis*.[23] Like the source, the Old English treatment is an unimpassioned catalogue of the sins, each of which is presented in a basic pattern: 1) introduction and description of the sin; 2) enumeration of other sins and faults engendered by the particular capital sin; 3) mention of the virtues and practices that can overcome the particular sin. While any elaboration Alcuin may have made on this pattern implicit in the *Liber* does not generally appear in the Old English, the homilist does add a few minor details. His most significant departure from Alcuin is the mnemonic emphasis in introducing each sin as a number in a series. The preparatory themes likewise show a dependence on tradition. The discussion of fasting and almsgiving is a commonplace, patristic in origin, and the story of Elias occurs in other texts.[24] Only four paragraphs, the first, the third, and the last two appear to be original. If it be granted that the structural pattern found in IX, X, and XIX is valid, then the structural originality of this homily lies in the substitution of exposition where a narrative or dramatic element might be expected. In a fundamental sense the homilist knows that sin has its own appeal and so uses the expectation of this *Kompilationspredigt* form for maximum effect. His exhortation to penitential practices and proper religious observances in the beginning of the homily thus becomes a natural antithesis to the treatment of the eight sins and not merely a collocation of worn themes. The crafty arrangement of the whole suggests a practical, self-conscious attempt by the homilist to confront his audience with the realities of the penitential season.

Despite its unique structural substitution XX must remain more crafty than artistic when compared to X because it lacks the variety of rhetorical resources found in that earlier homily. The transition to the center is abrupt and direct, e.g., *uton us georne scyldan wið þa ehta heafodleahtras,* whereas the listing of vices and virtues lacks the rhetorical purpose the technique of listing has in IX. The homilist chooses not to develop the theme *conflictus virtutum et vitiorum,* latent here and used in XIX; he seems more interested in discursive exposition for its own sake.

A similar tendency towards relatively unadorned and straightforward expression characterizes the portion of XXI that prepares for the structural center.[25] In exhorting his audience to Christian virtue the homilist relies on grammatical parallelism to enliven his style:

7 warnige ure gehwylc hine 7 georne nu ongyte gehwylc ure
hwæt be ðam earmun synfullum ys on Cristes bocum awriten

7 be ðam ofermodigu*m* 7 be ðam gytseru*m* 7 be ðam yfeldemum
and be ðam unrihthæmerum 7 be ðam arleasu*m* and be ðam ge-
dweolenum 7 be ðam forligergendru*m* and be ðam leas-
fyrhtu*m*
7 be ðam facenfullu*m* 7 be ðam andigum 7 be ðam þe yfel
ongean yfel agyldað 7 be ðam þe þearfum ænige teonan
gedoð.[26]

and

Men þa leofestan, uton efestan 7 uton gan þurh Godes wegas
þæt synt soðlice Godes wegas : riht geleafa 7 gewiss hiht 7
fulfremed soð lufu 7 þurhwunung on godu*m* daedum 7
godnes 7 anraednes 7 geþyld 7 liðnes 7 sybb 7 hyrsumnes 7
langsumnes 7 halig ymbhidignes 7 modes bigeng on haligum
smeaungum 7 cleannes 7 mildheotnes (etc.) . . .[27]

This limited rhetorical feature has, however, a part in a relatively
tight structure. The preparatory themes and motifs in this homily
anticipate a structural center which is a semipoetic representation of
the Last Days. The poetic rhythms exemplified above ready the
audience for the more heightened effects of :

se gesewena heofon	7 engla þrym
7 eallwihtna hryre	7 eorðan forwyrd,
treowleasra gewinn	7 tungla gefeall
þunorrada cyrm	7 se ðystra storm,
[þaera lyfta leoma]	7 þara liga gebrasl [28]

The moral themes the homilist articulates complement the style in
unifying effects in that every exhortation to Christian virtue comes
with a reference to *endedæg*. When the homilist develops *þa twelf
mægnu þære sawle*, his point is that on Doomsday the souls of the
righteous shine with these virtues in the sight of God. His contrast
between the heavenly and the earthly things men may do concludes
by recalling that Christ will give heavenly rewards for those prac-
ticing mercy. These recurrent references to the Last Days thus receive homiletic fulfillment in the portrayal of Judgment Day that
takes up most of the last half of XXI. Because XXI has numerous
preparatory motifs and themes that specifically anticipate the
center of the homily, it is all in all more satisfying than XX despite
its unadorned style.

What is significant about the Judgment Day portion of XXI is that it exists separately in the Vercelli Book as Homily II and also in other manuscripts.[29] Since a textual comparison of II and XXI indicates that these homilies are independent, there is no question that XXI is more than mere scribal conjoining of one homily with some other extant themes and motifs. Nothing in the manuscript suggests that the scribe was aware of the common material in II and XXI. Similarly the center of X exists as an independent homily in CCCC 302 and in Cotton Faustina A. ix.[30] While II antedates XXI, X is prior to its partial analogs. In the case of XXI it is certain that the homilist wrote a homily incorporating material he found in a vernacular source; in the case of X it is certain that a later redactor saw material that he could make into an independent homily. The textual history of X and XXI confirm the literary analyses above by demonstrating that a sufficiently full central episode or exposition can in effect be a homily within a homily and can also appear elsewhere with its own rubric. OE writers in different periods were aware of the structural feature called here the "center." In the genre of the *Kompilationspredigt* there is therefore a form one might label the "concentric homily," which consists of a number of motifs or themes that prepare for a narrative or dramatic center by anticipating the style and content of the center. What source or textual critics might see as a pastiche could very well have a unity obscured by a critic's overconcern with the antecedent parts of the whole. When a homilist uses traditional motifs and themes with rhetorical purpose and design, he is using an author's pen, not "scissors and paste." [31] The kind of critical examination of the structure of the *Kompilationspredigten* undertaken here should bring about a salutary reevaluation of the anonymous tradition.

The concentric structure is one significant response to the structural problems of the looser *sermo* form. No such problem of organization presents itself in the *homilia* proper, for there is always the impulse towards an overall coherence fastened by the biblical text that is to be explained. The author of XVI,[32] On the Epiphany, for instance, is beyond this problem of coherence when he interprets and elaborates on Matthew's account of the Baptism of Jesus, for the five-line biblical passage presents a well-wrought vignette that, as a self-contained narrative unit, has the kind of excellence which can only produce inspired exegesis. The quotation of the passage shows how a source can help a homilist:

> Then Jesus came from Galilee to John, at the Jordan, to be baptized by him. And John was for hindering him, and said, "It is I who ought to be baptized by thee, and dost thou come to me?" But Jesus answered and said to him, "Let it be so now, for it becomes us to fulfill all justice." Then he permitted him. And when Jesus had been baptized, he immediately came up from the water. And behold, the heavens were opened to him, and he saw the Spirit of God descending as a dove and coming upon him. And behold, a voice from the heavens said, "This is my beloved Son, in whom I am well pleased."
> (Matthew 3:13–17)

The first verse succinctly sets the scene. John's question makes explicit the dramatic tension that lies in the inappropriateness of the creature baptizing the Creator. Jesus' firm response leads to the expected narrative act, but instead of serving as the central action the Baptism yields to the higher significance of the miraculous manifestation.

Matthew's account naturally suggests a discussion of the nature of Christ's Baptism and an explanation of the Trinity, which exegetical and homiletic tradition makes virtually inevitable. What is important about XVI, however, is the homilist's development of the dramatic potential of the incident. John's attempt to hinder Jesus is a doctrinal point as well as a dramatic highlight. The homilist makes use of one of his favorite devices, paraphrase, to stress John's great anxiety:

> 7 he swa cwæð þæt Iohannes him andswerede 7 him to cwæð ðæt ðæt wære gedavenlicra þæt Crist hine gefulwade, ðeah þe he ða him to cwome, efne swa swa he cwæde: "Ic eom deadlic mann 7 gehrorendlic 7 þurh Adames scylde ic eom gebunden; 7 ic forðam hæbbe þæs fulwihtes bæð 7 þære cleansunge þearfe."
> (and in the next sentence)
> 7 ða andswarode him sanctus Iohannes 7 him to cwæð: "Ac

nis þe þæs fulwihtes bæð nan þearf forþan þu eart clæne 7
unwemme, 7 ealle clænnesse 7 ealle halignesse 7 ealle
soðfæstnesse gecyndelice on þe standað; ac ne meæg
ænig man þine clænnesse ne þine halignesse geiecan.[33]

In these expansive paraphrases, perhaps suggested by Pseudo-
Maximus, the homilist makes John the self-conscious representative
of corrupt humanity who expresses the great distance between the
mortal and the divine.[34] John's poignant confession of corruption
strikes no less an important note than the affirmation of Jesus'
blamelessness. After asserting the appropriateness of Christ's example for all mankind and stressing the rebirth that is Baptism, the
homilist draws out John's fear:

> Forþan þe se eadiga wer sanctus Iohannes ærest he wið-
> cwæð, forþan he cwæð þæt þæt he forhtode for þære myc-
> lan eadmodnesse, þe ure Dryhten Hælenda Crist hæfde; 7
> sanctus Iohannes he hæfde egesan to þan 7 him þæt þuhte
> þæt his gemet ne wære þæt se heofonlica Cyning under his
> handa gehnige.[35]

The homilist's use of John as a dramatic focus that brings the
audience into the action ultimately derives from the biblical source,
but his introduction and treatment of other themes make it clear
that dramatization is this homilist's preferred homiletic method.
When he discusses Christ's Baptism in the River Jordan, he points
out that the river acknowledged Christ in fulfillment of Psalms
113:5: "Why is it, O sea, that you flee? O Jordan, that you turn
back?" Developing a tradition found also in travel and geography
literature he tells us that the Jordan is a great body of water with
a strong, running current; when Christ stepped in, the river re-
versed its flow and stood still, not daring to move because of divine
fear. Christ's Baptism is at once heroic and miraculous. The Jordan's acknowledgment of Christ becomes a transition to a paragraph
drawn from Gregory's Homily X On the Epiphany wherein
Gregory develops a list of various elements of the universe that
gave witness that the author of their creation had come.[36] The
Vercelli homilist follows Gregory in the outlines of this list: the
heavens, the sea, the earth, walls and stones, and even hell acknowl-

edged and confessed Christ at His birth and death—all things confessed Christ except the hard-hearted Jews whose hearts were harder than any stones. The homilist then develops the Gregorian list in his own way. Gregory writes simply that "stones and walls recognized him because at His death they broke open." The Vercelli homilist writes:

7 hwæt! hine eac swylce wegas 7 stanas ongeaton; 7 swa we leorniaþ on bocum þæt ða wæs geworden in ða tid, þe he for mancynne geþrowode, þæt þæs temples in Hierusalem dæl on innan gefeol 7 manige stanas toburston.

7 Golgaðða þæt clif, þe he on ahangen wæs, þæt tobærst eall, 7 he ða byrþenne ahebban ne meahte, forðan he hit eallra gesceafta Scippend on him hæfde.[37]

To Gregory's statement that the sea made itself walkable for Jesus the Vercelli homilist adds the mention of Jesus' walking on water and the miracle at the Baptism. These elaborations, minor details added to the other elemental witnesses, together with the homilist's use of the interjection *hwæt* at several points, heighten the effect so that the Jews appear all the more horrendous for their disbelief. It is clear that the Vercelli homilist is primarily interested in evoking an emotional response from his audience.[38]

Later in Homily XVI the homilist shows that he can do more than dramatize events when he endeavors to explain the Trinity. He begins gently with a pastoral "my brethern, we have great need to learn something about the faith of God," but then chides and prods his audience in the mock exasperation of a teacher when he says that only a very unlearned person can say in his heart: "How can I understand anything about the Holy Trinity? There are three persons and yet one God and one Divine Substance."[39] This inner monologue has a light touch and a psychological shrewdness that combine to make the reluctant listener, reluctant only because the listener already knows the complexity of the doctrine, ready to accept the surprisingly homely analogy that will follow. The homilist tells his audience that "we see many things in this creation that are one thing and yet have three things in it." He points to the fire "we have before us" and enumerates three qualities in the one flame, namely heat, whiteness, and flaming light. A direct and immediate local reference of this kind is rare in Old English homilies and sermons. Even more rare is the apparently humorous or sardonic remark that the flame sometimes illuminates the *eorðærn* ("crypt," "tomb," "earthly place"?) more extensively than it should. Although Quodvultdeus provides the source for this passage on the Trinity, the author of XVI has selected but the monologue of the straw man and the analogy of fire from the African bishop; he does not follow him in mentioning biblical precedents or attacking the Arians.[40] The judicious selection retains the familiar, recognizable voice that with confidence and skill reaches out to the audience to help it understand a mystery. Theologians may question the validity of this demonstration, but the rhetorical technique of this mature teacher is quite effective.

In developing his homily the author of XVI does not stray very far from the biblical text. The running translation of Matthew in the opening and the recurrent use of paraphrase necessarily control any possible wandering from the point. In fact the homilist is so conscious of the biblical text that after he finishes his discussion of the "recognition" *topos,* he hastens to add, *Sceolon we nu eac, broðor mine, þone halgan godspel secgan 7 reccan þæt we ær ongunnon secgan.*

The author of XVII, on the other hand, creates an ordered exposition of a biblical text by other means.[41] His first two paragraphs briefly summarize what happened on the Purification, namely, that Christ's parents brought him to fulfill the Law requiring an offering of two turtledoves or pigeons for the first male-child and that there Simeon, inspired by the Spirit, met the consolation he had prayed for and worshipped Him. The homilist then chooses three points for elucidation: the Judaic Law, the allegorical meaning of Jerusalem, and the nature of the offering. He introduces each of these points virtually without transition, three times using the formula *us is nu to witanne* or a slight variant of it. Perhaps only the explanation of why Mary the immaculate virgin obeyed the commands of Leviticus 12 is absolutely necessary to understand Luke 2; the other two points the homilist offers suggest his interest in allegorical interpretations and in symbolism. Certainly the emphasis on Jerusalem as *sybbe gesyhðe* at first appears gratuitous and idiosyncratic, for there is no compelling reason to connect this traditional gloss with this particular text. Yet this gloss and accompanying explanation, ending with *Eadige beoð þa gesybsuman men forþon þe hie beoð Godes bearn genemde,* probably hold the conceptual key to the entire piece precisely because they appear at this point. The related concepts of *(ece) sibb, (ece) reste,* and *(ece) frofor,* expressed and implied in the exegesis of "Jerusalem" and in the discussion of the offerings, inform the rest of the homily and give it direction. Even in the discussion of Mary's observance of the Law the motif of peace is present. Mary obeyed the Law to fulfill Christ's words: *Ne cwom ic to þam in worulde þæt ic Godes æ towurpe 7 tobræce; ac ic cwom to þan þæt hie gefylde 7 getrymede.* The repudiation of the violence implied by the verbs *towurpan* and *tobrecan* states the key theme of peace.

The various themes in the biblical summary and in the subsequent exposition receive complete expression in the figure of Simeon. The homilist of XVII makes Simeon a *tacn* that embodies law, fulfillment, peace, consolation, and of course saintliness. In the summary, for example, the homilist adds a detail coming ultimately from the Apocrypha that Simeon was a priest of the Old Law. When he explains that the two birds given in offering betoken purity and innocence, he immediately states that Simeon *hæfde lifes clænnesse gehealden ge in wordum ge in dædum ge in geðohtum 7 eac in gesiehðe.* Simeon, the Bible says, prayed not for his own salvation, but for the consolation of all men; in that, he betokened that all should be of such mind and will. Just as the homilist of XVI uses St. John as a dramatic focus, the homilist of XVII uses Simeon for narrative interest. For the only time in the homily the homilist quotes the biblical text: *Nunc dimittis servum tuum, domine, secundum verbum tuum in pace, quia viderunt oculi mei salutare, domine* (Luke 2:29–30). In order to reinforce the impact of the Latin he translates the canticle straightforwardly and then adds an interpretive paraphrase:

Læt me faran of þære tyddernesse þysses meniscan
lichaman þe ic nu git on eom. Læt me geendian þis deað-
lic lif 7 læt me becuman to þam ecan life 7 to þære ecan
reste þe ðu þinum þam gecorenum 7 þam halgum ge-
gearuwad hafast, forðan þe ic þære andsware onfenc

þæt ic ne moste deaðes byrian ærþan ic ðe, Dryhten, min
eagum gesege 7 nu gesegon mine eagan
þine hælo ða ðe ðu geearuwadest to leohte 7 to frofre
manigum þeodum 7 to wuldre þines folces.⁴²

As the thematic heart of the homily the paraphrase gives the promise
of eternal life and peace for the righteous with the corresponding
implication of its fulfillment. To underline the joyous nature of this
fulfillment the homilist quotes the angelic *Gloria in excelsis* in Old
English and alludes to the tradition that angels became the friends
of men when the Lord became man. With this image of heavenly
harmony immediately present to the audience, the homilist asks
his hearers to recognize their need to live righteously and to pray
for the holy love that will lead to the holy kingdom. Coming as it
does beyond the mid-point of the homily after a number of preparatory themes, this portrayal of Simeon recalls the concentric structure
of the *Kompilationspredigten*. It may be that the author of XVII
had this more flexible structure in mind as a substitute for the
running gloss or the kind of structure found in XVI. Whatever the
case, it does appear that the author consciously avoided a number
of traditional Purification themes such as the prophecies of Simeon,
the witness of Anna, and the importance of Candlemas so as to
fashion a more general moral message grounded in a particular
liturgical occasion. Only a writer confident in his skill would have
attempted to blend features of the *homilia* and the *sermo* as they
are found in Homily XVII.

Unlike the authors who wrote the homilies and sermons discussed above, the author of Homily XVIII, the Vercelli life of St.
Martin, had to show his skill as an adaptor of a lengthy and
sophisticated Latin text, viz., Sulpicius's *Vita Sancti Martini* with a
portion of the *Epistola III, ad Bassulam*.⁴³ The Old English writer
gives evidence that, faced with a *Vita* numbering twenty-seven
chapters of varying length and with an *Epistola* containing the important and powerful account of Martin's death, he attempted to
select incidents from this basic text in Latin monasticism to focus
on Martin as a *vir dei*. He omits *in toto* the prologue and chapters I,
IV, VI, IX, XI–XIII, XVIII–XIX, and XXI–XXV of the *Vita*.
From the remainder he chooses judiciously. He avoids, for example,
Martin's clash with Julian the Apostate and gives only a sketch
of Martin's service with Hilary. Much of the omitted material con-

cerns the ecclesiastical and political struggles that beset Gaul in the later empire and moved Sulpicius to take an active role in the anti-episcopal party. The incidents selected by the Old English homilist portray Martin as a saintly man of God, working miracles, converting unbelievers, and teaching by word and deed. The retention of stories concerning Martin's campaigns against heathendom may have had particular point for the Anglo-Saxon audience. The homilist thus not only shortens his sources for the practical demands of reading or delivery, but he also attempts to define Martin more sharply as a Christian model for his audience and not as a controversialist in old disputes.

Since it appears that Sulpicius wrote his *Vita* while Martin was still alive and, after Martin's death, assembled a number of anecdotes, including Martin's rebuke of the devil at his deathbed, in the *Epistolae* and *Dialogi* that complete the record of Martin's life,[44] the Latin sources together present a unique problem for any adaptor. The literary genesis of the Latin forces the Old English homilist, who has a clear hagiographic need to show how his Christian model has died a Christian death, to deal with the final chapter of the *Vita* proper:

> Nemo umquam illum vidit iratum, nemo commotum, nemo
> maerentem, nemo ridentem; unus idemque fuit semper:
> caelestem quodammodo laetitiam vultu praeferens, extra
> naturam hominis videbatur. Numquam in illius ore nisi
> Christus, numquam in illius corde nisi pietas, nisi pax,
> nisi misericordia erat. Plerumque etiam pro eorum, qui
> illius obtrectatores videbantur, solebat flere peccatis
> qui remorum et quietum venenantis linguis et viperio ore
> carpebant.[45]

Quite obviously these sentiments and comments form an appropriate summary conclusion to the *Vita,* but the existence of the *Epistolae* and the *Dialogi* would appear to render them out of place except at the end of a version of a *vita Martini* that integrates all of Sulpicius's writings on the saint. Nevertheless the Old English homilist gives his rendering of chapter twenty-seven some three-quarters of the way into his *vita* in the place where the serial and linear selection of incidents would naturally allow.

Aelfric provides a singular contrast to the anonymous writer on this source problem. In his homily in the *Second Series* and in his piece on Martin in the *Lives of the Saints* Aelfric fashions a linear biography from the sources used in XVIII by the anonymous writer and additional material coming from Gregory of Tours's *Historia Francorum*, Sulpicius's *Epistola ad Eusebium*, and Sulpicius's, *Dialogi II et III*.[46] Martin's life unfolds as a narrative sequence of events because Aelfric simply eliminates Sulpicius's chapter twenty-seven and with it the hint that Sulpicius wrote the *Vita* before his other works on Martin. The seamless narrative argues that Aelfric has a greater command over his sources and a more independent perspective on his own role as a hagiographer that enable him to create a new *vita Martini*.

This comparison in favor of Aelfric assumes of course that a linear biography is preferable and necessarily so when it originates from a number of sources. The impulse of source criticism, it seems, is to reward the freer, more independent author. Without denying Aelfric's skill and art one might still perceive conscious purpose and design rather than slavish indebtedness to the Latin in the anonymous writer's retention of Sulpicius's chapter twenty-seven. As the above listing of chapters omitted suggests, the author of XVIII tends to be very selective. He accepts the premise of linear biography in that he stresses Martin's pagan birth and upbringing and in that he elaborates on Martin's death, but his selection of anecdotes from Martin's life is thematic. The anonymous author assembles enough stories to illustrate Martin's personal virtue and his miraculous powers. He thus summarizes Martin's virtuous life on earth with Sulpicius's chapter and even heightens the summary by pointing out Martin's healing powers once again and by calling attention to Martin's independence from secular authority. His flat-footed *þis is soðlice eadig wer* virtually announces to the audience that the hagiographic point has been demonstrated. What ended Sulpicius's *Vita* has become a major structural division in this Old English *vita*. The author of XVIII can now concentrate on Martin's last days, when Martin still displayed love and concern for his brethren in the face of his own illness and death and when he merited eternal salvation. The two-part structure for the whole becomes explicit in the homilist's closing statement:

Hwæt! we nu gehyraþ, men, hu haliglice þes eadiga wer
sanctus Martinus his lif for Gode lifde, þa hwile þe he
her on worulde wæs, 7 hu fægerum edleanum he þæs æt
urum Dryhtne onfeng.[47]

While Aelfric apparently saw the summary close of Sulpicius's
Vita as an impediment to his own *vita,* the writer of XVIII
retained it to give structural meaning. His audience can clearly see
Christian life and death in model form as well as Christian life and
its reward in bold relief.

Homily XXIII, the Vercelli *Guthlac,* differs from XVIII because it makes no attempt to present any kind of full-scale *vita,*
linear or nonlinear. Rather, XXIII is a presentation of chapters
four and five of the Old English translation of Felix's *Vita*
Guthlaci (London *Guthlac*); in the Latin this matter appears in
five of Felix's fifty-two chapters.[48] Without title, zoomorphic
initial, number, or any kind of device except a large *wynn* to begin
the first word *waes,* this extract has the marks of a scribal afterthought, either on the part of the Vercelli scribe or the scribe of
his exemplar. Lacking any prefatory or introductory statement,
XXIII simply begins to relate Guthlac's ascetic life in his barrow-
hut. The Old English redactor even allows the phrase *sprecenan*
iglande for *praedicta insula* in the first sentence, when, of course,
the island has not yet been mentioned. He recounts Guthlac's
religious observances, his religious despair and self-doubt, and his
eventual comfort from St. Bartholomew. The redactor follows
chapter five of the Old English translation in telling of two temptations: one by two devils who tried to lead Guthlac to excessive
fasting and another by a horde of devils who tried to frighten the
steadfast Guthlac by taking him to hell. Again St. Bartholomew
rescued Guthlac. The redactor now supplies a sudden close:

7 þa æfter þam fleah se haliga Guðlac mid þam apostole
sancte Bartholomei to heofonarices wuldre. 7 hine se
Hælend þær onfeng, 7 he þær leofað 7 rixaþ in heofonarices worulde a butan ende on ecnesse. Amen fiat![49]

Perhaps this abbreviated ending, clearly the Vercelli redactor's and
not that of Felix or the Old English translator of Felix, suggests

that the redactor has assembled these incidents from Guthlac's *vita*
as much for St. Bartholomew's glory as for Guthlac's. Since the
relationships of the London *Guthlac,* the Vercelli *Guthlac,* and
Felix's original do not give clear or easy evidence of the Vercelli
redactor's intention in other passages, it seems best to conclude
that XXIII is merely a prose piece on the temptations that Guthlac, comforted by St. Bartholomew, successfully endured. The
selection of incidents supports this reading. Bertram Colgrave
indicates that Felix's chapter xxvii, the starting point of the
Vercelli *Guthlac,* begins the second part of the *Vita* and that Felix
himself clearly regarded this chapter as the start of the *Vita*
proper. Felix relates many more examples of Guthlac's persever-
ance, but nowhere again does St. Batholomew appear, his mention
at the beginning of chapter xxxiii excepted. St. Bartholomew as
psychopomp is at least one unifying element in XXIII. Even
though the immanent intention is not very clear and XXIII is not
a *vita* in the manner of XVIII, one must note Colgrave's remarks
on the Old English translator's skill:

> This Old English translation is to some extent a simplification
> of Felix's elaborate style, and many of his difficult phrases
> and words are avoided by judicious omissions. But the main
> thread of the story is followed faithfully enough. Old English
> scholars have neglected this piece and have hardly done
> justice to the unusual skill of the translator, or the importance
> of the piece in the development of translation technique dur-
> ing the Anglo-Saxon period.[50]

The role of the Vercelli redactor is difficult to assess here because
of the likelihood that the many verbal differences between the
London *Guthlac* and the Vercelli *Guthlac* come from scribal transmission. The anonymous translator's successful encounter with
Felix's Hisperic prose, however diminished by the Vercelli
redactor's attempts to adapt it, is not an inappropriate ending to
the Vercelli Book.

As a prose and poetic miscellany or a "monastic reader," the
Vercelli Book provides an occasion for demonstrating the scope
and variety of Anglo-Saxon religious writing. The twenty-three
prose pieces in the collection give ample evidence that pre-Classical
Old English prose writers were skillful, and often artistic, in ful-

filling Bede's well-known dictum for church writers: *ad utilitatem ecclesiae Dei*. Not every item in the manuscript is an unalloyed success, but many homilies anticipate the structural and stylistic achievements found in the work of Aelfric and Wulfstan. Homily IX and particularly Homily X show that the *sermo* could satisfy the moral imperatives to persuade and exhort as well as the literary demands to accomplish the moral end with point and skill. Indeed the survival of X in many later versions can be no mere accident of chance. The various forms that the *Kompilationspredigt* takes thus make a strong argument for a confident and flourishing tradition. Homilies XVI and XVIII typify the achievement of earlier writers in the *homilia* and *vita* respectively, in that XVI is noteworthy for the clear pastoral voice that can explain mysteries and yet exhort gently at the same time, while XVIII displays the structural skill of a writer who has adapted a longer Latin masterpiece to his particular occasional need. If Aelfric and Wulfstan are the more accomplished writers, it is because such earlier authors have shown the way. There is every reason, therefore, to challenge C.L. Wrenn's comments on the *Vercelli Book* when he says that "there is not much literary interest in these sermons." [51]

NOTES

I would like to thank my colleagues Miriam Leranbaum and Norman Burns for many helpful suggestions in the preparation of this article.

1. For the dating of the Vercelli Book, see N.R. Ker, *Catalogue,* p. 460. G.P. Krapp summarizes the scholarship on dating in *The Vercelli Book, Anglo-Saxon Poetic Records* II (New York, 1932), p. xvi. For information on the Benedictine Renaissance, see Margaret Deanesley, *The Pre-Conquest Church in England,* 2nd ed. (London, 1963) pp. 276–302 and 303–27; see also David Parsons, ed., *Tenth-Century Studies* (London and Chichester, 1975).

2. Max Förster, ed., *Die Vercelli Homilien* (Hamburg, 1932;

rpr. Darmstadt, 1964) contains Homilies I–VIII (the
1932 ed. has the first ten lines of IX). My edition of IX–
XXIII will appear in the Toronto Old English Series.
Doctoral dissertations are: Paul Peterson, "The Unpub-
lished Homilies of the Old English Vercelli Book" (New
York University, 1951); M. Corfilia Pinski, "Six Unpublished Homilies in the Vercelli Manuscript" (University
of Ottawa, 1966); Lynn L. McCabe, "An Edition and
Translation of a Tenth-Century Anglo-Saxon Homily,
Vercelli X" (University of Minnesota, 1968). For a discussion of manuscript origins, see Donald G. Scragg, "The
Compilation of the Vercelli Book," *Anglo-Saxon England* 2
(1973): 189–207; R. Vleeskruyer, *The Life of St. Chad*
(Amsterdam, 1953), pp. 39–62.
3. There have been general notices in the standard histories, but
no particularly detailed analyses.
4. Fr. 61^r–65^r. The new facsimile is Celia Sisam's *The Vercelli
Book,* EEMF 19 (Copenhagen, 1976). It replaces Max
Förster, *Il Codice Vercellese* (Rome, 1913). Förster prints
this homily in *Festschrift für Lorenz Morsbach* (Halle,
1913), pp. 100–16.
5. Förster collates Bodley 340 art. 8 in his 1913 printing of IX.
Cotton Tiberius A. iii art. 18 appears in J.M. Kemble's
The Dialogue of Salomon and Saturn (London, 1848),
pp. 84–86. Fred Robinson's text and discussion supersede
Kemble; see *Neuphilologische Mitteilungen* 73 (1972):
363–71.
6. By way of comparison, Aelfric gives more variety to his brief
treatment of two deaths in Homily XI of Pope's SS II,
pp. 420–21.
7. Dom. J. LeClercq, *The Love of Learning and the Desire for
God* (New York, 1961), p. 171.
8. Margaret Deanesley, *Sidelights on the Anglo-Saxon Church*
(London, 1962), p. 65.
9. Pp. 147–48.
10. Ibid., pp. 250–65; ff. 65^r–71^r in the *Vercelli Book.*
11. See Klaus Ostheeren's bibliographical summary in the Dublin,
1967 reprint, pp. 355–57.

12. For Vercelli X I will cite the folio and give the reference to the corresponding page in Napier's edition; f. 66ᵛ, ed. Napier, p. 254. The source for the *daemon accusator* passage is Paulinus of Aquileia's *Liber Exhortationis,* cap. 62 (*PL* 104, 271–72). Wolfgang Becker has found another partial Latin source in the *Remedia peccatorum;* see his "The Latin Manuscript Sources of the Old English Translations of the Sermon *Remedia Peccatorum,*" *Medium Aevum* 45 (1976) : 145–52.

13. F. 67ʳ; ed. Napier, p. 255.

14. F. 68ᵛ; ed. Napier, p. 259.

15. F. 69ᵛ; ed. Napier, p. 261.

16. F. 70ʳ; ed. Napier, p. 263. For the *ubi sunt* theme, see J.E. Cross, "*Ubi sunt* Passages in Old English—Sources and Relationships," *Vetenskaps-Societeen i Lund Arsbok* (Lund, 1956), pp. 23–44; also I.L. Gordon, ed., *The Seafarer* (London, 1960), pp. 23–27.

17. F. 70ʳ; ed. Napier, p. 263.

18. F. 70ᵛ; ed. Napier, pp. 264–65.

19. See Scragg, "Compilation of the Vercelli Book," pp. 203–05; Paul Peterson, "Dialect Grouping in the Unpublished Vercelli Homilies," *Studies in Philology* 50 (1949) : 559–65.

20. Caesarius of Arles, *Sermo* 207, *De letania,* in *Opera Omnia,* ed. G. Morin, CCL 104, p. 829. For Caesarius in Old English generally, see Joseph B. Traherne, Jr., "Caesarius of Arles and Old English Literature," *Anglo-Saxon England* 5 (1976) : 105–19.

21. I discuss the Jonas passage in "Three Versions of the Jonah Story: an Investigation of Narrative Technique in Old English Homilies," *Anglo-Saxon England* 1 (1972) : 183–92.

22. See my edition, "Vercelli Homily XX," *Medieval Studies* 35 (1973) : 1–26 and corrections in *Medieval Studies* 36 (1974) : 493–94.

23. *PL* 101, 633–37.

24. See *Medieval Studies* 35 (1973) : 7–10.

25. Ff. 112ʳ–116ᵛ.

26. F. 112ᵛ.
27. F. 113ʳ.
28. F. 115ᵛ.
29. Ed. Förster, pp. 44–53. Förster collates II with the extant mss.
30. CCCC 302, art. 12, pp. 78–83; Cotton Faustina A. ix, art. 6 ff.
   27ᵛ–31ᵛ. Edited by Tolliver C. Callison, "An Edition of
   Previously Unpublished Anglo-Saxon Homilies in Mss.
   CCCC 302 and Cotton Faustina A. ix" (Diss., University
   of Wisconsin-Madison, 1973).
31. L. Whitbread, "Wulfstan Homilies XXIX, XXX, and Some
   Related Texts," *Anglia* 81 (1963): 36.
32. Ff. 85ᵛ–90ᵛ.
33. F. 86ᵛ.
34. Pseudo-Maximus, *De Baptismo Christi* I, *PL* 57, 290.
35. F. 86ᵛ.
36. *PL* 76, 1111.
37. F. 87ᵛ.
38. Aelfric provides a sharp contrast to the styles of this presentation in CH I, p. 108. For his own homily on the Epiphany
   he too borrows from Gregory, but impresses the passage
   with his characteristic restraint. Aelfric's Gregorian passage
   is essentially an unadorned close translation that merely
   relates the miraculous facts. He adds practically nothing to
   the list of the testifying elements, but makes his own
   contribution in his treatment of the Jews. Although he calls
   the Jews "impious" and "hard-hearted," Aelfric greatly
   reduces the anti-Semitic tone by ending the passage thus:
   "[The Jews] were not, however, all equally unbelieving, but
   of their race there were both prophets and apostles, and
   many thousands of believing men." This balanced comment
   takes away an emotional response from the audience and
   indicates that Aelfric is primarily interested in explaining
   the importance of the Epiphany and the doctrine of the Incarnation. The Vercelli homilist in contrast is primarily
   interested in moving his audience.
39. F. 88ᵛ.
40. *PL* 40, 658–59.
41. F. 90ᵛ–94ᵛ.

42. F. 93ᵛ.
43. Ff. 94ᵛ–101ʳ. XVIII is printed as Blickling XVII, which is defective and incomplete, by Morris in BH, pp. 210–27. The new Latin edition of Sulpicius's work on Martin is edited by J. Fontaine, *Vie de Saint Martin* I–III, *Sources Chrétiennes* 135–37 (Paris, 1967–69).
44. F.R. Hoare, ed. and tr., *The Western Fathers* (New York, 1954), p. 7, remarks that Sulpicius is "a literary log-roller of the most blatant type," who has exploited both his earlier success with the *Vita* and the memory of his saintly hero and friend.
45. Ed. Fontaine, I, p. 314.
46. Aelfric, CH II, pp. 498–519. See my dissertation, "Selected Vercelli Homilies," (Harvard University, 1968), pp. 151ff for source work.
47. F. 101ʳ.
48. For the Latin, see Bertram F. Colgrave, ed., *Felix's Life of St. Guthlac* (Cambridge, 1956) and for the complete OE version, see Paul Gonser, ed., *Das Angelsächsische Prosa-Leben des hl. Guthlacs,* Anglistisches Forschungen 27 (Heidelberg, 1909). Gonser prints Vercelli XXIII in parallel text, pp. 117–34.
49. Ed. Gonser, p. 134.
50. Ed. Colgrave, p. 19.
51. C.L. Wrenn, *A Study of Old English Literature* (London, 1967), p. 245.